THE GUINNESS BOOK OF
IRELAND

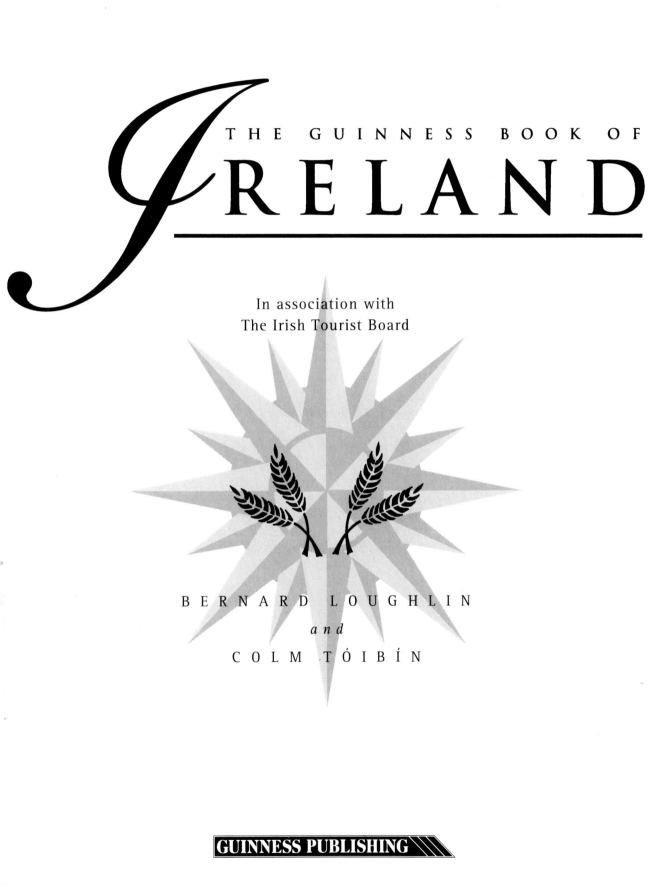

In association with
The Irish Tourist Board

BERNARD LOUGHLIN

and

COLM TÓIBÍN

GUINNESS PUBLISHING

In-house Editor: Roselle Le Sauteur
Design and Layout: Moondisks

Typeset in Rotis Serif and Frutiger by Ace Filmsetting Ltd, Frome, Somerset
Colour origination by Master Image, Singapore
Printed and bound in Italy by New Interlitho Italia SpA

ISBN 0-85112-597-2

The editors would like to thank Mark Cohen for his encouragement and patience in the preparation of this book.

Preface

by the Minister for Tourism and Trade, Mr Enda Kenny TD

The Guinness Book of Ireland is a well-timed publication – and not alone because it follows upon the best-selling *Guinness Book of Irish Facts and Feats*. That first volume, as its title conveys, is cast in the rewarding mould of *The Guinness Book of Records*. What we now welcome may be quite different, but complements perfectly what has gone before.

The two enlightened editors of *The Guinness Book of Ireland* seem to have given their head to a small but talented team of writers. The wisdom of that policy shines through in every page.

One becomes caught up in the thrill of a game of hurling, in the dreamy relaxation of cruising along the Erne and the Shannon waterways, in a sensitive retracing of the footsteps of some of Ireland's literary giants through the streets (and taverns) of Dublin.

Here, too, are glimpses of that shadowy Celtic civilisation whose heroes and epic struggles are remembered to this day in the folklore and the placenames of Ireland's four provinces; and, nearer our own time, some reminders that our history has more to it than memories of 'battles long ago', but also many beneficial legacies which are ours still to enjoy.

In every way, then, a timely book, earning full marks for Bernard Loughlin and Colm Tóibín and Guinness Publishing. For our visitors an ideal introduction to Ireland – all the better if it can be dipped into even before the holiday begins. For our own people, a book to be read with pleasure and a certain pride; and a distinct enouragement to all of us, in Ireland North and South, to set about knowing and enjoying to the full the company of one another.

Ireland

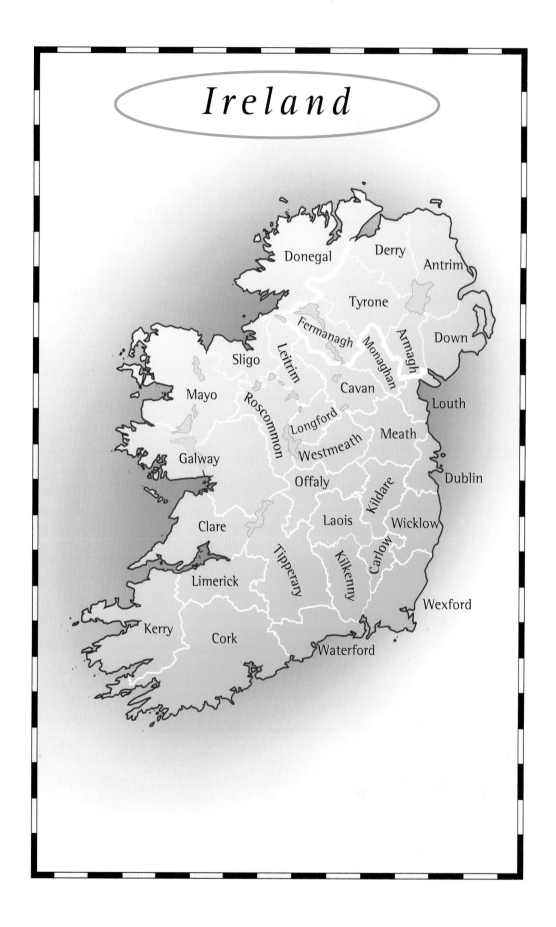

Contents

Preface   3

Introduction   6

Chapter One: *Dublin and The Pale* – Rosita Boland   8

COUNTIES DUBLIN, WICKLOW, KILDARE, MEATH AND LOUTH

FEATURE: THE DART LINE   31

Chapter Two: *The Southeast* – George O'Brien   36

COUNTIES WATERFORD, WEXFORD, CARLOW, KILKENNY AND TIPPERARY

FEATURES: THE COMING OF THE NORMANS   38
           PLAYING THE GAMES   50

Chapter Three: *The Southwest* – Sean Dunne   66

COUNTIES CORK AND KERRY

FEATURES: HURLING   76
           THE RING OF KERRY   80
           EMIGRATION   92

Chapter Four: *The West* – Michael Finlan with Bernard Loughlin   94

COUNTIES CLARE, GALWAY, MAYO AND SLIGO

FEATURES: THE ARAN ISLANDS   104

Chapter Five: *The North: Old Ulster and the Other Ulster* – Bernard Loughlin   128

COUNTIES ANTRIM, DOWN, ARMAGH, MONAGHAN, CAVAN, FERMANAGH, DONEGAL,
          DERRY AND TYRONE

FEATURE: THE GLENS OF ANTRIM AND THE ANTRIM COAST ROAD   152

Chapter Six: *The Erne and the Shannon* – Colm Tóibín with Bernard Loughlin   160

COUNTIES FERMANAGH, LEITRIM, ROSCOMMON, LONGFORD, WESTMEATH,
          OFFALY, CLARE AND LIMERICK

Index   187

Introduction

The Guinness Book of Ireland aims to prepare you for the adventure and the discovery of travelling in one of the world's most fascinating and complex islands. Written with the intelligent visitor in mind, whether first-time, native, business person passing through, or student with the whole summer before you and the rucksack strapped behind, this book will give you a sense of Ireland as it is today, and of all the historical peoples and events which have made it so.

The six of us who have written this book have sought out the superlative and the secret in the areas where we grew up or where we have spent most of our lives. We try to point you towards the heritage sites that must be seen, and the little-known, scarcely visited places that you will be thrilled to find for yourself. We have taken the country region by region, and tried to tell the whole island's history through the peculiarities of particular places. Thus, in each region the antiquarian and the contemporary jostle each other, the old history and the history that is still in the making.

We hope thereby to show you and tell you some of the things only a local can know, the intimate details of the everyday that reveal the country's soul. It might be an inscription on a stone, a quotation from a poem, a story from the newspaper, a chance acquaintance on the road, a sudden revelation in the pub. These epiphanies, to use the Joycean word, can often say more than a thousand pages of scholarly explanation ever could.

For the best perspective on Ireland is the local one. This has been the making of many of our great writers: the Dublin of James Joyce was, in one sense, a metropolis – the fifth city of Christendom as he never tired of calling it – but, with a population of only 300 000 at the beginning of the 20th century, it was also a village and could readily be encompassed, as it was by him, in one day's peregrination. In the 1950s Patrick Kavanagh made County Monaghan his universe, as John B. Keane has the Kerry of today, for in these small places they have found all the imaginative sustenance an artist needs. Seamus Heaney has Ardboe, Kate O'Brien Limerick, W.B. Yeats Sligo, Sean O'Faolain Cork, Edna O'Brien Clare, and Roddy Doyle the suburbs of Dublin. Even the most sophisticated of our expatriate greats – Oscar Wilde, who made London high society his parish, George Bernard Shaw, who found his congregation in the theatre, and Samuel Beckett, who placed his famous tramps in the middle of a Wicklow bog – have known how to recreate the distinctive intimacy and directness that are essential Irish traits; the result of the smallness of the place and the bigness of imagination it has engendered.

Apart from the enduring works of these men and women, there is a rich literature of the local all over Ireland. In small town bookshops and newsagents, even in the butcher's and the grocer's, you will find booklets on proud display that describe the immediate area or some aspect of its history and traditions. If you stop to talk to a farmer in a field or a woman in a shop, fall into conversation with a sage in a pub or a priest on his rounds, they will all have some story to tell or some site to show you that will illuminate that particular place. The people of Ireland treasure the most minute details of her history, both the big events that decided national destinies and the doings of more local heroes and villains whose fame does not extend beyond the parish boundaries. Irish folklore, both the epic sort of the early Gaelic tales and the more domestic kind that is conjured out of the quotidian, remains the birthright of a people who have always liked to talk and to hear other people talking.

Not surprisingly, Ireland is well endowed with local museums that are always worth a visit, especially the more eccentric ones run as much on amateur zeal as professional know-how. Some of the outstanding historic sites have recently had interpretative centres grafted on to them, which prepare the visitor for the wonder they are about to see and the knowledge they are about to receive. Yet the most moving experiences may come from visits to places which have no more than a small, weather-worn plaque proclaiming them national monuments, and little else to intrude between you and the pure experience. Here you can be alone with the place, and with the people who made it.

For all that Ireland's land area makes it one of the smallest countries in Europe, it has managed to pack and preserve a lot of past within its stormy shores. Our island's geographical situation has at different times placed it at the centre or at the edge of things. Hence our history, and our society indeed, are more complex than is often credited. This is perhaps why debate on contemporary moral issues, with which the Irish newspapers and airwaves are full to overbrimming, is conducted with all the vigour and viciousness of a family that is not yet quite done growing up. Through the great changes of the last couple of decades – as exemplified in the election of a liberal socialist as the first female President of the Republic – a new *modus vivendi* is emerging that will allow us all, progressives and regressives, Catholics and Protestants, atheists and dissenters, rock 'n' roll and country and western fans, to share the same island.

While Ireland is not one of the richest countries of the world in terms of its Gross National Product, it has always been one of the most resilient in making a virtue of poverty and doing the best with what resources there are. For all that both parts of the country are now well and truly in the consumerist mainstream of the European Community, there is still a great respect here for things like fresh air, clean water, uncluttered landscapes, good company on a day out, a song well sung, old friendships – all the honest pleasures that an easy-going place affords.

Emigration has made Ireland's people one of the most dispersed on the planet, but deep bonds tie all its sons and daughters, grandsons and granddaughters, unto many generations, back to the motherland. Ireland is a way of life you absorb not only from living here, but from all the songs and stories and nostalgia in which the memory of it is steeped. For those who have never been here but still claim Irish ancestry, who now number in their tens of millions throughout the world, Ireland is a *Tir na nOg*, an island of eternal youth, a free-floating fantasy that still has room for all our dreams.

Just as we have become restless travellers in the great world, at home, too, we are still discovering the island we inhabit. In the old days you went away to 'Amerikay' and never returned. Nowadays emigrants come and go with the jumbos and the ferry boats that they use like their parents' generation used buses. When we do return we travel in our own country with the eagerness with which we explore our countries of adoption.

All of the present writers have travelled widely in the world beyond Ireland's shores. We bring to our homeplaces the perceptions of returned wanderers. All of our stories are different, written from different points of view, but together, we hope, they tell as much of the real story as a real traveller needs to know – enough to pass yourself, as they say.

1 Dublin and The Pale

Rosita Boland

COUNTIES

DUBLIN

WICKLOW

KILDARE

MEATH

LOUTH

Dublin is a city folded under the seagull's wing. These raucous scavengers scour its salt-rimed streets day and night, foraging in all the broad sweep where the Liffey washes granite silt out into the bay that Bray Head and the Hill of Howth embrace with open arms.

The Irish Sea forms both boundary and gateway to the capital of Ireland. The Vikings were the first to settle Dublin as a frontier port at the end of their long sea road. Ever since, the sea has lapped within the collective consciousness of its inhabitants: its diverse currents and influences can be heard in their voices, and descried in their faces, the colour of their hair, their names and their genealogies.

Yet Dublin as capital is also very much open to the interior of the island. The flagship Eason's bookshop and newsagency on O'Connell Street stocks over seventy provincial newspapers. The names of these papers offer clues to their origins, ranging from the *Clare Champion* to the *Donegal Democrat*, from *Kerry's Eye* to the *Tuam Herald*. Every Friday there is a mini exodus as scores of buses and trains travel out of Dublin, bringing country people back home. Such commuting between urban and rural Ireland makes Dublin a city very much attuned to the rest of the country.

What makes a true Dubliner? Those who have been born within the circumference of the two canals lay rightful claim to the title, even to unbroken lineage with Molly Malone herself, yet, eavesdropping on Dublin streets, an attentive ear will quickly detect a surprising variety of accents for such a small city. Waves of migrants from the Irish countryside have contributed their own local rhythms and pronunciation to the making of a Dublin voice. In turn, the Dubliners, or 'Jackeens', coined the word 'Culchie' to describe the migrants. It seems the word may derive from 'agriculture' since most of the migrants came from a farming background. It is suggested that 'Jackeen' denotes the common man, Jack, with the diminutive 'een' added to give a note of cosy disdain.

And yet for the Dubliners who stay, the city has a vibrancy and texture which belies its size. The centre is compact enough to be explored on Shanks's mare. In the street names, Irish history achieves an easy unity. O'Connell, Parnell, Pearse and MacDermott are commemorated in the same white lettering on a green background as the Duke of Grafton, King George and Queen Anne.

Dublin is a city of one million people in an island population of five million. People in the public eye are far more visible here than in other capitals. It is not unusual to see a government minister strolling down Grafton Street or a famous rock and roll star standing in South Anne Street having a chat with friends. The city is small and intimate and yet has the buzz of a metropolis, with stories and gossip harvested daily from a wild and unruly grapevine. Governments change because of a whisper passed through the streets and open secrets sparkle in the weekend papers. Within a few days, a visitor can experience a sharp sense of belonging in the city as faces in the crowd appear and reappear, giving a sense of *déjà vu*.

The Customs House dominates the tidal reaches of the River Liffey, Dublin City.

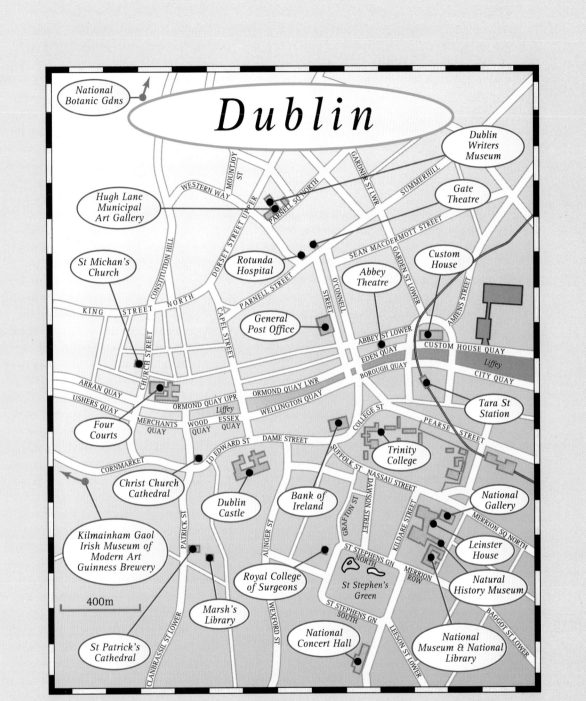

All map artwork by Drawing Attention © Guinness Publishing

'The Medieval Town in the Modern City' is the name of an intriguing map which shows the original boundaries of the capital superimposed over the city centre of today. In this *trompe l'oeil*, the medieval town emerges in vivid colours from the muted monotone of the modern city, seeming more like the blueprint for a new development than an informed guess at the layout of the first settlement. What is most startling in the difference between these two Dublins is how much wider the River Liffey was a thousand years ago. Among the first rules of Trinity College, Dublin, was one forbidding undergraduates from diving into the river off the college walls. The Liffey is now a long way from Trinity's hallowed walls, safely restrained within its narrow quays. When James Joyce (1882–1941) came to write *Finnegans Wake*, he also superimposed the ancient river on to the modern, and a purely Dublin goddess was born – Anna Livia Plurabelle – wise, loquacious and unfathomable. In medieval times there existed a large network of overground tributaries to the Liffey, including the aptly named Poddle, which now is almost completely culverted beneath the city. The underside of Dublin is only vaguely mapped and continues to hold its own secrets.

When the Vikings first settled on the river's banks in the latter part of the ninth century, they chose a site east of an ancient crossing place which gives Dublin its Gaelic name, Baile Átha Cliath, or 'the town of the ford of the hurdles' from the rough wooden stakes that would have made the Liffey crossable. Today you can visit this place just west of Father Matthew Bridge and imagine the Norsemen's longships swaying on the water like sea creatures from another realm.

At the junction of Hawkins Street and Townsend Street there stands a small monument with two Viking faces carved on the stone base. One stares outwards to the river, the other is turned inland to the city. On this spot the Vikings erected a *steyne* or standing stone to mark the first place they landed. Thirteen feet high, the stone stood as a testimony to their might and right until the 17th century, when it disappeared.

From Dublin the invaders sent out raiding parties across the country, sacking monasteries and looting villages. In 902 a brief respite from the Viking menace was gained by an alliance of Irish kings in battle. Then, in 918, the dreaded longships sailed into Dublin Bay once more. This time the Vikings were not to be banished. The Battle of Dublin in 919 was a decisive victory for the seafarers, a victory they consolidated by fortifying the city. Their stronghold was moved to the strategic high ground on which Christ Church Cathedral is now situated. From here any threat of attack could be easily spied long before it became dangerous. Formidable battlements were built along the Poddle and the Liffey – which at that time flowed inwards as far as Fleet Street on the southern bank. A large pool formed at the bottom of the hill, where Liffey and Poddle met. Its water must either have been dark in colour or a place of murky happenings, because the name given to it was the black pool or *dubh linn*. These two words elided to form the name Dublin.

The Viking fort was thus protected on three sides by water and, on the fourth, a steep embankment guarded against attack from the rear. Additional protection was given by an inner wall that ran east-west through the settlement. This was refortified many times over the ensuing centuries. Within these walls, the Vikings created the diminutive nucleus of what is now a sprawling, modern city whose suburbs extend miles south to Loughlinstown, west to Tallaght and Blanchardstown and north to Santry.

Today the walls of this original enclave are mapped out by stone markers in the area of Dublin Castle, Wood Quay, Christ Church and Cook Street. Each marker carries a bronze plaque with a plan of how the walls fit into today's city. An afternoon spent tracing the outline of the citadel brings the lost world of the Vikings to life.

Excavations by the Office of Public Works and the National Museum in the 1970s uncovered so much of Viking Dublin that it would have been possible to reconstruct some of the post and wattle houses and create an open air museum *in situ*. However,

Christ Church Cathedral, built on the site of Dublin's earliest church.

bureaucracy prevailed over history and Dublin Corporation remained determined that Wood Quay would be the site for its new Civic Offices. The decision could hardly have been more controversial. Thousands took to the streets in protest but the Corporation went ahead, cementing over the excavations and building two of the anticipated four tower blocks on the site, with the rest being added in the 1990s. The grey functional buildings obscure a fine view of the cathedral from the north side of the Liffey. Designed by Sam Stephenson and nicknamed 'The Bunkers', the towers hold the dubious distinction of being the most disliked buildings in Dublin, if not in Ireland. It is a pity that such unromantic buildings be allowed to squat above Fishamble Street, a street where, in 1742, Handel's *Messiah* first stirred the air.

Yet there is one poetic artefact hidden away in the new Wood Quay. Shored up in the car park beneath Block 2, a piece of the old city wall stands testimony to the perseverance of the original Dubliners. Two other fragments of the original walls remain. One can be found on Cook Street, although this has been so heavily restored that it has lost much of its mystery. The second lies within the precinct of Dublin Castle and is by far the more remarkable. When the castle was built in the early 13th century, it was cannily positioned on the south bank where the Poddle joined the main river so that the rivers might afford protection on two sides. A moat along the remaining two sides, with stout towers at each of the four corners, completed the defences.

During excavations at the Powder Tower in 1986 it became apparent that its builders had used a pre-existing stone embankment as part of the foundations. This Viking bank is the only one of its kind, as all those uncovered at Wood Quay were made of earth. Also found in the excavations was part of the original moat and the third extant piece of the city walls. Descend beneath the Powder Tower and you will find yourself in a dim, cool cavern crisscrossed by the original stonework of the city (a suitable place to revel in the mystery of Dublin's beginnings). The Poddle still seeps through a tall stone arch that must have been a gateway for small boats carrying provisions upriver to the castle. The steps in the moat wall at which they docked can still be seen from the metal walkways suspended above the site.

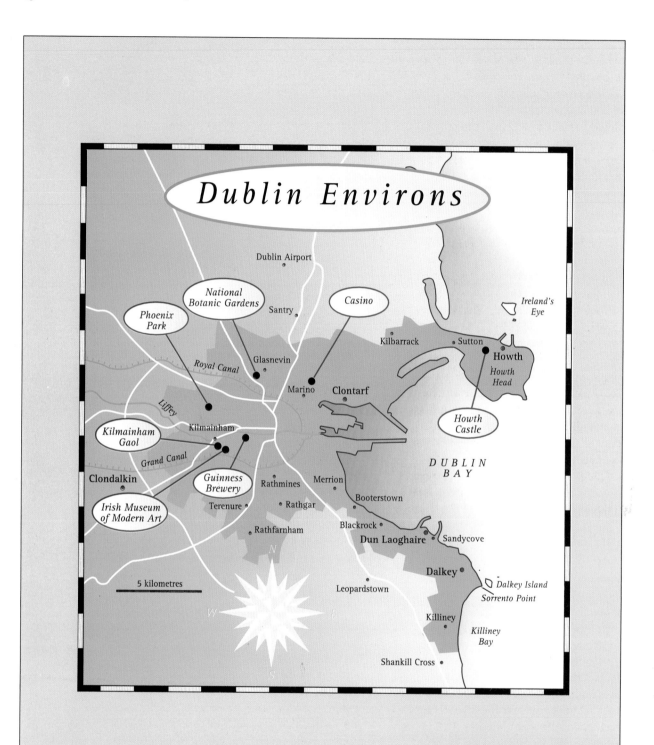

Dublin Environs

Dublin Airport

National Botanic Gardens

Casino

Ireland's Eye

Phoenix Park

Santry

Kilbarrack

Sutton

Howth

Royal Canal

Glasnevin

Howth Head

Liffey

Marino

Clontarf

Kilmainham

Howth Castle

Kilmainham Gaol

Grand Canal

DUBLIN BAY

Clondalkin

Guinness Brewery

Rathmines

Merrion

Booterstown

Irish Museum of Modern Art

Terenure

Rathgar

Blackrock

Sandycove

Rathfarnham

Dun Laoghaire

Dalkey

Dalkey Island

Sorrento Point

5 kilometres

Leopardstown

Killiney

Killiney Bay

Shankill Cross

N
W
E
S

During the excavations of Wood Quay, the remains of over two hundred houses started to emerge from the heavy clay soil. Also discovered were utensils, jewellery, weapons, toys and shoes, things discarded or lost over the ages that revealed the intimate details of the Vikings' rough-and-ready lives in simple, straw-thatched buildings. It seems the foundations were so shallow that, when a house fell down, another would be built directly over it. On one site in Fishamble Street a dig revealed 13 different houses, built one on top of another like a collapsed structure of cards.

In the National Museum on Kildare Street, a profile of what each house looked like can be found along with other Viking relics. The exhibits are accompanied by descriptions of what each tool was used for and, over the course of a visit, a clear picture of the Viking civilisation emerges from the glass cases. Spaces and places may change beyond recognition but the leather boots and wooden combs, glass gaming pieces and beads provide tantalising and tangible links with the first inhabitants of Dublin.

Studying some of these findings, Seamus Heaney (1939–) ignites them into poetry in 'Viking Dublin: Trial Pieces':

> *And now we reach in*
> *for shards of the vertebrae,*
> *the ribs of hurdle,*
> *the mother-wet caches –*
>
> *and for this trial piece*
> *incised by a child,*
> *a longship, a buoyant*
> *migrant line.*

Dublin's first church was built in 1038 on the site in High Street which is now occupied by Christ Church Cathedral. However, the medieval churches of St Audoen's and St Michan's on Church Street are the oldest churches still in use. In the belfry of St Audoen's are the three most ancient bells in Ireland, dating from 1423. St Michan's was founded in 1095 and is the oldest building on the north side of the Liffey. Its squat, square tower is a local landmark and the vaults are famous for the strange preserving quality of the air. All the bodies interred here have

mummified naturally in the dry atmosphere and constant temperature.

Preserved in one of the vaults is an odd quartet. Parish records reveal that the oldest of them is a crusader who died 800 years ago. His companions, who joined him 400 years later, are said to be a nun – who reputedly lived for 111 years – a thief and a stranger. The nun's fingernails are still weirdly intact but the thief is missing a hand and both feet. It is thought they were cut off as a punishment for stealing.

Mummies preserved by the dry atmosphere in the vaults of St Michan's Church.

In the church itself can be found the organ Handel played while he was in Dublin. The front of the organ gallery displays a remarkable carving which features 17 musical instruments. From this single piece of oak emerge violins, flutes, trumpets, a mandolin and a harp. This last instrument is the symbol of Ireland and its music is soft as the mist that blows in from the sea. In the Harp Room in the National Museum, the ancient instruments are taken out from time to time and played to keep the strings and wood fluent with music. A tape recording of these strange recitals resounds through the air of the Harp Room like the lost songs of extinct birds.

As Dublin expanded beyond its walls, a second cathedral was required for its zealous citizens. In 1191 St Patrick's was built on what is now Patrick Street. A fierce rivalry sprung up between the two cathedrals. This was only ended in 1300 when a papal decree recognized Christ Church as having the superior claim. It is here that thousands of Dubliners gather each 31 December to hear the bells ring in the New Year.

After centuries of rebuilding, St Patrick's is now the largest church in Ireland, with the tallest spire in the country. Yet it is not for its architecture that St Patrick's is most famed but for its Dean, Jonathan Swift, who penned acerbic satires here between 1713 and 1745. Swift came to Dublin after failing to win the political commission he sought in England. The relationship between the author of *Gulliver's Travels* and his adopted city was a complex and fiercely ambivalent one – an ambivalence which is reflected in his most outrageous satire, *A Modest Proposal*, in which Swift proposed that Dublin's food shortages and overpopulation could be solved by selling babies for food. He is buried in the cathedral next to Stella (Esther Johnson), one of his two loves. Vanessa (Hester van Homrigh), his other love, is buried in St Andrew's Church on Suffolk Street. So great was the dislike Dubliners held for this 'other woman' that her grave is unmarked.

Tucked away behind St Patrick's Cathedral opposite the Choir School is Marsh's Library, the oldest public library in the country. This exquisite Queen Anne building dates from 1701 and has a stock of over 25 000 books. When Marsh's first opened, books were still rare and expensive and thus available to very few. Consequently, scholars and readers were locked into cages with the tomes they were studying, giving new meaning to the saying 'chained to your books'. Three of these strange cages still survive.

Rambling away from the cathedral across New Street, you find yourself in an area of small alleys and redbrick terraces called the Liberties – the first major expansion of the city beyond its walls – so called because it was then outside the city's jurisdiction. The tangle of streets, lanes and alleys form such an intricate pattern that a first-time explorer may need a ball of string to escape from the maze. The street names here read like a Dickensian litany: Back Lane, Black Pitts, Bull Alley, Copper Alley, Cornmarket, Cow Parlour, Golden Lane, Marrowbone Lane,

Marsh's, the oldest public library in Ireland, with its quaint 'reading cages'.

Ship Street, Skipper's Alley, Weaver's Square and Engine Alley. This last is so beautifully incongruous that one of Dublin's many rock bands took it as its name.

There remains a strong tradition of trade in the area, with the stalls lining Thomas Street selling everything from fruit and vegetables to china and shoes. The fish market is still here and nearby on Francis Street are the Iveagh Markets. This cavern of a building (another of the many built in this area through the benevolence of the Guinness family, one of whose aristocratic titles is Iveagh) overflows with bundles of old clothes and bric-a-brac. Armchairs with the stuffing spilling out at the seams may obscure beautiful, if battered, rosewood tables and Georgian dining chairs. This flea market was the bazaar in 'Araby', the first story in Joyce's *Dubliners*. The Joycean sixpence will have to be replaced by a shiny pound coin, but for that a frock-coat or a piece of frail and lovely china may be yours.

A far more raucous market can be found across the river in Moore Street. Every morning at five o'clock the women stallholders wheel their prams and barrows off to Smithfield Market to buy the day's supply of fruit and vegetables. By nine o'clock Moore Street is bustling with morning shoppers attracted by such cries as 'five for fifty the oranges' and 'cabbages, lovely cabbages'. The pitches are passed down from mother to daughter, and guarded fiercely. The quick witticisms and rainbow array of flowers, fruit and vegetables make a visit worthwhile, even if you are staying in a hotel and have no need of potatoes and turnips and carrots. If you are staying longer, it is better to establish patronage at one particular stall rather than spreading your buying power throughout the street, for, eager to keep your custom, an extra bunch of parsley or a choice lettuce may be added gratis to your shopping bag by the motherly dame in charge.

One of the most memorable things about Dublin is the wonderful smell that floats downriver when the prevailing wind blows from the west. It is strong and pleasant, lingering warm and thick in the air, a little like freshly brewed coffee. This is roasting barley and hops, the aroma that wafts from the immense Guinness Brewery at St James's Gate. The brewery was founded in 1759 by James Arthur Guinness to develop a recipe invented by his father when he was butler to the Archbishop of Meath. Guinness is now a word synonymous with Ireland. Its emblem of a harp is also the official symbol of the Irish government in what is a perhaps coincidental show of solidarity with the national drink. The brewery can produce around four million pints of Guinness a day and is the world's largest producer of stout. Purists argue that Guinness does not travel, and every initiate into its mysteries has his, and increasingly her, own opinion as to what constitutes a good pint. However, there is no doubt that the beer's home town of Dublin is the best place to sink a pint of 'plain'. Although Guinness is now produced using sophisticated modern machinery, the ingredients have not changed since the 18th century: hops, barley, yeast, malt and water are magicked into the distinctive black and white elixir that you are guaranteed to see on the counter of every Irish pub. The pub is the hearth of Ireland. It is here that people come to exchange news, listen to music and watch sporting events or theatre performances. Drink is important but the community is vital. Even in the relative sophistication of Ireland's capital, there are pubs to be found that would not look out of character in the smallest village.

The oldest pub in Dublin is the Brazen Head in Lower Bridge Street, which dates from 1668 but is built on the site of a 12th-century public house. The smallest pub is the Dawson Lounge, situated in a basement on Dawson Street. Each pub has its particular clientele: Mulligan's in Poolbeg Street is where journalists and printers converge from nearby newspaper offices; The Norseman in Temple Bar has an upbeat mixture of musicians and artists; Doheny and Nesbitt's on Lower Baggot Street is where poets and media celebrities exchange jokes with stray politicians and barristers. You should also look in on Kehoe's of South Anne Street, The International on Wicklow Street, The Palace in Fleet Street and Toner's of Lower Baggot Street. All of these have unique interiors that

have escaped modernisation and yet also managed to resist ossification as museum pieces, but there are hundreds of others which all have their own charm for their own devotees, who are fiercely loyal to their chosen chapel and its 'curates', an old Dublin word for 'barman'.

After having a drink in the Brazen Head, the historically inclined should wander up to nearby Dublin Castle. The castle has been extended and rebuilt over the centuries, so now the Castle Yard has an eclectic mix of Anglo-Norman and Georgian buildings. In the main building are the State Apartments which have recently been restored to their former splendour. Here, too, is St Patrick's Hall, where all the presidents of Ireland have been inaugurated. Their term of office is seven years, with a maximum of two terms being served by any one person. The inauguration in 1991 of Mary Robinson as Ireland's first woman President was a landmark in Irish history that sent waves of optimism throughout the country.

The first major public building to be built after Dublin Castle was Trinity College. It was established as All Hallows College in 1592 under charter from Queen Elizabeth I and remained a Protestant enclave until very recently. Nothing remains of the original college buildings today, but the space at the centre of Dublin that Trinity has always occupied is probably the most intellectually charged in the city, having absorbed 400 years of tutorials, scholarship and debate.

Anyone who has seen the film *Educating Rita* will recognise Trinity from the moment they set shoe on its cobblestones. College lore has it that a student overheard one such visitor exclaim, exasperated, 'with all the money in this place, you'd think they could afford to tarmacadam it!'

The oldest buildings on campus, the redbricked Rubrics on New Square, dating from 1712, are still in use as student rooms. The college buildings open to the public include the multi-denominational chapel, the Douglas Hyde Gallery of Modern Art, home to both national and international exhibitions, and the Long Room of the College Library. The best time to visit Trinity is during term when the torpor of the long summer vacation gives way to scurrying, vibrant undergraduate life and noticeboards are layered with a palimpsest of posters for plays, debates, parties and meetings, some of which are open to the general public.

Edmund Burke (1729–92), Oliver Goldsmith (1728–74), Bishop Berkeley (1685–1753),

The Long Room of the Old Library, Trinity College, home to the world-famous *Book of Kells*.

The entrance gate of Trinity College.

Jonathan Swift (1667–1745), John M. Synge (1871–1909) and Samuel Beckett (1906–89) were all alumni of Trinity. Perhaps the most appropriate – albeit inadvertent – tribute to such distinguished graduates is the lecture theatre known as the Samuel Beckett Room. This is a raw and windowless space, lit by fluorescent strip lights, strangely appropriate to the famous playwright of the absurd.

The most famous book in Ireland is on display in the Long Room of Trinity's Old Library. This is the *Book of Kells*, the Irish equivalent of the Louvre's *Mona Lisa*. This eighth-century manuscript contains the Gospels and was written by monks on thick vellum. It is illuminated throughout and capital letters are elaborately patterned with swirls of intricate tracery. Cavorting through the text are greyhounds, hares and strange creatures with a life purely in the imagination of those who drew them. The margins contain the occasional doodle or fragment of poetry, penned by a monk taking time off from the intricate calligraphy. The *Book of Kells* was rebound in the 1950s and split into four volumes, two of which are always on display. The mystery and beauty of *Kelly's Book*, as it is disrespectfully known to the students, are revealed by a careful attendant in white gloves turning one page a day.

The other main university is University College, Dublin, or UCD. Originally located on Earlsfort Terrace at the heart of the town, the campus moved to Belfield in the suburbs during the sixties. Built after a wave of student riots, the college buildings were designed to prevent large numbers of students assembling at a central point. It has a shallow lake set at the heart of the campus, rather than the usual quadrangle. The lollipop-shaped water tower of the college is a distinctive addition to the silhouette of Dublin's skyline.

UCD's most famous graduate is James Joyce (1882–1941), who scraped together the money to attend the university in its Earlsfort Terrace days. During his years of self-imposed exile, Joyce recreated Dublin in the pages of *Ulysses*, thereby making of the trivial and local incidents and characters of his hometown a universal city of all cities.

With his sight failing rapidly, Dublin's streets and voices in his memory became more real to him than the squares of Trieste, Paris and Zürich in which he lived. Fiction is now literally superimposed on the city, as a *Ulysses* trail has been marked out by bronze plaques, bearing quotations, set into the pavement at various key locations. On 16 June every year, hundreds of pilgrims take to the streets in Edwardian costume to retrace the fictional steps of Leopold Bloom and Stephen Dedalus as their paths crisscross the Dublin streets and watering holes whose immortality is now ensured.

Also on Bloomsday, readings are held at the Joyce Museum, a Martello tower in Sandycove a few miles south of the city. Despite the fact that Joyce spent less than a week here in 1904 as the guest of Oliver St John Gogarty (1878–1957), the building is now always called the Joyce Tower. On display in the museum are first editions of his work, letters and various belongings, such as a waistcoat with a few grains of tobacco speckling the button holes. Having climbed the narrow stone stairs, the panorama from the top of the windswept tower is the nearest you will get to a three-dimensional insight into the opening pages of *Ulysses*, one of the seminal books of the 20th century.

Dublin's reputation as a literary centre has spawned a large compendium of bookshops. From the long-standing Greene's of Clare Street with rare books squirrelled away in its upstairs rooms, to the lively Books Upstairs with its wide range of literary reviews, every taste and curiosity is catered for. Second-hand bookshops, beloved alike by impecunious student and bibliophile, crop up along the backstreets all over the city. The most charming location of any bookshop is the Winding Stair second-hand bookshop and café on Lower Ormond Quay. Here you can browse away peacefully or linger over a mug of coffee, contemplating the Ha'penny Bridge and the rooftops at the other side of the Liffey. These days you no longer have to pay the halfpenny toll demanded in 1816 when the bridge opened, which gave the bridge its name, though its real quaintness derives from its eccentric and distinctive ironwork.

Another worthwhile point on the literary pilgrimage is the Dublin Writers' Museum on Parnell Square. Opened in 1991, it is located in a restored Georgian house and has a wide range of writers' memorabilia on permanent display. You may also catch a reading by one of Ireland's standing army of poets, or join in a heated debate on the role of the writer in today's society, in the Writer's Centre next door.

Over the last decade, several old buildings in Dublin have been converted in this way, their solid structures having outlasted the functions for which they were once purpose-built. The most ambitious conversion has been that of turning the Royal Hospital at Kilmainham into the Irish Museum of Modern Art, known as IMMA for shortness and greater ease of memory. The building was originally erected as a home for retired soldiers in 1680 and was used as such until 1922. With the departure of the British Army, the Royal Hospital became a storeroom for the overflow from the National Museum. Maurice Craig, in his *Dublin 1660–1860*, wrote in 1952 that 'The latest tenant of the Hall is Queen Victoria in bronze from Leinster House, whom I found glaring out at me through a window the last time I visited the Hospital.' This same statue has travelled far since then: it was presented as a gift to the Australian people from the Irish people for the 1988 Bicentennial celebrations and can now be seen in Sydney, outside the Queen Victoria Buildings. Her Imperial Majesty, who still arouses controversy in Ireland, now resides on a plinth into which is set a piece of stone from Blarney Castle in a happy – if somewhat ironic – petrification of Anglo-Irish relations.

Now that the clutter of soldiers and museum pieces has been swept from the building, the Royal Hospital is home to modern artworks that are displayed in both the long corridors and in what were once the soldiers' bedrooms. This mixture of very fluid and very contained exhibition space gives a refreshingly flexible gallery space and allows a radical and challenging artistic programme that is always worth a visit.

The centre of Dublin as we know it today was primarily shaped during the 18th century. While Dublin is famous for its Georgian townhouses with their panelled doors and elaborate fanlights, the two most important single events in the development of the city's layout were the building of James Gandon's Custom House and the establishment of the Wide Streets Commissioners. Gandon's beautiful and palatial Custom House was completed in 1791. It replaced the old one which had been further upriver at Essex Quay. With this move, the focus of the city's commercial life shifted east to the dockside around these splendid colonnades and halls, where exporters and importers shuffled forms with His Majesty's custom officers. The building has recently been cleaned and its Portland stone gleams as whitely now as when Gandon himself first viewed his completed masterpiece.

The Martello tower in Sandycove, home to the Joyce Museum.

The knot of narrow streets which wound through Dublin was an affront to the Georgians who believed in elegant and classical proportions as the key to beauty. The Wide Street Commissioners set out to untangle the city and create the gracious boulevards of Parliament Street, Dame Street, O'Connell Street and the triangle of D'Olier and Westmoreland streets that now form the city's main axes. Apart from making the city a more spacious one to live in, this development effectively brought together the areas of expansion on both sides of the Liffey.

The Liffey has always been Dublin's unofficial equator. The popular fallacy is that the southside is pretentious and affluent and the northside is a rough diamond hewn out of poverty and native wit. Contributing to the endless and somewhat fruitless debate, the journalist John Waters has coined the phrase 'Dublin 4' to describe the influential middle class who supposedly reside in this southside postal district. His theory that the country is effectively governed by this elite has provoked much discussion and the phrase has now entered the public domain.

The Ha'penny Bridge spanning the River Liffey.

O'Connell Street was originally designed by Luke Gardiner as a leafy mall, a showpiece for one of the United Kingdom's most gracious Georgian cities. It is Dublin's widest street and still its main thoroughfare. It is wonderfully eclectic, with amusement arcades and fast-food outlets wedged between McDowell's Happy Ring House, the Gresham Hotel and other more venerable institutions. Notable buildings include Cleary's, Eason's, and the General Post Office, or GPO as it is always called. This was the first purpose-built post office in the British Isles. 'I'll meet you

under the clock at Clery's' has long been a phrase used by lovers and parents anxious to make a readily recognisable rendezvous with children getting their first taste of independence.

Up at the north end of O'Connell Street, on Parnell Square, is the Rotunda, erected in 1748 as the first purpose-built maternity hospital in the British Isles, which drew an income from the concert rooms that were built as part of it. Part of the concert rooms premises has become the Gate Theatre, founded by Micheál Mac Liammóir and Hilton Edwards, for long one of Dublin's premier playhouses and recently rescued from a slow decline to become, once again, a showplace for classic plays and the great European dramatic tradition.

When the term 'Georgian Dublin' is mentioned, the image conjured up in most minds is that of the grand residential squares built by the Protestant ascendancy: Merrion, Fitzwilliam, Mountjoy and Parnell Squares are all still impressively elegant if somewhat down at heel. Through the hard work of the Georgian Society and Students Against the Destruction of Dublin, attention is now being focused on restoring Mountjoy and Parnell Squares to their former glory. In spite of the fact that many of these houses were converted into flats and bedsits over the course of the last century, beautiful plasterwork and marble fireplaces still remain in many of them. It is often more informative to examine the back of these houses than the front since, to create a uniform impression, all the façades had to look the same even though they were often built at different times. The inventive architects found scope for individuality in other ways: idiosyncratic designs for doors, fanlights, and street furniture such as coal-holes and boot-scrapers distinguish one house from another.

One of the few original Georgian houses which the casual visitor can inspect is 29 Lower Fitzwilliam Street. The Electricity Supply Board, who own the building, have restored it as the typical merchant's home of its first owner, Olivia Beatty, and her three children. Everything in the house is on loan from other houses of the period or from the

National Museum. Stucco, floors, drapes and wallpaper are exact copies by modern craftsmen. It is a charming museum with everything on a manageable scale, from the kitchen through to the master bedrooms, making it seem a comfortable home rather than an imposing mansion.

A substantial number of the Georgian townhouses are now nearly derelict from years of neglect and Rachmanism. The ghosts of once-splendid houses line the streets parallel to O'Connell Street, kept alive by the frequent turnover of students and young people attracted by the low rent, who experience the romance of high ceilings and bare floorboards, of corniced plasterwork and shuttered windows – at least for as long as they can endure the cold that accompanies such cavernous rooms.

Stories about these houses infiltrate the city like urban myths. Henrietta Street was once the most coveted address in the city and is now a ragbag of a street where enormous Georgian houses survive in wildly different states of repair. A recent resident was rumoured to be stabling his horse in a top storey, much to the disbelief of all on the street, until the day the unfortunate beast jumped out through a window. One story that

is certainly true is of the young man who secretly built a plane in the bedroom of a rambling old house in South Frederick Street. It was only when he had to knock down part of a wall to remove the plane that his secret got out.

Recently, to add to the street mythology, a number of sculptures have appeared at various locations around the city. All of them have attracted comment and Dubliners have translated their official titles into wicked nicknames. Perhaps the oldest statue to have the popular honour of a nickname is that by Edward Delaney of Wolfe Tone which stands on the southwest corner of Stephen's Green. Behind Tone are a number of tall standing stones, thus the nickname of 'Tonehenge'. The first of the new wave of sculptures in the late 1980s was a piece called 'Anna Livia', or the Spirit of the Liffey, by Eamonn O'Doherty. Islanded in the middle of O'Connell Street, a strange woman in bronze reclines in the flowing water. This has been called variously 'The Floozie in the Jacuzzi', 'The Mot on the Pot' and 'The Hoor in the Sewer'. 'Floozie' and 'mot' are both Dublin argot, meaning loose woman and girlfriend respectively. Opposite the floozie, on the corner of North Earl Street, is a statue of James Joyce by

Georgian doorways in Dublin City.

Marjorie Fitzgibbon, looking preoccupied as he leans on his walking stick. This representation of the famous writer is known as 'The Prick with the Stick'. Close to the Ha'penny Bridge are the figures of two women with shopping bags, resting on a bench. This sculpture by Jackie McKenna is officially entitled 'Meeting Place' but is known to all as 'The Hags with the Bags'. At College Green is the ill-fated Molly Malone who, according to the street ballad, 'wheeled her wheelbarrow through streets broad and narrow' until she 'died of a fever'. Jeanne Rynhart's statue of Molly, complete with wheelbarrow and plunging cleavage, was instantly rechristened 'The Tart with the Cart'.

Leinster House, which is home to the Irish parliament, was originally built as a private house in 1748 for the Duke of Leinster and was the most extravagant city mansion of its time. Refurbishment under Charles Haughey's government earned the adjoining government buildings the nickname of 'Charlie's Palace' or 'Taj Mahaughey'.

The Irish parliament has two houses, Dáil Eireann, the House of Representatives, and Seanad Eireann, the Senate. The 166 Dáil members (Teachtai Dála) are voted in by the general electorate in 41 constituencies. Of the 60 members of the Seanad, six are elected by the universities, eleven by the Taoiseach and the remainder by the incoming Dáil and outgoing Seanad, County Councils and Borough Councils.

The three main political parties are Fianna Fáil, or soldiers of destiny, Fine Gael, or Irish family, and the Labour Party. The rest of the house is made up by Progressive Democrats, Independents, Democratic Left and Greens. In recent years, with no one political party gaining an overall majority, coalition governments have become an increasingly familiar phenomenon. Whichever party gains a majority then elects a Taoiseach or Prime Minister. General elections are held at least every five years.

Gathered around this redoubt of Irish politics in Leinster House are four treasure hoards: the National Library and National Museum on Kildare Street and the National Gallery and Natural History Museum on Merrion Street. You can obtain a visitor's day pass for the domed Reading Room of the library and thus gain access to the best collection of old newspapers and maps in the country, much perused by writers chasing scraps of information vital to their research and visitors trying to untangle their roots.

Across the way at the National Museum, there are pieces of jewellery from the Bronze Age and precious ecclesiastical objects from the eighth and ninth centuries. The Celtic collars, earrings, hair ornaments, dress fasteners and bracelets – golden jewellery that has been beaten, twisted and smelted into shapes that are perfect in their simplicity – wink and glint as brightly as the day they were first worn. The eighth-century Tara Brooch is the most famous of all the pieces; intricately decorated on both sides, it is the equivalent in metalwork to the delicate illuminations of the *Book of Kells*. Exhibitions of these unique wonders have travelled the world as 'Irish Gold' and 'The Treasures of Ireland'.

Much of what is to be seen in the museum was discovered in the bog, whose soft, peaty earth swallowed these secret hoards of chalices, pattens and pieces of jewellery that were buried in the bog for safekeeping, but for some reason never collected. Items drift to the surface of the earth every now and then, to be found by turf-cutters or farmers working the land. The spectacular Ardagh Chalice was found in this way. The most recent addition to the Museum Treasury, the Derrynaflan Chalice and Patten, was found in 1980 by the more modern device of a metal detector.

The interior of the Natural History Museum is a piece of pure Victoriana, all stout mahogany showcases, metal turnstiles and grilles in the ornately tiled floor. The stuffed animals are all so old that everything has faded to brown and grey. The giraffe, too large to fit into a case, has had the hide of its legs rubbed away by the exploratory hands of generations of curious children. The birds in glass cases on the top walkway create an exotic and wholly unexpected splash of colour, like the inhabitants of a silent, petrified woodland.

There are some extraordinary things to be seen in the museum – the blade of a swordfish that sliced through a piece of ship's timber; the well-worn clothes of Irish explorers; a fossilised bird's nest; row upon row of brightly coloured insects and reptiles preserved like strange jewels in old glass jars. Most curious of all is the bird's nest that was discovered sealed inside a tree trunk by someone who was chopping it up for firewood. A card explains: 'The nest was made by a Blue Tit and was also used by a Coal Tit. A little later the tree must have grown in such a way as to completely close the hole, leaving portions of the eggs of both species in the nest.'

In the National Gallery across the way, the rooms are decorated in colours as rich and glowing as those of the paintings they contain; a visual surfeit of crimson and burnt orange, aquamarine blue, tawny gold and emerald green. The colours in paintings by Goya, Fra Angelico and Rembrandt contrast with the soft hues of sea-washed landscapes and clouds in work by the Irish artists Paul Henry (1876–1958), Walter Osborne (1859–1903) and Sir John Lavery (1856–1941). Jack B. Yeats (1871–1957) has an entire room to himself, a strange deep pool of energy and changing light. A recent sensation has been the restoration and authentication of 'The Taking of Christ' by Caravaggio, now one of the gallery's chief treasures. Each January the gallery shows its collection of Turner watercolours. They can only be displayed for one month in winter, when the light is palest and will do the least damage to Turner's frail and beautiful work.

As well as the National Gallery and IMMA, there is also the Hugh Lane Municipal Gallery of Modern Art at Parnell Square North. Sir Hugh Lane's gift of 39 Impressionist paintings to help establish a gallery of modern art in Dublin had a complex history, provoking Yeats to write the bitter lines:

> *You gave, but will not give again*
> *Until enough of Paudeen's pence*
> *By Biddy's halfpennies have lain*
>
> *To be 'some sort of evidence',*
> *Before you'll put your guineas down*

> *That things it were a pride to give*
> *Are what the blind and ignorant town*
> *Imagine best to make it thrive.*
>
> *Your open hand but shows our loss*
> *For he knew better how to live.*
> *Let Paudeens play at pitch and toss,*
> *Look up in the sun's eye and give*
> *What the exultant heart calls good*
> *That some new day may breed the best*
> *Because you gave, not what they would,*
> *But the right twigs for an eagle's nest!*

When the *Lusitania* was torpedoed off the Old Head of Kinsale in 1915, Lane went down with it, leaving a controversial will behind him. He had bequeathed the paintings to 'the Nation'. But which nation? Ireland and England both claimed ownership, with the result that the Dublin and London national galleries each display half the collection and every few years swap the paintings, the most famous of which is Renoir's *Umbrellas*.

At the Hugh Lane you can find paintings by Manet, Monet, Degas, Renoir, Ingres, Whistler and Picasso along with those of contemporary Irish artists. Perhaps the most outstanding Irish exhibit is Harry Clarke's (1889–1931) astonishing stained-glass interpretation of Keats's 'The Eve of St Agnes'. Illuminated from behind, the intricately decorated pictures look more like precious jewellery than painted glass.

These days, giving the lie to the myth that the Irish are visually illiterate, there are as many artists as there are writers in Dublin, hence a number of galleries to rival the number of bookshops. Galleries to wander through, coveting and wishing your wallet were fatter, include the Kerlin, Rubicon, Taylor, Douglas Hyde, Project Arts Centre, City Arts Centre and Temple Bar. These galleries all display work by both established and emerging artists.

Other interesting buildings which survive from the Georgian period are the Four Courts on Inns Quay and the Bank of Ireland on College Green. The enormous rambling bank was Dublin's Parliament House until the 1800 Act of Union, when Ireland and Great Britain were united under a single London-based parliament. Since 1802 the Bank of Ireland has been conducting business within its marble halls, the hum of commerce echoing around lofty ceilings that were meant to ring with high oratory.

The Liffey bisects the city and the Royal and Grand Canals arc round it. Created in the 18th century as liquid roads for cargo to the midlands, the only traffic on the canals today is the occasional narrow-boat and families of swans, ducks and moorhens. As the poet Patrick Kavanagh (1904–67) wrote in celebration, the Grand Canal's green and shady tow-path is 'leafy-with-love'. Kavanagh lived nearby, at Pembroke Road, and found the canal a place of inspiration and joy. He is remembered by two benches on the canal banks. On one of these is a bronze, life-sized statue of the man himself, feet stretched out, arms folded and face preoccupied. Dubliners have given this work of art by John Coll the wryly affectionate nickname of 'The Crank on the Bank'.

Along with the canals, St Stephen's Green is one of the favourite strolling grounds in the city. Usually known as 'the Green', the park was a gift to the people from Arthur Guinness in 1880, a gift almost as popular with generations of Dubliners as the famous pint itself. The Green is the biggest and oldest of the city's central parks and is always a place of calm amid the city's traffic. Occasionally, the traffic will be held up by a sharp-eyed pedestrian who has spied a stray mother duck and her brood emerge from the park railings and wander in confusion across the road.

'Dublin', a well-known song enthuses, 'can be heaven with coffee at eleven and a stroll in Stephen's Green.' The coffee at eleven in the lyrics could well refer to the Dublin institution of Bewley's. There are a number of Bewley's Oriental Coffee Houses around the city: in South Great George's Street, Westmoreland Street, Mary Street and Grafton Street. All who spend time in Dublin have loyalty to one particular branch of Bewley's, but the flagship café on Grafton Street is a grand place to start exploring the manifold joys of the 'legendary, lofty, clattery café'.

The Grafton Street café spreads through several levels but the hub of activity is on the ground floor where it is always toasty-warm, with open fires blazing in winter, and myriad conversations humming through the air. The outstanding feature of this Bewley's is the stained-glass windows by Harry Clarke, whose vibrant tangle of birds, butterflies and flowers glows throughout the café.

Buskers in Grafton Street.

All the branches of Bewley's are renowned for their range of teas and coffees, the rich aromas of which are deliberately wafted out into the streets to tantalise the passer-by. Newspapers, chessboards and Scrabble can all be borrowed from behind the desks. The best thing about Bewley's is the unwritten rule that you will never be hassled to move on once you've finished eating or drinking. This is the place to come and gossip, play chess, work on your novel, write letters, read the paper, take stock or thaw out by the fire. As long as you sit there, no waitress will collect your drained cup or empty plate, which will sit before you as token of your immemorial right not to be moved.

For refreshments in a very different setting, afternoon tea overlooking the Green in the front hall of the Shelbourne Hotel is a must. The Waterford glass chandeliers, the comfortable armchairs and the exquisitely presented tea trays all give a sense of decadent occasion to the ancient institution of afternoon tea. Popular opinion has it that as much business is carried out by politicians in the Shelbourne Bar as in Dáil Eireann, a conveniently short amble away. The Shelbourne is also where many business people and lawyers do their wheeling and dealing, so that it always has about it a tantalising sense of important conversations being discreetly held just out of earshot.

Outside Bewley's the pedestrianised Grafton Street is Dublin's most chic shopping area, yet very much a street that still belongs to the people. Flower sellers, buskers, newspaper vendors, jewellery sellers and performance artists compete with each other for attention. Grafton Street absorbs all kinds of people and is the closest thing to a public stage that the city possesses.

The Phoenix Park is the largest green space in greater Dublin and one of the most extensive city parks in Europe. It was opened as a public park in 1747. Its boundary wall is seven miles long. Within its nearly 2000 acres are woods, ponds, pathways, fields and hollows; places to get lost in, and places to play games such as football, hurling, cricket and polo. The names of areas within the park are open invitations to be explored: Tinkler's

Path, the Hollow, the Furry Glen and the Wilderness.

The park has two distinctive landmarks. A giant cross soars surreally over the area known as Fifteen Acres. It was installed for a Papal Mass in 1979 and remains a memorial to that day when Pope John Paul II came to visit his enormous and enthusiastic Irish flock. The Wellington Testimonial, or the Obelisk as it is called, was erected in 1817 to honour the Duke of Wellington. It is said to be the tallest monument in Europe, standing at 205 feet. Beloved by children who scramble up its many sloping steps to gaze out over Dublin, the obelisk spikes the skyline and is the first landmark you see when approaching the city from the west.

As well as sheltering a herd of fallow deer, the park is home to the menagerie at Dublin Zoo, and you could well be serenaded on a morning jog by the distant roaring of lions or trumpeting of elephants. The zoo's most famous resident was the lion named Caibre which snarls at the beginning of every MGM movie.

Islanded within the park are the official residences of the President of Ireland and the American ambassador. Aras an Uachtaráin, the President's home, was originally built as a residence for the park ranger in 1751. In the 1780s the building was bought by the English government and converted into a summer house for the Lord Lieutenant. It thus became the Vice-regal Lodge, a title it bore for the next 150 years. Painted a dazzling white like its famous American counterpart, the Irish presidential palace has always been known simply as 'The Aras'.

From 1782 Grattan's parliament had ensured the Anglo-Irish ascendancy a substantial measure of political independence from the Crown. With the Act of Union, such independence came to an end. Irish domestic affairs were brought under Westminster's control and Dublin's 18th-century expansion was abruptly curtailed. The large landowners left the city they had constructed as their own for the brighter prospects of London; the fanlights and panelled doors fell into disrepair as the once elegant houses became tenements for the city's poor.

Walking into a Parnell Square house in the early part of this century, you would have seen a large family living in each of the rooms, with washing strung in lines from chandelier to window sash. Today this world of bittersweet laughter and hard endurance lives on in the plays of Sean O'Casey (1880–1964). Tuberculosis spread quickly in such cramped conditions and in the first decades of the 20th century Dublin had an infant mortality rate second only to Calcutta's. It was not until the Minister for Health, Noel Browne, introduced a TB eradication scheme in the 1950s that this disease was finally defeated.

The phrase 'England's disadvantage is Ireland's opportunity' once more rang true in the Easter Rising of 1916. Against the background of World War I, the Rising was born out of a combination of intrigue, poverty and desire for home rule independent from England. Several buildings in Dublin were seized by the Irish Volunteers, among them the Four Courts and, most famously, the GPO, the headquarters for the Rising. There was intense fighting in the city centre for five days. Many people died and several buildings were destroyed, but nobody really knows for certain how many were killed in the Rising. If you look up at the winged figure at the base of the Daniel O'Connell monument by John Henry Foley (1818–74) on O'Connell Street, you can see a tangible reminder of the fighting in the bullet hole one of the angels has through her breast.

The leaders of the Rising were all held at Kilmainham Jail. Fifteen of them, including Padraic Pearse, James Connolly and John MacBride, were later executed. Their 'blood sacrifice' was the subject of W.B. Yeats's celebrated poem 'Easter 1916'. The jail buildings have been preserved as a museum of the War of Independence. It is a horribly fascinating place, cold and echoing. You can peer into the cells in which these men spent their last night, and then walk through the yard where they were executed by firing squad.

Today the GPO forecourt is still an important space in the continuing history of Dublin. It is a meeting place for public rallies

The Daniel O'Connell monument on O'Connell Street.

and is also the starting point for marches through the city, so the building continues to have a social and political resonance. It is entirely fitting that a post office should be the centre stage of popular politics, for the Irish abroad have contributed much to the shape of our national identity.

There have been three renaissances in the country's literary history. The first was that of Gaelic bardic poetry written in the 16th and 17th centuries by the dispossessed Irish. The second was an 18th-century renaissance of philosophy and novel-writing by the English settler clan, and the third was the Gaelic revival which infused the rhythms of the Irish language into the literature of Hiberno-English. Lady Gregory (1859–1932), William Butler Yeats (1865–1939), George Moore (1852–1933) and Edward Martyn (1859–1923) turned to national legends such as the Cattle Raid of Cooley for inspiration. In the heroes Cuchulainn and Finn MacCumhaill, Yeats found an ennobling metaphor for the politically stable but dull years of the 1890s and early 1900s.

In 1904 the Abbey Theatre was founded as Ireland's National Theatre. Its stated policy was to stage only plays of direct Irish relevance, a policy which led to much discussion as to exactly what was 'Irish'. When W.B. Yeats met J.M. Synge living in Paris in search of inspiration, he curtly instructed him to go to the Aran Islands and write of what he found there. Out of this sojourn came *The Playboy of the Western World*, which became infamous on the opening night when the audience rioted, supposedly offended by a reference to Irish women 'standing in their shifts'. It is more likely that the idea of a small western community making a hero out of a man guilty of patricide was the cause of the offence. Sean O'Casey's *The Plough and the Stars* provoked equal controversy with its revisionist view of the all too recent Easter Rising.

New plays by Irish writers continue to be commissioned by the Abbey and the Irish theatre-going public continues its traditional love-hate relationship with its National Theatre. The present building on Lower Abbey Street dates from 1966 and houses two theatres. In the main auditorium, plays by established writers are performed. Downstairs, in the smaller Peacock, emerging talents are showcased. Vibrant new works in the last few years include Tom Murphy's *The Gigli Concert*, Frank McGuinness's *Observe the Sons of Ulster Marching Towards the Somme* and Sebastian Barry's *Prayers of Sherkin*. Brian Friel's *Dancing at Lughnasa* packed the theatre for months before going on to London's West End and New York's Broadway, where it was showered with awards.

In 1964 Dublin got its first and only high-rise building, Liberty Hall on Eden Quay, headquarters of the Irish Transport and General Workers Union, a soaring glass office block with a fluted green roof that looks like a modernised Japanese pagoda. It is still the tallest building in Dublin. Two years after it was built, the IRA blew up Nelson's Pillar on O'Connell Street. It was a curious way to mark the 50th anniversary of the Rising, since the Pillar had long been a landmark for Dubliners and is mentioned in countless novels and plays. It is one of those spaces in the cityscape that somehow continues to reverberate with associations and memories.

Another idiosyncratic addition to the Dublin skyline is the red- and white-striped chimneys of the ESB power station at Poolbeg. The tallest structure in the city at over 680 feet in height, Poolbeg is the last thing to disappear from sight on days when the sea mist drifts across Dublin Bay and the tang of salt is carried into the streets.

Dublin's fourth renaissance is in rock music. Thin Lizzy and U2 really put Dublin on the rock pilgrim's path, but the city's unofficial title of 'rock capital of the world' was conclusively established by a fictional band, The Commitments, heroes of a film scripted by Roddy Doyle, one of the new breed of Irish writers who describe the country and its people very much warts and all. Notable music venues include Whelan's of Wexford Street and the rough-and-tumble McGonagles of South Anne Street. The Tivoli in Francis Street and Place of Dance on Hawkins Street are recent additions to the city's night life.

A few years ago, David Bowie gave a surprise performance at a Blue Angels gig in The Baggot Inn. Similarly, The Hothouse Flowers, Christy Moore and Sinéad O'Connor have made unscheduled guest appearances at Mother Redcaps, Midnight at the Olympia and other venues throughout the city.

There is now a 'Rock and Stroll Tour' for dedicated 'musoes' to follow through the city. Places of rock-historical interest are marked by plaques in the shape of a record. Some are cheerfully tenuous in their interest: outside The Bad Ass Café in Crown Alley a plaque baldly states 'Sinéad O'Connor once waitressed here.'

Someone is always starting up a new band somewhere in Dublin: rock, traditional, jazz, techno or a combination of all these. Those who look like making it have to endure the inevitable pundits' verdict of 'the best Irish band since U2', a cliché as smothering as 'the best Irish poet since Yeats'.

Much of the musical and artistic life of the city now revolves around Temple Bar, a warren of streets between the Central Bank on Dame Street and the quays. This area has been rescued from a 1980s plan to transform it into a central bus station and is currently undergoing the most ambitious urban redevelopment undertaken in Dublin this century.

The Temple Bar project is both imaginative and exciting. Streets have been re-cobbled and the new Irish Film Centre has opened in the light and airy Quaker Meeting House on Eustace Street. There are plans to create living accommodation for two thousand people and to develop areas of wasteland into public spaces. Hyped as the Left Bank of Dublin, the ever-changing area is densely textured with offbeat shops, pubs, restaurants and galleries.

By 1996 Temple Bar will be resplendent with a mixture of inventive new buildings and streetscapes among its old alleys and pubs. It is already the alternative centre of Dublin with a wide variety of shops selling everything from comics to Venetian glass beads, from fishing rods to second-hand clothes, 60s records to the wildest shoes you'll find this side of San Francisco. On summer evenings the hippest cats in town can be found hanging out between The Temple Bar and The Norseman pubs.

Yet to get a complete sense of Dublin, you should journey outside the centre. Over the course of two generations, villages to the north and south have become Dublin suburbs, yet Dalkey, Rathfarnham, Balbriggan and Skerries have all preserved their own distinctive characters and are well worth exploring. Ireland's Eye and Dalkey Island, north and south of the bay, carry the silhouette of the soft Dublin mountains into the sea. Georgian streets direct the eye to magnificent vistas of Three Rock Mountain, the Sugarloaf and the glory of the Wicklow hills. The city escapes into this landscape, as the mountains and sea are never more than half-an-hour's drive from its centre.

At Glasnevin, on the banks of the Tolka, are the country's Botanical Gardens, founded by the Royal Dublin Society. In 1987 'the Big Storm' of Hurricane Charlie ripped through the grounds and uprooted swathes of fine trees. Despite this destruction by the wind, the gardens are still home to over twenty

thousand species of plants, flowers, trees and shrubs. Miniature gardens give a sense of intimacy to the whole and the rose, bog and water gardens all provide places of sanctuary from the city's bustle.

Richard Turner, who also designed the hothouses at London's Kew Gardens and the Botanic Gardens in Belfast, is the architect of the Great Palm House here, a beautiful kite-like structure of iron and glass. Entering it, the visitor is dwarfed by the tropical plants which press their huge leaves against the misty glass like the hands of some gigantic creature imploring to be let out.

Another architectural gem of the north side is the Casino at Marino, an elaborate *trompe l'oeil*. From the outside this Palladian building looks like one large room perched atop a flight of granite steps. Once inside it becomes apparent that there are two storeys, disguised in the façade by dummy windows. What looks from the outside like a folly turns out in the perfect proportions of the interior to be a sizeable house, with kitchens, pantry and wine cellars in the basement, study and saloon on the ground floor and bedrooms and dressing rooms on the first floor. Each unexpected room is small and exquisitely decorated. The house is alive with architectural tricks: the stone urns on the roof, for example, are really chimneys. This

The *trompe l'œil* façade of the Casino at Marino.

double-sided marvel was designed by Sir William Chambers and was constructed in 1762 from blueprints sent over by him from England. Originally the building was set amid rolling parkland, part of the Marino House estate, and the country residence of the Earl of Charlemont.

The extraordinary Chester Beatty Library and Gallery of Oriental Art has recently moved from Shrewsbury Road to Dublin Castle. Chester Beatty made his money in diamonds and his name by gathering one of the finest Islamic and Eastern manuscript collections in the world. The museum contains jade books from Japan, illuminated Books of Hours, Egyptian papyri and early manuscripts of the Koran. When he died in 1968 the fruits of his lifetime's passion were donated to the state along with the library building in which they used to be housed.

About a mile outside the fishing village of Malahide on the north coast of Dublin is Malahide Castle, an impressive mixture of medieval tower embellished with Gothic turrets. The castle was home to the Talbots from 1185 to 1973 when the last direct descendant of the family died. The main reception rooms are painted Tudor Orange, reflecting the family's loyalty to King William of Orange at the Battle of the Boyne.

Malahide Castle made sensational literary news in 1924 when a visiting American academic discovered bundles of letters written by James Boswell, the biographer of Doctor Johnson, that had been in the family for years. They were found stuffed into an ebony cabinet as part of the flotsam and jetsam that accumulates over the centuries in big houses.

Nearby Laytown Strand resembles a small village in summer with row upon row of parked cars guarding each picnic spot. In July or August, depending on when the tide is lowest, horse races are held along the beach. It is quite a carnival, with a 'Nuns Only' race which sees habits and prayers flying as the sisters gallop along the wide sands.

Hikers should don their backpacks and strike out along the Wicklow Way, Ireland's first official trail. It winds for over eighty miles along bridle paths and old military roads through the Sally Gap and past Lugnaquilla. The starting point is Marley Park in Rathfarnham. Three or four exhilarating days later you should arrive in Clonegal on the Wexford border.

Wicklow is known as 'the Garden of Ireland', not because of its domesticity but because of the huge variety of landscapes it contains. Expanses of bog cover the higher slopes of the mountains in ever-changing hues. In autumn, as the grasses wither and the heather blazes, the Featherbed and Sally Gap glow purple and gold like the threads of a glorious tweed. The mountain tarns of Lough Bray and Lough Tay are so cold and deep it is said that any swimmer rash enough to venture into them will be pulled down by a hand from below. In the valleys, ruined castles provide shelter for the hardy local breed of sheep and the tea-coloured rivers are teeming with trout. It is this mercurial Wicklow landscape that fascinated Synge and was as much a source of inspiration to him as the Aran Islands. In the Shadow of the Glen, an uncomfortable, brooding morass of a play, captures superbly the peculiar mystery and energy of the place.

The flinty character of Wicklow granite must have inspired the hermit St Kevin to situate his sixth-century monastery in remote and lovely Glendalough. This 'Valley of the Two Lakes' still inspires poetry such as Omeros, the epic poem by Nobel prizewinner Derek Walcott, who was born in St Lucia in the Caribbean. The round tower, built as a refuge from the Vikings who looted Glendalough at intervals from the ninth century onwards, looks as if it has grown out of the very earth itself.

Close to the round tower is St Kevin's Church with a 12th-century bell tower projecting from its roof. The bell tower is oddly shaped and resembles a chimney stack, thus the colloquialism of St Kevin's Kitchen. This domestication of the ancient landscape extends to a cave, called St Kevin's Bed, hidden in the cliff above the upper lake, where St Kevin is said to have slept. Also overlooking the Upper Lake is a small restored oratory, Teampull na Sceilge or 'the Church of the Rock'. The Bed and oratory are

THE DART LINE

The DART line (short for Dublin Area Rapid Transit) runs between Bray and Howth. It is a good way to see the wide sweep of Dublin Bay and all the varied landscapes it embraces, including Killiney Bay which is often compared to the Bay of Naples on account of the villas scattered along the hillsides. Here, the vast horizon of sea and sky stretches out beside you and changes by the minute as the sun is reflected off the water and the clouds.

Those who do not have to make the 9 o'clock start in the morning should take time to walk along the path from Balscadden Bay to Sutton around Howth Head, where fulmars and kittiwakes wheel along the cliffs below you and Dublin's seafront stretches as a backdrop to the passage of yachts and cargo ships making their slow way into the city's docks. To the north you may see the faint outlines of the Mourne Mountains, grazing the horizon beyond Dundalk. On an exceptionally clear day you may be able to make out the mountains of Wales to the east.

Howth Castle has been in the St Lawrence family for around eight hundred years and is still their private residence. The gardens should be visited in May, the time of year when Molly declared her assent to Leopold Bloom – 'yes, I will yes, yes' – amid the famous rhododendron groves.

Travelling back into the city, the DART line passes through the functional station of Kilbarrack which has found unexpected fame as the fictional station for Barrytown in Roddy Doyle's trilogy of novels, and was used in the movie of *The Commitments*.

To the south of the city, the line runs alongside the bird sanctuary at Booterstown Marsh. Oystercatchers, redshanks, curlews and other waders winter here, while kingfishers dart along the streams inland. Charts on the station platform help passengers to identify the birds that fly past while they are waiting for the train.

Dún Laoghaire is a town in its own right yet, since it is physically so close to Dublin city, has about it the strange, somewhat insubstantial atmosphere shared by towns on the peripheries of cities. Dún Laoghaire, or Kingstown as it was named under British rule, was originally a seaside resort where wealthy Victorians would come to take the waters. At weekends families converge to stroll along the piers that jut out into Dublin Bay. The Maritime Museum on Haigh Terrace documents Dún Laoghaire's long maritime tradition.

Apart from the James Joyce tower, Sandycove's other main attraction is the Forty Foot, a bastion of male privilege. This is where Buck Mulligan and countless other men since have taken their constitutional dip in the nip. Of recent years some brave women have also been asserting their right to plunge nude into the icy Irish Sea.

Dalkey is the next stop and a good place from which to walk along the cliff path to Killiney or Shankill stations. Dalkey feels like a smugglers' village, full of alleys and stone cottages. Fish can be bought straight from the trawlers at Bulloch Harbour and boats hired at nearby Coliemore to bring you to the small church at Dalkey Island.

From Sorrento Terrace, one of the most desirable addresses in Dublin, drawing room windows open out onto Bray Head, which rests like the snout of a sleeping whale on the boundary between counties Dublin and Wicklow. Inland, the peak topped with white quartzite is called the Sugarloaf, from the time when sugar was sold in tall cones from which pieces would be chipped when needed.

Ballad singing at the Abbey Tavern in Howth, County Dublin.

accessible by boat; passage over water seems to have been a ritual of monastic settlement.

St Kevin himself, if legends evolve from truth at all, may have been a deeply religious man but seems to have been less than enamoured of womankind. An enduring legend is that of a young woman who climbed up to this cave to plead with the hermit to be her lover. She found him there at prayer but, enraged by her shameless temerity, St Kevin shoved her into the lake below. This ambivalent relationship between Catholic church and sexual morality still persists in Ireland today.

Along the Wicklow rivers, the Protestant Ascendancy, the ruling class in Ireland during the centuries of British rule, built their stately residences. In the grounds of these houses you will appreciate how the county got its sobriquet as the 'Garden of Ireland'. Avondale, once the seat of Charles Stewart Parnell (1846–91), the Chief who galvanised the Irish Home Rule movement in the 1880s, is now owned by the Forestry Commission and has a magnificent arboretum, with gigantic Californian redwoods among its specimens.

The Sugarloaf mountain rises above the picturesque gardens at Powerscourt, Enniskerry, County Wicklow.

The Powerscourt estate at Enniskerry has gardens overlooking the adjoining hills. Designed by Richard Cassells in 1740, the house was gutted by fire in 1974 and now only its shell remains. Terraces run down from the façade to the huge lilypond, bedecked with fountains and balustrades beyond which the Sugarloaf rises like a heroic monument to Cassells' genius. Grottoes, ornate statues, a walled garden and a Japanese garden contrast strikingly with the wild mountain slopes. Four miles away, Powerscourt waterfall tumbles down over a cataract of fool's gold. It is the highest waterfall in Ireland and one of the county's most spectacular sights.

Less formal than those at Powerscourt, Mount Usher Gardens near Ashford seem to have been allowed to sprawl naturally along the Vartry river, though there is in fact an underlying structure that keeps the first owner's passion for collecting new species under check. This garden is at its most resplendent in spring, when thousands of naturalised bulbs set off the nascent leaves of the hundreds of varieties of shrubs and trees.

Russborough House near Blessington is a fine Palladian house, renowned for its collection of paintings by Goya, Velázquez, Gainsborough, Murillo, Rubens, Vermeer and other old masters. Most of them were left to the nation by Sir Alfred Beit (1903–94), whose family amassed a large fortune mining diamonds in South Africa in the late 19th century. Sadly, most Irish people associate Russborough with two famous robberies. Sixteen paintings slashed out of their frames in 1974 were recovered, but in 1980 part of the collection was raided again and only some of them have been recovered so far.

The most imposing house in Ireland is Castletown House, a stone extravaganza with palatial wings. It was built in 1722 for William Conolly and modelled on an Italian palace. Conolly was Speaker of the Irish House of Commons and the richest man in the country at the time. Glass chandeliers were imported from Venice and the famous Francini brothers commissioned to do the plasterwork. Rescued from almost certain destruction in 1967 by the Irish Georgian

The Palladian
splendours of
Russborough House,
County Wicklow.

Society, who kept it going by every means, including annual charity dances held in the capacious ballroom, it has now been handed over to the state. Throughout the summer, classical concerts take place in the house, part of the Music in Great Irish Houses series.

Two miles away is Conolly's Folly, a 140-foot-high crazy display of obelisks, arches and urns that balance on top of each other. Built under the direction of Lady Louisa Conolly in 1739, it was and is an entirely useless structure, one of the many follies in Ireland whose construction provided much needed wages for local men in hard times, even before the Great Famine.

The owners of these great houses would have gone often to the Curragh at Kildare, a place-name synonymous with horses and horse-racing, where there are two racecourses, the Curragh and Punchestown. The flat season opens in April and reaches a climax in June with the Irish Derby.

A day at the races is the best way to get a complete picture of Dublin society. Men in trilby hats and Church's shoes step gingerly across the turf carrying race cards in their right hands, binoculars in their left. Women in preposterous hats stand around the paddock assessing the condition of the horses as they parade past. Small children scuffle along with pages of *The Field* tucked underneath their elbows, eyes peeled for accidentally discarded winning slips. Self-important bookies stand around the ring, fluttering their cards at the punters and shouting 'Twenty to one the field'; outside, hefty women sit on orange crates and call 'Race card, race rating'. These chants echo weekly from Leopardstown to Fairyhouse, from Navan to the Curragh, and around the dozens of other racecourses that all have their own festivals throughout the long season.

It is said in a legend that St Bridget was given as much land as her cloak could cover. The wily woman laid her cloak down on a small portion of the Curragh, whereupon the garment billowed over the entire plain. This is the centre of the horsebreeding industry in Ireland, of which the National Stud is the showpiece. It was from here that the famous racehorse Shergar, winner of both the Irish and Epsom Derbies, was stolen. Shergar's fate is still a mystery. Despite a nationwide search for many weeks, no trace of the wonder-horse was ever found. After his disappearance, a competition was held to choose a name for the last foal he sired: the winning entry was the prosaic and predictable 'Missing Poppa'.

About an hour's drive north of Dublin lies the historically rich Boyne Valley. Here at Oldgrange, in 1690, possession of the English Crown was fought out between James II and William of Orange. The latter emerged victorious, a victory still celebrated every Twelfth of July by the Orange Order in Northern Ireland.

West of the battle site and close to the course of the Boyne is an extraordinary concentration of over forty prehistoric passage tombs, with the three best known being Newgrange, Dowth and Knowth. These tombs are part of a network of satellite tombs, some of which have been dismantled over the centuries, their stones being used to rebuild boundary walls in nearby fields.

Older than the pyramids, Newgrange is a passage tomb with three burial chambers. However, such is the size and complexity of the structure that it is suggested these were more than just graves, and were in fact temples for some inauguration or ritual. The mound that swells up from the green and fertile landscape has an astonishing retaining wall with a façade of white quartz. The nearest source for the quartz is Wicklow, which means that it must have been brought here by a highly organised transport system. The water-rolled granite could be from Dundalk or even the Mourne Mountains, again indicating a great feat of carrying to get it here. The Irish name for quartz is *clochan na liath* (sun-stone) and the glittering circle of Newgrange would have been visible for miles. The granite stones look like blank

dark eyes. Possibly they once formed a pattern but there is now no way of discovering what, if any, this was and so they have been replaced at random.

Many of the kerbstones that necklace the mound are decorated, most notably the entrance stone. Spirals, chevrons, circles, lozenges and triangles are carved into the rock. These continue to mystify archaeologists, who speculate about the meaning of these symbols that are older than any form of writing. Some of the stones weigh as much as ten tons. It is thought they were brought to the site on log rollers, necessitating a staggering amount of manpower.

Throughout the interior of the passage, there are more decorated stones. Some of these are visible; some are concealed, decorated side furthermost. This has given rise to the theory that the stones were decorated for the eyes of a God, not for those of man.

Over the entrance is a lightbox, whose function has only recently been discovered. On the morning of the winter solstice and for a few mornings either side of 21 December, the sun's rays are aligned with the entrance, so that the sun gleams in through the lightbox and down the slanting passage, filling it with a powerful ancient magic that marks the return of life after the darkness of winter. For visitors, at other times of the year, the solstice effect is simulated by turning off the lights within the tomb, allowing absolute darkness to seep throughout. In that total blackness, it becomes possible to forget that

The decorated entrance stone at the Neolithic site of Newgrange, County Meath.

there are other people close by. A lamp is turned on at the entrance to the passage and as it glows, it slowly becomes possible to believe one is witnessing a prehistoric dawn.

Stone structures created by man are an inherent part of the Irish landscape. The monastic site of Monasterboice in County Louth alone has the remains of two churches, a round tower, an ancient sundial and three high crosses. In a time when few people could read and write in Ireland, the two faces of high crosses were divided into panels decorated with carvings depicting scenes from the Bible, making the Christian story accessible to all. The clergy would have used the crosses to explain the Christian message, with the carvings an indelible reminder of their teaching. Amongst the scenes on Monasterboice's Cross of Muiredach are those of Eve tempting Adam, the Three Wise Men bearing gifts, and the Last Judgment. Carved deeply into the stone, the images on the Cross of Muiredach have weathered extraordinarily well, making it one of the best examples of an Irish high cross.

They belong in the open: to place them in a museum would be to take them out of context with their setting and thus to lose much of their meaning. Rooted in the earth like petrified trees, these stone crosses have survived a thousand years outdoors. They are as old as the city of Dublin itself.

The story of Ireland could be told through stone alone – the drystone walls that vein the country, the dolmens and passage graves, the castles, cottages and churches, the round towers, high crosses and the city walls.

But perhaps the truest experience of Ireland is one of return. Joyce and Beckett may have chosen exile, but today, as the poet Thomas Kinsella has commented, 'Irish writers no longer emigrate; they commute.' This observation is equally apt for most Irish people. In a country whose citizens have been crossing the water since time immemorial, homecoming and return is part of Irish life, and much of this to-ing and fro-ing passes through Dublin and its hinterland, enriching them with the traveller's age-old store and lore.

MUSTS IN DUBLIN AND THE PALE

* Ryan's of Parkgate Street, one of the finest Victorian pubs, just across the river from the Guinness Brewery, guaranteeing a perfect pint, and just down the road from the Phoenix Park, for somewhere to walk it off.
* The trip by boat to Dalkey Island for a picnic.
* Any Bewley's Café – now also available in Belfast, Cork, Galway, and the Dublin suburbs.
* The Clarence Hotel, U2 Prop., one of the most fashionable haunts in the city.
* Leo Burdock's Fish and Chip Shop, near Christ Church Cathedral.
* The Dublin Corporation Fruit and Vegetable Market, its early-opening pubs and its rough-and-ready eating houses.
* The Guinness Hop Store and Brewery.
* The National Concert Hall, Earlsfort Terrace, for anything from pop to classical music.
* The Iveagh Gardens, hidden away behind the Concert Hall. An achievement just to find and enter.
* The Dublin Sculpture Trail, guides available from tourist offices, or just to come across along the way.
* Bloomsday on 16 June, for aficionados and illiterates alike.
* The Dublin Theatre Festival, every autumn.
* The Kilkenny Design Centre, Blarney Woollen Mills and other emporiums of good Irish taste.
* The Powerscourt Townhouse Centre, for shopping with ambience.
* The Huguenot Cemetery on Merrion Row.
* Thomas Read, Dublin's oldest shop, a cutler's founded in 1670, in Parliament Street, near the City Hall, now a bar and museum.
* Dublin Castle.
* A walk on the Bull Wall, one of the arms of Dublin port keeping it from silting up.
* A walk on Dún Laoghaire Pier.
* A walk along the Grand or Royal canals.

2 The Southeast

George O'Brien

COUNTIES

WATERFORD

WEXFORD

CARLOW

KILKENNY

TIPPERARY

The Southeast is different. It manages to avoid the ways that other parts of the country are defined. It has cities, but none of them is big enough to dominate the region. It has a *Gaeltacht*, an Irish-speaking area, around the fishing village of Ring, County Waterford, but it is the West of Ireland that everybody believes is the home of the native Irish and the Irish language, not the Southeast. As typical of the Southeast as its minute and virtually forgotten *Gaeltacht* is the unique linguistic enclave along the south County Wexford coast which also had its own language. Known as *Yola*, it sounded like Flemish and was a mixture of Old Irish, Old French and medieval English.

Nor, unlike Ulster, can religion be used by way of introduction to the area. All sorts and conditions of Christians are represented across the southeastern landscape by high crosses dating from the ninth century, 12th-century monasteries, Romanesque chapels and early Gothic cathedrals. Many of the Catholic churches in the towns sprang from the drawing board of the 19th-century English architect, Augustus Pugin. In the 1780s rebel Calvinists from Geneva were invited to establish a New Geneva at the village of Passage, on the Suir estuary. At the other, western end of County Waterford, a small sect called the Cooneyites maintain their low-church communitarian observances under the jurisdiction of their elected bishops, who to all appearances are commonplace yeoman farmers.

The Southeast is a mixture. It has broad beaches of silver sand and golden sand. It has mountains celebrated for their scenic prospects, like the Knockmealdowns north of Lismore, County Waterford. And it has mountains famed in song and story, such as Slievenamon, in eastern Tipperary. The rocks around Kilmore Quay, County Wexford, are the oldest in the country. The most ancient human remains yet found in Ireland were

unearthed in a cave at Kilgreany, in the Nire valley, in west Waterford, with bones 4500 years old. The town of Wexford was known to Ptolemy of Alexandria, who named it Menapia on the earliest known map of Ireland. At Hook Head, on the southwestern tip of County Wexford, there is the descendant of a lighthouse whose existence travellers first recorded in the 12th century.

The countryside around it, and on the other side of the Suir estuary, abounds in passage graves and other evidence of prehistoric settlement. Even the quiet County Carlow offers spectacular evidence of those impenetrable times with its Browneshill Dolmen, the highest in Europe, two miles east of Carlow town. There is an ancient relic five miles east and north of Dungarvan, County Waterford, known as Cloc Labhrais, a talking stone. Just outside the town on the west side, there is a monument revering a greyhound. Castlecomer, County Kilkenny, was laid out

Hook Lighthouse, Hook Head, County Wexford.

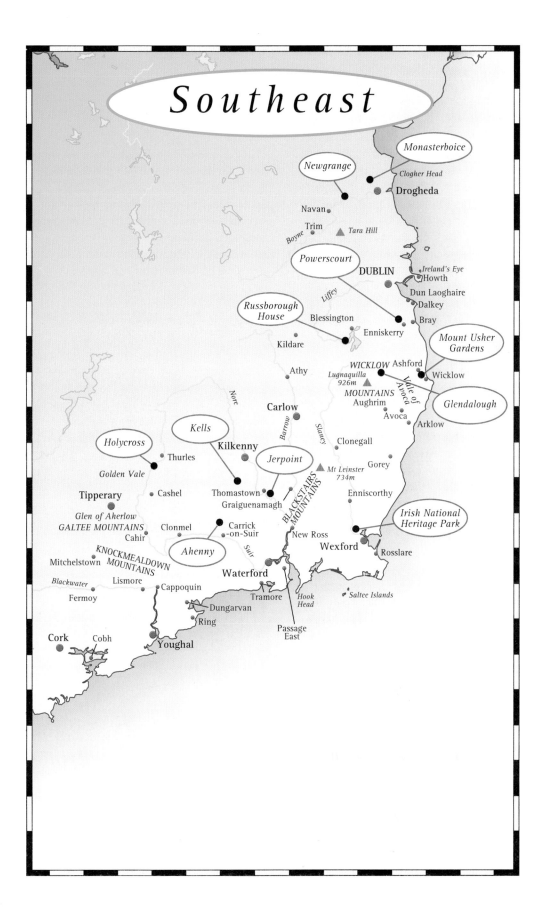

Southeast

Monasterboice

Newgrange

Clogher Head

Navan

Drogheda

Trim

Boyne

▲ *Tara Hill*

Powerscourt

DUBLIN

Ireland's Eye

Howth

Liffey

Dun Laoghaire

Dalkey

Russborough House

Blessington

Bray

Kildare

Enniskerry

Mount Usher Gardens

Athy

WICKLOW

Ashford

Wicklow

Lugnaquilla 926m ▲

Vale of Avoca

MOUNTAINS

Glendalough

Aughrim

Carlow

Avoca

Arklow

Nore

Kells

Clonegall

Holycross

Kilkenny

Jerpoint

Gorey

Thurles

Barrow

Slaney

Golden Vale

▲ *Mt Leinster 734m*

Tipperary

Cashel

Thomastown

Graiguenamagh

BLACKSTAIRS MOUNTAINS

Enniscorthy

Glen of Aherlow

GALTEE MOUNTAINS

Clonmel

Carrick -on-Suir

New Ross

Irish National Heritage Park

Cahir

Suir

Ahenny

Wexford

KNOCKMEALDOWN MOUNTAINS

Mitchelstown

Rosslare

Blackwater

Lismore

Cappoquin

Waterford

Fermoy

Tramore

Hook Head

Saltee Islands

Dungarvan

Cork

Cobh

Ring

Passage East

Youghal

in the 17th century to correspond as precisely as possible to the Italian town of Alsinore, though it is much more closely associated with the anthracite mine on which it sits and with the socialistically inclined Welsh miners who were brought in to work it.

In the Southeast, various cultural and historical elements vie. But none has the upper hand, none imparts to the region a definitive stamp. What binds the southeastern mixture together, holds it fast and makes it distinctive is the land. The Southeast is the green place. On the road from Dublin, between Athy and Kilkenny, the rich plains of Meath and Kildare can be seen funnelling down through Carlow and breaking at the foot of Mount Leinster and the Blackstairs Mountains to spill into the granary counties of Wexford, Kilkenny and Tipperary, culminating to the west of Cashel in the Golden Vale. Down here, Ireland is more pastoral than picturesque, reveals more of the continuity of husbandry than the barrenness of dispossession. In 1185 Giraldus Cambrensis, one of the first travellers to write

about the country, saw what still remains to be seen hereabouts:

> The land is fruitful and rich in its fertile soil and plentiful harvests. Crops abound in the fields, flocks on the mountains, wild animals in the woods. It is rich in honey and milk.

This is where the lush valleys and the slow-moving rivers are: the Slaney, the Suir, the Barrow, the Nore, the estuarial Blackwater. Cattle take their ease in the still water-meadows. The roads are lined with lime trees, chestnuts, sycamores, beech, and on the meandering minor routes there is still life to be seen in the hedgerows. The locals speak in soft accents. The atmosphere is tacit, placid. Acres of barley and oats are hinted at through gaps in the foliage.

Ireland's membership of the European Union has brought an economic revolution to these fertile valleys. Every townland has a fine crop of bungalows. Satellite dishes sprout like extraterrestrial mushrooms from backyards, lawns and gables. Farmsteads seem more cared for here. Outbuildings are

THE COMING OF THE NORMANS

It all started with a Leinster king called Dermot MacMurrough who made off with Dervorgilla, the wife of another king, O'Rourke of Breifne, to the north, where Cavan is now. This was in the year 1152. The following year the lady was recovered by her husband, but the humiliation festered. So, in 1166, when O'Rourke and MacMurrough found themselves on opposite sides in the continual internecine feuds of the time, O'Rourke took the opportunity to avenge himself, sacking MacMurrough's castle at Ferns, County Wexford, and forcing him to flee and find allies to recover, in turn, his loss.

No less an ally than King Henry II of England was whom MacMurrough had in mind, and he travelled to France to swear fealty to Henry on condition that the necessary assistance would be forthcoming. Henry gave MacMurrough leave to enlist men to accompany him back to Ireland. He found what he was looking for in Wales, in

the person of Richard FitzGilbert de Clare, Earl of Pembroke, known to history as Strongbow. This Norman leader had conditions of his own, among them the hand in marriage of MacMurrough's eldest daughter, Aoife, and the right to succeed to the kingship of Leinster. MacMurrough agreed. At the beginning of May 1169 the first brigades of Normans landed at Bannow Strand, on the south coast of Wexford. A further force landed at Baginbun, further west along the same coast, and overcame a defending force in an engagement the earthworks of which are still to be seen. Before the summer was over Strongbow himself had landed at Passage East, Waterford had fallen, and Aoife had been given to Strongbow in marriage. King Henry landed in Waterford in 1171 and accepted the pledges of fealty from the country's rulers. By the middle of the following century most of Ireland was in Norman hands, and the complexities of modern Ireland followed.

in good repair and painted. There are more new farmers' houses, all two storeys and with slate roofs. The thatched cottage is a thing of the past, and the Mercedes-Benz has ousted the Austin and the Ford, though not necessarily the ass-and-cart.

Angling has always been well catered for here, and to go with the new prosperity there has been a proliferation of golf courses, many of championship standard. The terrain is hospitable to cyclists as well, virtually all of whom sport French flags, Dutch flags, German flags somewhere on their kit, since the locals have been motorised to a man. They always seem to be pushing on regardless, but they do suggest the way to see the Southeast, which is not a sequence of vistas and venues: the pleasure of travelling the region comes from seeing it as an intricate network of little trips. Days out with picnics in fields by a river, afternoons with four o'clock tea in small rooms whose new windows let light pool on old stone floors, a meandering drive on a long summer evening through quiet by-ways: these are the approaches the Southeast repays.

The settled and productive air of life here, the sense of continuity and community, say that here we are several cuts above topography and mere scenery. This is land worth fighting for, worth owning. The Normans thought so, 800 years ago. Others before them also thought so. But the Normans are the ones who count. They not only settled the land, they turned it into history, and made the Southeast the cradle of modern Ireland.

Formidable as was the force of Norman arms, military might seems at this remove to be the least of what they introduced to the country. They imposed themselves not simply as an army, but as a race. Their aquiline features, long jaws and close-set eyes are equally visible in the stone work and statuary which are the Normans' greatest artistic legacy and in the faces of passers-by. They brought surnames which are now at home everywhere in Ireland – Barry, Butler, Burke, Fitzgerald, Roche. And they brought surnames which are still largely confined to their original landfalls – Power in Waterford,

Synott in Wexford, Rocket in south Kilkenny. Their forenames were absorbed into Irish. Jean became Sean, Guillaume Liam. And French *histoire* turned into Irish *stair*. Even the rough guttural of the French 'r' can still be heard in the voices of the townlands between Waterford and Dungarvan, although regional accents are dying out: there was a time when their inflections and timbres seemed to change with every bend of the road.

With the Normans, Europe, never all that far away, was brought back to Ireland with renewed zest, most notably in the form of architecture. The innumerable Norman towers which dot the countryside – square and squat, in contrast to the round towers of an earlier era – express very well the new style and new ways with materials. Their very number shows the degree of penetration achieved by Ireland's new rulers. But the proliferation of defensive buildings needs to be put alongside that of abbeys, churches and friaries in order to appreciate the completeness of the new polity's impact. Where Normans conquered, monks waged peace. Not all the clerical establishments date from the coming of the Normans, and many of the sites occupied by the new orders were already age-old holy places, often marked by high crosses ornamented in the Celtic style. The best examples of these in the Southeast are at a place called Ahenny, on the Kilkenny side of Carrick-on-Suir in southern Tipperary.

The ornamented High Cross at Ahenny, County Tipperary.

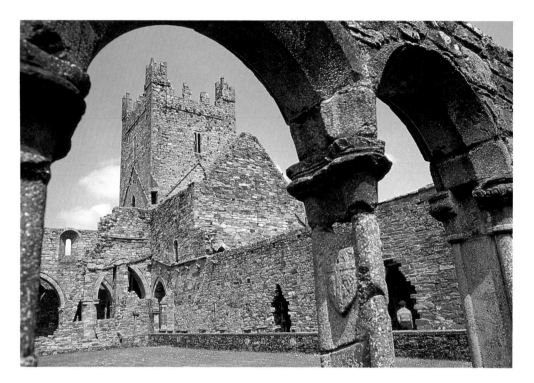

The 12th-century remains of Jerpoint Abbey, County Kilkenny.

But the great expansion in church building, and the place in Irish life of such orders as the Dominicans, the Franciscans and the Cistercians, dates from the age of Norman supremacy. Those days can be reached between lunch and teatime in south Kilkenny. Three sites, all dating from the 12th century and within easy reach of each other in a straight line running east–west in southern County Kilkenny, give an arresting sense of what the Normans fostered, once what a later writer called a 'quiett and welthie estate' was imposed and the monasteries were able to play their full economic as well as devotional roles. These are the Cistercian abbey at Jerpoint, the Augustinian priory at Kells, and Duiske Abbey at Graiguenamanagh.

The first of these, Jerpoint, on the main Kilkenny–Waterford road, took its present form in 1180, and is one of the most eloquent remains of the period in the whole country. Its engineering work alone gives some sense of the builders' dedication, while the cloister's stone effigies convey the period's spirited measure of the human, none more so than the carving of the man with the bellyache. This medieval dyspepsia victim keeps company with knights, ladies and eminent churchmen, an unlikely but very simple and effective reminder of the unpompous but not undignified tenor of the times. It is fascinating to glimpse the worlds of difference between these figures and the Christ, Apostles and Old Testament representations on the Ahenny crosses.

The Augustinians found a high cross at Kells, and established themselves in its name at about the same time as the development of Jerpoint. There is a greater variety of buildings here, giving something of a sense of what elaborate communities these monastic settlements were, and of what it must have taken by way of manpower and material to support them. Tucked out of the way in a meadow by a stream, its location is more appealing than Jerpoint's, and its environs harbour something of the silence and awe which the ruined past can inspire. If Kells were nearer a main road it would have attracted the attentions of the restorer, as Jerpoint has. As it is, the spacious site remains detached from, and indifferent to, Volvo 18-wheelers thundering towards the port of Waterford on their way to the European continent and beyond.

For what can be accomplished in the way

of public restoration, Duiske is the place. Here, purpose as well as fabric has been preserved, and engineering has become the handmaid of homage. The Abbey's dignity as a place of worship is as intact as ever. The name Graiguenamanagh means, roughly, 'monks' grange', which is certainly what the place was, since Duiske, founded early in the 13th century, was the largest Cistercian monastery in the Ireland of its day. Also known as the Black Abbey, its appearance on the outside is unprepossessing. But the interior contains some architectural gems, among them the clerestory windows and the great processional door. The effigy of the knight at the main entrance seems appropriately custodial. And then there is its dignified calm. Compared to the Southeast's

The interior of Duiske Abbey, Graiguenamanagh, County Kilkenny.

other elaborately restored Cistercian church at Holy Cross, near Thurles, County Tipperary, Duiske is an impressive tribute to simplicity, with none of the aggressive piety of Holy Cross's modernised precincts.

The elaborateness and proximity of these three settlements are a striking illustration of the newcomers' impact. This picture can be easily enlarged by venturing slightly further afield. Within twenty-five miles of Jerpoint are the remains of many other settlements, each noteworthy and distinctive. A drive that takes in Tintern Abbey by Bannow Bay in south County Wexford and nearby Dunbrody Abbey, then via St Mullin's through south Kilkenny and ending up at Fethard, County Tipperary, is just one of many ways that this part of the world can bring the landscape of Norman monasticism into focus. Some of this tour is already available to walkers in the form of the South Leinster Way. The route is a stimulating reminder that what are now remote sites and minor roads were once quite otherwise. And at unassuming Fethard can be seen both a Templar's Castle and a *sheelagh-na-gig*, a very candid Celtic female fertility symbol, which together serendipitously keep the mixture rich.

And the Normans brought trade, and a coinage, and a strong sense of organisation. Bridges were built, woods came down, markets sprang up, mills ground into action. Stone became vital and the land was cleared. Of late, some of that same land has been reforested, and these official plantations provide places to picnic, good walking on clear trails, and pleasant viewing points. One of these new, or renewed, woods is at Kilcash, on the slopes of Slievenamon, a place remembered for a well-known poem in Irish lamenting the decline of Kilcash Castle. Its opening lines go:

> *What shall we do now for timber?*
> *The forests all over are down.*

The Normans brought new, centralised forms of administration. Sheriffs were appointed and trial by jury was introduced, as was a certain kind of parliamentary representation. Ultimately the Norman writ was unable to run, resulting in the ceding of their power to England. But initially the Normans adapted very well to their new colony, assimilating largely thanks to intermarriage and a shared religion. Over the course of a couple of centuries, their integration gave rise to the most notorious cliché of Irish history – they became more Irish than the Irish themselves.

The confident, jaunty rhythms of a 13th-century poem 'The Walling of New Ross' project the joy of Norman feudal harmony at work. The whole of the town's population, regardless of rank or other distinction, are presented as willing contributors to the task at hand:

> *Then on Sunday there came down*
> *All the dames of that brave town . . .*
>
> *In all the lands where I have been,*
> *Such fair dames working I've not seen.*

And the Norman heyday caused at least some parts of the country to be sufficiently prosperous and at peace to inspire a 14th-century Kildare monk to compose a poetic fantasy called *The Land of Cockayne*. In this opus, clerical vows of chastity are more honoured in the breach than in the observance, and the architectural achievements consist of:

> *. . . bowers and high halls,*
> *And of pasties are the walls,*
> *Of flesh and fish and of rich meat,*
> *All the best that men may eat.*

Yet not all that long after this song of the merry monk, the Statutes of Kilkenny were enacted, proscribing among other things Irish dress and the Irish language, in an early effort to introduce apartheid between settler and what was officially identified as 'the Irish enemy'. The effort was not a success, but the Statutes remained on the books nevertheless and, like a lot of laws, became pretexts for various cruelties, injustices, and segregationist habits of mind which died hard, when they died at all.

'The Walling of New Ross' is something of an anthem to the Norman energy that cut the stones and carved the gamut of humanity in the cloister at Jerpoint. But it also underlines the Normans' most important legacy, the towns. The Normans did not invent the town in Ireland. Wexford and Waterford – Weissfjord, Vadrafjord – were foremost among the Norsemen's thriving Irish trading posts. They did, however, unite economics with politics, so that Waterford and Kilkenny became their twin turbines in the Southeast. But there was a time when New Ross, stimulated by the attentions of William Marshall, husband of Isabella, daughter of Strongbow, rivalled them in wealth and significance. An impressive display of civic treasures in the *Tholsel*, or toll house, makes the point.

New Ross is, uniquely in Ireland, a river town, an inland town whose wealth comes not from the land but from the river which is navigable to this point. It is not just on the river, but of it, its face turned to the river's flux rather than to the land's firmness. The face is not very prepossessing, and the town seems to have been as much scarred as enhanced by the ebb and flow of trade. It appears quite out of keeping with the monastic settlements with which it was surrounded and for which it was an important centre. It seems much less demure a place for not being merely another market town, perhaps because in the quays it has the kind of clamorous workplace that in Ireland is almost entirely confined to cities.

And the fertiliser factory has almost as much a claim to fame as the church that Marshall built, St Mary's, still intact among the ruins of yet another abbey. It was at that factory that John F. Kennedy, on a presidential visit to the home place, said he might be working if his forebears had not gone to Boston from nearby Dunganstown. That townland is where the connection between the President and the area is commemorated by an imposing arboretum stocked with some five thousand varieties of trees and shrubs donated from around the world. The other recent American President with southeastern associations is Ronald Reagan, whose people have been traced to Ballyporeen, at the foot of the Galtee mountains, west and south of Cahir, County Tipperary. The 'Ronald Reagan' pub is here.

The Nore and Barrow merge just above

New Ross, so that the town is a starting place for trips either on the water or along the banks, up river or down. The rivers flow seaward to meet the Suir at Cheekpoint, a little to the northeast of Waterford City. This act of kinship has earned the rivers the nickname 'The Three Sisters'. From Cheekpoint Hill, above the meeting place, the wooded river valley can be seen broadening into the splendid estuary, with Waterford City at one's back and the dark green and pale yellow plain of south Wexford spread before. Nearby is the village of Passage East, now the western terminal of the very handy ferry across the river from Ballyhack. Passage is where Strongbow and the Norman juggernaut proper landed. Now it is an adventure to sail

The Kennedy homestead, New Ross, County Wexford.

The limestone effigies of Piers and Margaret Butler, St Canice's Cathedral, Kilkenny City.

in the other direction, inland from Dublin to the sea via the Grand Canal to near Athy and along the Barrow from there to New Ross and the tide.

Another trip with New Ross as base is upstream by the Nore towards Kilkenny. Here are some fine, quiet stretches of slow water and sleepy villages: Thomastown, Inistiogue, Bennettsbridge. Of these, Inistiogue is the picturesque legacy of an improving landlord, with its riverside lawns and shady square, although, compared to most Irish villages, prim to the point of artificiality. And charming as it is, this village also has its ghost. This is the shell of Woodstock, the landlord's house, burned like many another of its kind during the War of Independence in 1921, notable now for having been neither razed nor restored.

'Move, if you move, like water', Thomas Kinsella commends in his poem 'Tao and Unfitness at Inistiogue on the River Nore'. Pleasant as the river looks, though, it also inspired one of Ireland's foremost painters, Barrie Cooke, to produce, when based at Thomastown, a series of huge, nightmarish canvasses depicting the Nore's strangulation by pollution. Plastic grocery bags inhabit trees. Car repair shops in the middle of nowhere look like pastoral slums. New housing estates are inflicted upon hillsides like careless scars. To these smirches on the quality of modern Irish life, the Southeast is no exception.

The capital of Norman Ireland was Kilkenny, and its centrepiece remains the cathedral of St Canice, the saint for whom the city is named, and who fathered the names Kenneth and Canning. The cathedral is on a hill, which was how capitals used to assert themselves, at least in Ireland, as Tara, Dublin, Armagh and Cashel attest. A day's outing in Kilkenny should begin in the grounds of St Canice's – or better yet, on top of the round tower to which it is attached – whence the eye is drawn as much out over the city to the castle's storybook setting by the river as it is down into the city. There is a vague sense of one eminence calling to another, of Butler soul addressing Butler body. The Butlers held land for fifty miles around, so that the establishments of church and state can be mistaken for monuments to their temporal and spiritual greatness.

But the city's rich historical mix is by no means confined to monuments. On the contrary, it is very much part of the general fabric of the community, which may be one reason why it is so well preserved. On the face of it, the prevailing muslin-grey tone of the buildings is not immediately conducive to the idea of richness and diversity. But first impressions are almost invariably insufficient in Ireland, and Kilkenny is no exception. The colour is that of the local limestone. When polished, it becomes blacker and shinier than a raven's wing, and is called marble. That is what the striking effigies of Piers and Margaret Butler in St Canice's are made of, and is the reason for Kilkenny's nickname of the Marble City.

What lies between the cathedral and the castle, which the continuing reconstruction of the city wall helps to frame, is packed with interest. From Irishtown, which is the area directly overshadowed by St Canice's, to the city centre with its array of public buildings from all phases of the city's eminence as a seat of civil and clerical authority, Kilkenny offers provincial Ireland's richest assemblage of unmummified history. Here the richness is of intact remains, not merely, as so often in Ireland, a richness of associations. Note the scarcity of plastic fascia and illuminated signs on the High Street, and how fresh the paint is on the old shop fronts.

As the bustling centre of Kilkenny shows, people still come to town to shop, to meet by accident, to gossip over cups of tea. The shopping centre has yet to make its mark in provincial Ireland. Supermarkets, chain stores and fast food outlets may be squeezed in between a thriving bakery and a down-at-heel shoemaker's. Even now family-owned businesses are in the majority. High Street is the social hub, the major venue for local accents and community banter, for the singing milkman and the whistling window-cleaner, who still may be heard holding their own despite the greatly increased volume of canned music that wafts from the more modern shops.

The expanses of plate glass in the shop fronts, and the recessed shop doors, have a miniature arcade effect and suggest the lure and intimacy of shopping in another age. This design is to be found still in all the more substantial market towns and Kilkenny has some excellent examples of it. It seems a little odd to rent a video, book a holiday in the Bahamas, or inspect the latest in designer jeans behind these shop fronts. But such incongruities are part of the mix of Irish social life, expressing an unconsciously ironic awareness that the contemporary is only skin deep. The absence of standardisation is refreshing, though there are signs that it will not last.

There was a famous theatre in Kilkenny in the late 18th century, when the city rivalled

Street Scene in Kilkenny City.

Dublin as a place to see and be seen. Among those who trod the boards here were Thomas Moore (1779–1852), who wrote such celebrated Irish melodies as 'The Last Rose of Summer', and his contemporary, Wolfe Tone (1763–98), who invented a rather different version of Irishness by becoming the founding father of the country's republican, separatist, political tradition. The site of the theatre is occupied now by the local offices of the Internal Revenue Service, a development which, as many cynics have pointed out, puts the recent course of civilisation in a nutshell.

The tax office is on the Parade, the broad approach to the castle. By the time it is reached, most of official Kilkenny will have been encountered, including the original tax office, the *Tholsel*, on the High Street, and the veritable choir of churches which seemingly attend St Canice's. Most notable among these is the 13th-century Black Abbey, still occupied by the order which founded it, the Dominicans, for whom the sole remaining city gate nearby, the Blackfriars gate, was named. Also noteworthy are the various Tudor dwellings, more so for their survival and their rarity in Ireland than for their current contents. Chief among them are the Shee Alms House, where the Tourist Information Centre is housed, and the Rothe House, which typifies early burgher well-being in the city, and which is actually an amalgamation of three houses. The Rothe House is now the home of the Kilkenny Archaeological Society, an organisation whose own history conveys much about recent cultural life in Ireland. Some of the story has been recounted by the eminent essayist and cultural historian, Hubert Butler, who played an active part in the Society, and whose writings give a rich and informed view of life in modern Ireland.

But best of all in Kilkenny is to wander off the main streets down the alleys and around the lanes or along the path by the Nore under the castle walls. These by-ways are the little veins and ligaments which make the city work. They bring out the layers of architectural tissue which have accumulated in the rise from the riverbank and reveal unselfconsciously the lives the locals make –

including how they manage to drive cars in the most unlikely and narrowest places. All of these little passages seem to lead to Kyteler's Inn, owned by Dame Alice Kyteler in the 14th century. If there were any justice, the inn would be named for Dame Alice's maid, Petronilla. Because, when charged with witchcraft, heresy, and doing away with four husbands – each offence enough to make the lady fit for burning – Dame Alice fled to Scotland, leaving Petronilla to die at the stake in her place. It is said that on certain nights Petronilla still visits the scene of her betrayal and cries out under a gibbous moon.

The river path leads to the castle grounds, a fine open acreage of parkland, to which access was presented to the city and people of Kilkenny in 1967 by the sixth Marquess of Ormonde. Ormonde, a corruption of the Irish for east Munster – *iar Mumhan*, pronounced 'ear moon' – is the titled name of the Butler family, who have called the castle home since 1391. It was in this castle that some of the deliberations of the Confederation of Kilkenny took place. This was a parliamentary conclave which attempted to preserve the Royalist cause in Ireland and, with it, the integrity of the old Catholic aristocracy. But in 1648, after six fraught years of trying to govern in the wake of the carnage of the rebellion of 1641, the old order disintegrated. The Norman era finally came to an end, and the next thing the country knew was Cromwell.

The castle's most imposing feature is the long picture gallery, containing portraits by, among others, Lely and Van Dyck. The Butler Gallery, in the castle basement, has regular exhibitions of contemporary art, much of which is produced locally. Kilkenny became an arts and crafts centre during the 1970s thanks to an initiative which provided painters, jewellers, and potters with work space in the Kilkenny Design Workshops. The workshops were housed in what originally were the castle stables which circle an elegant courtyard opposite the castle's main entrance. Now the artists and craftsmen have mostly dispersed to studios of their own in the countryside, leaving the Kilkenny Design Shop to exhibit and market their wares.

After its eclipse as a political and administrative centre, Kilkenny's name continued to be prominent culturally, owing in some degree to Kilkenny College, which within a short period educated two students as different from each other as Dean Swift (1667–1745) and Bishop Berkeley (1685–1753). Now the city hosts an annual Arts Festival at the end of August, which is distinguished by a strong contemporary emphasis, particularly on music, painting and poetry. Pride of place among the festival venues goes to St Canice's and the castle.

> *At the creek of Baginbun*
> *Ireland was lost and won.*

So goes an old rhyme on the Normans' first Irish landing on the southern coast of County Wexford. And while that may very well be the case, paradoxically enough County Wexford is not really the place to look for proof. Even if the Normans were introduced to Ireland by a chieftain whose seat was at Ferns, and the county's nickname, The Model County, speaks of the exemplary care that has been taken of its fertile land, rather than its scenic attractions, history and husbandry only go so far. A tour of the county suggests that it is more County Kilkenny's opposite than its counterpart.

The county's agricultural pre-eminence was officially recognised by the siting of the Irish Agricultural Museum at Johnstown Castle, not far outside Wexford town on the Rosslare side. The museum emphasises the agri- more than the culture. But, in addition to a full range of exhibits representing the various aspects, ancient and modern, of working the land in Ireland, the castle is set in extensive, well-maintained and horticulturally lavish grounds. Not very far down the road from the museum is the Irish National Heritage Park, at Ferrycarrig, which is an informative complement to some of the materials displayed at Johnstown. Particularly worthwhile are the models of different types of ancient Irish life. The fact that the park's chronological terminus is the arrival of the Normans is, under the circumstances, intriguing.

Nevertheless, despite such official gestures,

Interior of St Canice's Cathedral, Kilkenny City.

Wexford is perceived not as a place of settlement but as land sacred to the memory of the ousted and usurped, a place of blood and peasants, defiance and defeat. Although its occupation and development generally follow the southeastern pattern, geographical factors played some part in keeping the county at the periphery of the Norman world. The silting up of Wexford harbour inhibited the county's commercial development. Also, it may have been that the Blackstairs Mountains and the obstacles of the Nore and the Barrow acted as something of a limitation to the county's connections.

In the shadow of the Blackstairs, and due east of Kilkenny, Bunclody is one of the Southeast's best examples of a landlord's town, a town that reveals the hand of a so-called improving landlord. Once known as Newtownbarry, the pleasing proportions of its layout distinguish it from the seemingly haphazard straggle of streets that make up most small towns, and make an attractive base camp from which to attempt a climb of nearby Mount Leinster. An 18th-century gentlewoman, Lady Lucy Maxwell, liked to view the pleasant scenes of these parts while being borne aloft in her sedan chair, an approach which Mount Leinster's hospitable slopes do not really favour. The chair survives, and may be seen in the County Wexford Historical and Folk Museum in Enniscorthy. There is another rewarding climb not very far to the east at Tara Hill, near Gorey, a town whose wide, straight streets are the main evidence remaining of its translation by its 17th-century proprietors into the town of Newborough ('new' in an Irish name is a complex code-word). Rather higher than the prehistoric Irish capital which is its County Meath namesake, this Tara Hill offers a panoramic view from its summit.

The most renowned hill in County Wexford, though, is an unprepossessing knuckle on the outskirts of Enniscorthy: Vinegar Hill, where, in the poet Seamus Heaney's words, 'the fatal conclave' ending the 1798 rebellion took place. The ruined tower on the hill is the remains of the old windmill which was the rebel headquarters. The hopelessness of the odds against the rebels and the size of their defeat have given 1798 a long half-life in the hymnal of popular 19th-century ballads claiming to recapture the insurgent spirit. There is a ballad which asserts that 'The boys of Kilkenny are stout, roving blades', but they are nothing in Irish popular memory compared to the boys of Wexford, 'who fought with heart and hand', inspired by Kelly, the boy from Killann and his 'long-barrelled gun from the sea', and led by 'brave Father Murphy' of Boolavogue.

This townland and many of the others which featured prominently in '98 – Oulart, Killann, Scarrawalsh, The Harrow – are all within a 10-mile radius of Enniscorthy. The violence here was very local, very intimate. These place-names even now evoke a certain amount of complicated nationalist sentiment. The quiet fields of the gentle Slaney valley are not quite what they seem. This is 'croppy' country, croppies being what the rebels were called, because as they marched by they cropped the heads of the young corn and, as legend has it, from where the casualties were buried a new crop grew. Their image appears in bronzes like the one in Enniscorthy's

Market Square of an erect youth with what was often the rebels' only weapon, the pike. This eloquent statue and its twin in Wexford town are the work of Oliver Sheppard (1865–1941), sculptor-in-chief to the new Irish sensibility which arose at the end of the 19th century and achieved its rebellious apotheosis in the Easter Rising of 1916.

'A rebel band set the heather blazing'. This line from the ballad 'Boolavogue' unintentionally sums up the character of the 1798 rebellion. But its seeds bore fruit in Easter 1916, when a band of Enniscorthy rebels became the most prominent participants in the Rising outside Dublin. In the 1970s, in honour of this, the Sinn Féin masterplan for a 32-county republic nominated Enniscorthy as one of the four provincial capitals. But what the town celebrates best now are strawberries. Thanks to light soil and mild climate, including – for what it's worth – Ireland's lowest rainfall, Wexford has the country's earliest strawberry harvest. For palates made wooden by freezers and supermarkets, these berries have the taste and freshness of another time.

The history of the Enniscorthy rebels of 1916 forms the centrepiece of the Enniscorthy museum, which is located in what used to be

The memorial to the rebels of 1798, Enniscorthy, County Wexford.

the local castle, once owned by Edmund Spenser (c. 1552–99), author of the Elizabethan epic *The Faerie Queen*, much of whose imaginative landscape draws on his time in Ireland as a servant of the Crown. The castle overlooked the river crossing. Safe crossings must have been rare, otherwise such a hilly site would not have been built on, but Enniscorthy rose from the river and thrived, and has a square to prove it. A square means not only a plan with a view to a future, it also speaks of a present need, usually for a space big enough to hold a market.

The wide range of materials on display in the museum pays ample tribute to the ardour which drove these amateur rebels of 1916. On view are the cavalry manual from which they learned the art of war and the devotional objects painstakingly carved in the internment camp at Frongoch in Wales, where they awaited their fate until, contrary to expectations, they were amnestied. Another room has a display of American police badges and medals. Almost as arresting as this room is the one next door to it, which contains an exhibit of hurling sticks autographed by the Wexford greats of the game. The vast majority of these players were members of the team which swept all before it in the early 1950s, many – but by no means all or necessarily the greatest – from Enniscorthy. Not quite the equivalent of international 'caps', these hurleys nevertheless have a representative and collective significance, evoking not only championship levels of attainment but some of the elements of local myth. The county was unified in these names. Distinctions dissolved between club rivals, between town and country, between bank clerk and lorry driver. And one of the results was to play in Dublin before politician and prelate and a crowd of forty or fifty thousand. And to win. To win the All-Ireland. To secure a national place for local energies. In the 1950s, when there was no television and soccer was hardly worth bothering about, that was really something.

The Slaney valley is at its most restfully scenic between Enniscorthy and Wexford town. Wexford is one of the Southeast's oldest communities. In its cramped, meandering Main Street and the lanes that sprout off it, the skeleton of Viking town planning may be detected. This Main Street is virtually an exhibition of small shops and, given the way the street totters on and on, it is appropriate that every other one of them seems to be a pub. Better yet, these are pubs of the old school, for the most part, with the best of them offering little more than dark interiors, grimy appointments and limited menus. Wexford has not been able to escape the vogue that has given bars elsewhere the pretensions of bistros, but it has done more than its fair share to resist it.

The lanes climb up above the town and from the top of them it is possible to see, more intimately than from the cathedral in Kilkenny, the various layers of the town. There are the English-sounding Westgate and Cornmarket. There is Selskar Abbey, where King Henry II spent Lent on retreat in 1172 after the murder of Thomas à Becket. Facing the harbour is The Crescent, an imposing but out-of-place slice of Georgian architecture. And the ancient quays are called the Woodentops. But such features of the town as these have been overshadowed in the popular mind by one notorious event, a massacre by Cromwell's troops in 1649. The venue for this atrocity was the Bull Ring, in those times one of the town's places of entertainment but now almost invisible. On the October day in question, the vast majority of the Catholic population was put to death. Some accounts put the number of victims as high as two thousand. About a hundred Wexford townspeople were murdered by the rebels in 1798 in the long inheritance of blood memory that has always coursed through Irish history.

The statue in The Crescent is of Wexford town's most famous son, Commodore John Barry (1745–1803), founder of the United States Navy. President Kennedy unveiled it. The irony of its overlooking a harbour notorious for silting has not been lost, and perhaps the Slaney estuary's dun mud reflects the town's air of being a port and a county town, but also rather a backwater. Still, in yet another of those instances of new provincial

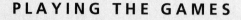

PLAYING THE GAMES

In Hayes's Hotel, Thurles, County Tipperary, on 1 November 1884, a famous meeting was held. It had no official or ostensible political purpose; sport was the topic on the agenda. Yet this, the inaugural meeting of the Gaelic Athletic Association, was to have a major effect on the development and expression of a nationalist sensibility, particularly in rural Ireland. As well as being the oldest organisation associated with the growth of cultural nationalism in the generation of 1916, the GAA is by far the country's most successful cultural institution. Even in today's international environment, it can boast of a high level of popular support at the local and county level. This degree of affiliation is matched by a highly evolved administrative network.

The GAA is the governing body and administrative sponsor of what are called Gaelic games. These games embrace four codes, and three of them are field games: hurling, which is an informal and accelerated version of hockey; Gaelic football, the nearest equivalent of which is Australian Rules football; and camogie, which is hurling, with modifications, for women. The fourth game, handball, is a barehanded cousin of pelota or jai alai or squash, and requires a court, or alley. For the field games, competition is organised along age lines, known as minor games, and along lines of skill, senior and junior games. There are various intra-county club competitions, and more prestigious competitions for representative teams from eligible counties. The most important of the latter competitions is the All-Ireland Championship.

Local team names generally echo nationalist motifs, such as Thurles' Sarsfields, or Waterford City's Erin's Own. Alternatively, club names may honour the local saint, such as St Aidan's, Enniscorthy, or St Molleran's, from the Carrick-on-Suir area. Team names such as Cahir Slashers, Clonmel Commercials, or Faythe Harriers, from Wexford Town, are rare. From the outset the GAA sought the patronage of the Catholic Church, initially in the inspiring person of Archbishop Croke of Thurles. It is for him that the organisation's Dublin headquarters, Croke Park, is named. The games themselves, particularly hurling, are played at an exhilarating pace and are well worth seeing not only in their own right, but for the insight they provide on the ebb and flow of Irish provincial life in one of its most intense local concentrations.

A hurling final between Wexford and Cork at Croke Park, Dublin.

self-respect in Ireland, even a backwater has been found to have its poetry. Life in the small shops – the bookie's, the barber's, the snooker hall – has been revealed to audiences at London's Royal Court Theatre and Dublin's Peacock in the plays of Billy Roche (1950–). More revealingly, perhaps, the plays have also had packed, admiring houses here in Wexford. There was a time when a writer who drew back the veil on local life would have been far from welcome in his native place. It is strange and piquant to think of this plain, unexceptional town producing not only its own laureate in the playwright, but also the most exquisite Irish novelist of his generation, John Banville (1945–).

Despite its overall facelessness, Wexford deserves credit for being one of the first provincial towns in Ireland to open its doors to a wider world. Every October since 1951 the Wexford Opera Festival has welcomed scholars, music professionals and opera fans from far and wide, drawn not only by the novel venue but by the festival's repertoire. The inspired concept which has guaranteed the festival's success is to stage either little-known, seldom-performed works by the great composers, or works by composers who are less well known. This approach makes virtually unavoidable a sense of surprise and delighted discovery, which is added to by performers who for the most part are unknowns just beginning their careers. These attractions, plus the intimate confines of the Theatre Royal, the smallness of the town, and an active festival fringe, create one of the genuine highlights of the cultural year in Ireland.

Even the silt has proved good for something. It has created the natural treasure-house of the Slobs. There are the North Slobs and the South Slobs, which together form the Wexford Wildfowl Reserve. Here many species rare to the British Isles may be observed, including white-fronted Greenland geese, spotted redshanks and blacktailed godwits. The Slobs, the Barry statue, the estuary, the trawlers in the harbour, are all tokens of strong maritime connections. Sir John McClure (1807–73), discoverer of the North-West Passage, is

another famous Wexford seaman. Town and county are rich in everything that brings people to the ocean, from beaches to a proud record in the lifeboat service, and from lightships to a now faded reputation for wrecking. The county's east coast is virtually an unbroken string of strands, from Ballymoney to Rosslare. The most popular are Courtown Harbour and Curracloe, the latter notable also for its exemplary, eco-sensitive Nature Trail. In addition, the coast near the village of Blackwater has some superb secluded beaches. It was around here, in the 19th century, before the cliffs were quite so eroded, that the wreckers worked.

The south Wexford coast has equally broad and sandy beaches at Fethard-on-Sea, Carne and Booley Strand, near Duncannon, the only difference being that these tend to be used rather less. One partial exception to the sandy rule here is Kilmore Quay with its imposing cliffs. This attractive fishing village is the point of embarkation for the Saltee Islands, Ireland's most important bird sanctuary, and a vital land-fall for migrating birds. A stonier venue is the Hook Peninsula in the opposite corner of the county. Against its exposed tip of bare, ancient stone the ocean beats in constant drama. It offers panoramic vistas of bay after bay of the Waterford coast, all the way to the beached-whale shape of Helvick Head, west of Dungarvan, some forty miles away. On the way to the officially designated Hook Drive there is the most expensive wedding present in Irish history, Loftus Hall, built in the 1820s by a member of the Loftus family for a bride who, according to legend, never arrived. She should have. She too would have praised the beaches, relished the seafood, and been diverted by the birdlife that makes the Model County the Southeast's premier holiday place.

And so to Waterford. If the city of Kilkenny was the centre of the Norman political world, the city of Waterford was its commercial hub, and as such retained its eminence throughout the political upheavals which culminated in the yielding of the Norman hegemony to the English. And upheavals there were, what with Fitzgeralds rising against the king and other families fighting among themselves, and restless natives, and questions of legitimacy and authority almost continuously in the balance. Small wonder that it seemed to the merchants of Waterford that the best plan was to keep one's head on one's shoulders and make, not war, but money. In 1487 Lambert Simnel, pretender to the English throne, was crowned king in Dublin. Four years later another pretender, Perkin Warbeck, stuck his neck out. Waterford would have nothing to do with either of them, and by way of thanks received the sobriquet *urbs intacta*, the virgin city, from King Henry VII. The city had been taken once, by Strongbow. Once was enough. Waterford was content to abide by the marriage of interests which the wedding of Strongbow and Aoife seemed to represent. Centuries later a flourishing trade sprang up with Newfoundland, where a large number of inhabitants are descended from fishermen who came from villages along the Wexford and Waterford coasts.

It was Cromwell who put paid to the first phase of Waterford's commercial significance. The city successfully resisted his siege of it in 1649, a unique event in the Lord Protector's Irish campaign, surrendering the following year only on the promise of advantageous conditions by General Ireton. Soon, though, it was decreed that only somebody who was 'a freeman and of the English nation' could be a merchant. The result was that many merchant families left to settle in those European cities with which they had traded. Partly because of this connection, perhaps, persecuted Huguenots made their way to Waterford at the end of the 17th century. Where they worshipped is still known as the French Church, originally Greyfriars, established by the Franciscans in 1240. And Waterford is known as a community in which Quakers worshipped and prospered.

It was not until the 18th century that Waterford regained its mercantile name. One reason for its rehabilitation then was the foundation by the Penrose brothers of the Waterford glass factory in 1783. The secret manufacturing process ensures lead-crystal glass which is not only of great purity but also of great thickness. Thanks to the latter,

The mercantile port of Waterford.

ornate designs can be deeply incised in it, resulting in the complex interplay of facets and refractions which give the glass its world-renowned brilliance. A superb local example of 18th-century Waterford glass is the chandelier in the City Hall. But, successful as the original glass company was, it closed in 1851, and only since its re-opening in 1947 and the development of the North American market have Waterford and glass become inextricably associated in the international mind.

The city retains some impressive evidence of its 18th-century rehabilitation. The tall town houses and wide streets such as The Mall date from then, although efforts to preserve the houses seem to have been very hit-and-miss. The public buildings of the period have fared better. Foremost among these are Christ Church Cathedral, City Hall and, in particular, the Chamber of Commerce with its elegant staircase, all designed by a local architect, John Roberts. Churches seem to have been his speciality. Waterford rivals Kilkenny in their number and variety, and is also noteworthy for other important clerical connections. Luke Wadding, a noted 17th-century Jesuit theologian and missionary to Mexico, was born here, and Mount Sion school, in Barrack Street, was the Christian Brothers' inaugural establishment. Church pews throughout the Southeast bear a little oval disc with 'Hearne, Waterford' on it. And though there may be no necessary connection, it seems strange that a place the size of Waterford does not have a brewery.

Architectural credentials notwithstanding, Waterford is no Kilkenny, nor does it pretend to be. It is less easy to amble around Waterford: the traffic is too heavy and the street plan is a bit too much like that of its Viking cousin, Wexford. The people here walk briskly, like city people. And there is the obvious difference that Waterford has remained a successful port, and is inevitably a more bustling place, with a fuller sense of present possibilities in the air. England and the Continent are actively in the offing. Here is the grit and grime, the engines and the offal, of an Ireland that is seldom thought of, a place with workers in it.

Kilkenny is as elaborate and implicit as the law. Waterford is as blunt as commerce – one reason, perhaps, why socialist politics have long had a vocal role here. And when soccer teams were rarely found outside Dublin and Cork, Waterford had a very successful one, complete with legendary players and a public who supported 'the Blues' through hail, rain or snow. W.B. Yeats found himself reflecting on the consequences of being 'a sixty-year-old smiling public man' in the poem 'Among School Children', inspired by a visit to St Otteran's Montessori School here. But there is little sign of it left. St Otteran's is the name of the mental hospital now.

What catches the eye in Waterford is not so much the evidence of any one phase of its development but the cheek-by-jowl existence of its different phases. Extensive remnants of both the Viking and the Norman city walls have been uncovered, and as a centrepiece to the city's heritage stands Reginald's Tower, dating from the early 11th century, in which can be seen an array of royal charters, including the most impressive Charter Roll, dating from the reign of King Richard II (r. 1377–99). But these architectural remains, partly because they are not overwhelmingly pre-eminent, seem less representative of the life the city has known than the way Lombard Street runs into The Mall, and how a Parnell Street consorts with a Garter Lane, and a Parade Quay with a Barronstrand Street. It is intriguing to imagine the renowned exponent of hard-boiled detective fiction, Raymond Chandler (1888–1959), walking through this mixture of the ancient and the barely modern as a child on holiday with his mother's family, the Thorntons, law practitioners in Cathedral Square.

What grand opera is to Wexford, light opera is to Waterford, which has its own successful festival to prove it. The composer William Wallace (1812–65), best known for *Maritana*, was a Waterford native. So, too, is Val Doonican, the entertainer. Edmund Kean (1789–1833), the great Victorian actor, was born here. It is the kind of city from which one would expect a rock 'n' roll band with a hefty beat to hail. But Waterford has seen nothing like that since the fabulous days of

the Royal Showband in the early 1960s, which swept through the dancehalls of the country with a live-wire vocalist, a high-energy horn section and a rage to be young. Instead, the city boasts of one of the country's most successful provincial theatre companies, the evocatively named Red Kettle, among whose achievements are plays based on the lives of Waterford's workers.

One of the strange aspects of Waterford city is how cut off from the county it is. This is partly owing to the fact that it has remained a municipal borough unto itself, rather than the county's administrative centre, as Wexford and Kilkenny and most county towns are. County Waterford people typically regard the city as the place with the hospitals to which serious cases are brought, or the long train-stop on the way to Rosslare Harbour and the emigrant boat to England. Even the local bishopric is a reminder of a separation, being known as the diocese of Waterford and Lismore.

The Suir valley is Waterford city's natural hinterland. Though less well known than its sister valleys, a drive along it shows at once that it matches them in scope and bounty, ruins and beauty, particularly if a geographical point is stretched and Cashel is included. The patient cattle, the glimpse of mansions, the intermittent spires, the points of scenic uplift: the mix of elements in southeastern pastoral is as intact here as anywhere. And to form a striking complement to, in Edmund Spenser's phrase, 'the gentle Shure', there are the mountains. From east to west, the Comeraghs, the Monavullaughs and the Knockmealdowns run the length of County Waterford; arbiters of weather, creators of swift-changing cloudscapes, they are obtrusive colourists with their heather and bracken and stands of pine. The homely quilt of rich County Tipperary farms spreads out as far as the eye can see. There are fields here defined by fences, rather than the more usual hedges and banks, and in them can be seen svelte horses. The Irish name of Clonmel, the valley's major town, is *Cluain Meala*, which means 'honey meadow'. It speaks for the whole area.

River and mountain blend winningly

around the village of Portlaw. In the early 19th century a Quaker family named Malcolmson set up a mill here and ran it along lines which shared something of the ethos of the early socialist Robert Owens' New Lanark. Although it is difficult to see now, the village itself was designed in the shape of a hand and fingers, denoting both benevolent employer and willing worker. Much more visible, and rather more characteristic, is Curraghmore House on the village's west edge. This is the seat of the Lords Waterford, the Beresford family, prominent Tories at the time of the Patriot Parliament in the 1780s, who were rewarded with a peerage for facilitating the passage of the Act of Union which abolished that parliament. The house expresses their status very well, not least in the way it incorporates the Norman home of the La Poer family – in English, Power – and its holding of portraits by, among others, Gainsborough and Reynolds. A much more striking instance of an architectural mixed marriage is nearby at Carrick-on-Suir, where what is Ireland's most imposing Elizabethan house can be seen emerging from the remains of an earlier castle. Legend has it that Anne Boleyn was born here in 1507.

South of Carrick there is a peak in the Comeraghs called Coumshingaun. There a mountain lake bears the name of the 19th-century highwayman, Crotty, who had a cave by its shores. This retreat had a peculiar modern counterpart on the County Waterford side, where in a mountain townland called Leacandara an anchorite resided, though he was law-abiding. Leacandara Jim had his story told in *Wide World* magazine, and there was a photograph of a dusty, minor road, and bleak furze-covered land, and a man with a large beard standing at the mouth of his abode. But caves proper, miles of them, in the shadow of the Galtees, south Tipperary's continuation of Waterford's mountain chain, provide Ireland's premier speleological treat. Known as the Mitchelstown caves, they are on the Cork road between Cahir and Ballyporeen, and are so called because they are on land which, at the time of their discovery, was owned by the Kingston family,

owners of Mitchelstown.

The Suir is tidal as far as Clonmel. But the trade the tides brought to the town – on the strength of which it once regarded itself as the capital of Tipperary – is gone now, leaving only deserted quays, and the shells of warehouses and merchants' homes, as reminders of how substantial it was. The Suir has become an amenity, its banks providing very pleasant walks. In its river life, as well as in its origins, Clonmel resembles New Ross. But it grew much larger, much more loyal to the Crown, and so much more prosperous until, like Waterford city, that loyalty drew the attention of Cromwell. The siege of Clonmel, to which the Ironsides applied themselves after their Waterford rebuff, was equally unproductive from a military standpoint. The Irish garrison even managed to slip away before the end and, when the end came, town and people were spared. But they lost the peace. The face of the new order can be seen in the severe cut of the stone in the façade of the Main Guard, though at least this building is genuine, unlike the heavy-handed pastiche of the unavoidable West Gate.

The terrace of 18th-century houses off the quay reveal that Clonmel, too, had its heyday. And in 1815 the town found a new source of success, thanks to Carlo Bianconi, who inaugurated and headquartered his coach service here. The roads were narrower then, and there was no county council, much less an EC Structural Fund, to pave or widen them. The only thing that was the same was the fickle weather. The Lombardy coachman was asking for trouble. But before they were finished, the 'Bians', as they were called, had made the country smaller, serving not only the travelling public but delivering newspapers and mail, not to mention welcome consignments of gossip. Although Bianconi is buried in the north of the county, in a place called Boherlahan (the translation of whose Irish name is 'wide road'), Clonmel is as proud of him as if he were a native. Less seems to be made of the fact that Laurence Sterne, of *Tristram Shandy* fame, was born in the town in 1713, as was his mother before him.

Its success in trade has ensured Clonmel's reputation for being what is called in that part of the world a 'good town', a phrase whose ostensible simplicity covers a multitude of nuances. 'Good' means not only commercially active but good for artisans too, a place where things are made with pride. There was a time when the mark of a good town was that soft drinks were manufactured in it. Cities were responsible for breweries and distilleries; towns should know their place by being no more than founts of orange crush and red lemonade. Lorries laden with the stuff blazed down largely empty roads, their cargoes jingling all through summer, the milk-floats of *Tir na n-Og*, land of eternal youth. The names on them seemed as large and colourful as boasts: Dwan's of Thurles, Lett's of Enniscorthy, Magner's of Clonmel. But then Clonmel is also the Irish home of Bulmer's Cider, an altogether more intoxicating brew.

A more complex sign of a good town is that it has an Irishtown. These are areas which were originally outside the walls, where the natives lived, the people who became the town's maids and labourers. Kilkenny has one. The one in Enniscorthy is on the Vinegar Hill side of the river. It is called the Shannon, a mocking allusion to the river beyond which the expropriated Irish were driven as a result of Cromwell's incursion. They are not exclusive to towns. The village of Lismore, County Waterford, has a quarter known as Botany. Its official name is New Street, but locals thought it more appropriate to refer to it as a replica of the Australian landfall of transported criminals. Irishtown in Clonmel is beyond the West Gate, in the general direction of the mountains. Its appearance is flattened, and its history mollified, by the raw-looking housing estates straggling over the hilly land behind it.

One feature of a good town which Clonmel lacks, though, is a square. Squares became prevalent in the 19th century, the brainchild usually of some improving landlord back from a European tour and full of the joys of space and light. Instead the compact interconnectedness of the town's streets, and the way in which they reveal how ancient landmarks have been negotiated, offers the feel of an excursion. This can be agreeably carried out on foot, Clonmel being as stroll-worthy as Kilkenny, with the eye alert to the mix of styles that occur above the fascia, and an outlook disposed to play with resonances.

The lush beauty of the Glen of Aherlow, County Tipperary.

The Comeragh Mountains in Waterford.

And in the evening there are restaurants where the food is fresh, the cuisine not terribly pretentious, the wine is nondescript, and the majority of the diners are earnest young professionals. Or, if such company does not appeal, there are the dogs. Clonmel is one of greyhound racing's shrines, and passions excited by local favourites add to the evening's voltage, already high with the big money that is changing hands.

The other Suir valley town is Cahir. Smaller in size and significance than Clonmel, it is much more typical of the average Irish market town, particularly the kinds that abound in the Southeast. These towns owe their present-day look to landlords, and made a name for themselves by having a tannery or a bacon factory or, as in the case of Cahir, a flour mill. Usually these towns' most imposing building, besides the church, houses the bank.

The square in Cahir was installed in the early 19th century by one of the earls of Glengall, whose former town house, now a hotel, fronts it. Perhaps it was because of the square's novelty that the first run made by a Bianconi coach was along the river as far as Cahir, though the riverscape is still enough to make the drive worthwhile. The local Protestant church dates from the same period, and was built to a design of John Nash (1752–1835), the architect of Regency London. On the outskirts of the town, part of the Glengall estate has been made into a very pleasant park. In addition to walks and vistas, the park also contains Swiss Cottage, a kind of Regency folly, in the design of which John Nash is also said to have been involved. A picture of tweeness on the outside, its rooms are delightfully light and airy, clad with wallpaper that is hand-painted.

As a capstone to the intimacy that existed here between landlord and tenant, a World War I memorial stands in the square, dedicated to the Tipperary to which it is 'a long, long way' – though most of the servicemen who sang about it thought the name of the place was Tipperairai, a mythical place in France. This monument is more notable for its existence than for any particular artistic merit. It is estimated that some two hundred and fifty thousand Irishmen served in the Great War, and the names of their units – the Royal Dublin Fusiliers, the Royal Inniskilling Fusiliers, the Connaught Rangers, the Royal Munster Fusiliers and, above all, the 36th (Ulster) Division – are inseparable from the carnage and heroism of that conflict. But public monuments in Ireland commemorating this fact of modern Irish history are not nearly as numerous as such a commitment might be thought to warrant.

Long before their lordships of Glengall, though, Cahir was a place thought worth defending, as its castle by the ford asserts. A Butler stronghold, its oldest stones date from the 14th century, and it is the largest castle in Ireland of its period. The building itself is something in the nature of a palimpsest of architectural styles, having been extensively remodelled virtually once a century since its foundation. But recently many of the most egregious stylistic anachronisms have given way to more authentic restoration, one instance of the large number which could be cited of a greater degree of official commitment to the preservation of the physical past, as distinct from its ideological shadow.

Cahir is also convenient to the Glen of Aherlow, one of the Southeast's most celebrated beauty spots, a little way to the north and west of the town. The route of a circular drive around the glen is well signposted, but its scope can be more fully appreciated by doing a bit of climbing. One of the climbs is called Paradise Hill. Beyond the heavily wooded slopes is the spread of the Golden Vale, an inland sea of lushness and fertility, and the most westerly pocket of rich farmland in the country. Near here, at a place called Soloheadbeg, the shots were fired in 1919 that killed two policemen and began the War of Independence. A monument marks the spot. Leaving Cahir to the southwest on the road to Ballyporeen will lead to the spectacular ruin of Burntcourt Castle, a relic of Cromwellian times. Its owner, Sir Richard Everard, took part in the Confederation of Kilkenny. The big house's gaunt walls are as chilling as the sight of a skeleton.

Another reason to circle the Glen of Aherlow is that it means approaching the Rock of Cashel from the northwest, which is not the best approach; though the rich land leading this way to the Rock suggests a crude, common-sense, economic reason for this famous ecclesiastical site, undoubtedly a gem of European importance.

It is worth going out of the way to make the best approach to it, which is from the north on the main Dublin road, round an unremarkable bend to the left – and there the Rock is, unique, immediate and complete. The lump of limestone is 200 feet high and is said to hail from the Slieve Bloom mountains thirty miles to the north. Legend has it that the devil took a bite out of these mountains and, finding that it did not agree with him, spat it out. It landed at Cashel. The gap left by the bite, known as the Devil's Bit, can be clearly seen from the top of the rock.

This place was in the forefront of Irish ecclesiastical and political history for a thousand years before a long period of neglect set in during the 18th century. Evidence of its secular past is sparse, but this is more than compensated for by the grandeur of its spiritual remains. These are not only of great variety as to period, but the crowding together on one rather small and awkward site of such distinctive architectural representatives of each period is also homage of a kind to the site's commanding location. The view from the summit is an enticement to imagine what can be seen from the top of the round tower which, as at St Canice's in Kilkenny, seems anachronistically to be the cathedral's sentry post.

To a considerable extent, the history of the Rock is the history of its great cathedral. In the 15th century one of the Earls of Kildare set fire to the cathedral on the pretext that he thought the archbishop was inside. A couple of hundred years later it was burned again by the Earl of Inchiquin, one Murrough O'Brien, nicknamed Murchadh na Doiteain ('Arson Murrough'). And, for good measure, he slaughtered those seeking sanctuary inside. Then, a hundred years later, an archbishop stripped its roof off. But, despite war, fire and weather, it remains very much an heirloom,

with an almost providential number of its ornamental features still intact.

The cathedral overshadows Cormac's Chapel, but does not eclipse it. What the cathedral is to the Rock historically, Cormac's Chapel is aesthetically. Dating from the 12th century – which makes it older by a century than the cathedral – the chapel is significant not only for being the first Romanesque church built in Ireland but the best preserved. The European influence on its design, and the fact that a number of its most outstanding features argue strongly for its debt to European craftsmen, are intriguing glimpses of Cashel's medieval standing. The chapel's size and its state of preservation enable its striking integrity to be appreciated in full, and the details of its stonework – the head and the fabulous beasts, as well as the seemingly more ordinary ornamentation – are a rare treat. See, particularly, the quality of the detailing on Cormac's tomb. Also not to be overlooked are the family plots of locals mixed in amidst the grandeur. Homely almost to the point of seeming incongruous, they add a welcome human touch.

Few towns would be able to offer anything to compete with a neighbour like the Rock of Cashel and Cashel seems to know better than to try. There are, however, a number of other worthwhile places to see in the town and surrounding area. Most of these have ecclesiastical associations, such as Hore Abbey, the ruin right at the foot of the Rock, and the bishop's palace in the town itself that has been converted into an hotel. The most illustrious of the Protestant bishops of Cashel was Theophilus Bolton whose 18th-century collection of manuscripts and various other literary riches may be viewed at the library that bears his name. It is said that, while in the service of one of the bishops of Cashel, Robert Guinness, father of Arthur, discovered what it is that makes that drink of theirs so distinctive.

By turning to the left on the western edge of Irishtown in Clonmel, it is possible to defer a visit to the upper Suir Valley and head for a valley which seems to be its opposite. This is a much more literal kind of valley, a slit between the shoulders of the Monavullaghs and, to the west, the Knockmealdowns, with the road snaking up and around and through it as best it can, while on the valley floor the little river Nire gurgles along busily. The road to which the Nire Drive signs point is noted for its mountain views. Before the signs were put up, the townlands here used to be bywords for remoteness. All around was one of the last 18th-century redoubts of the Irish language in the Southeast. A poet ran the local school and, true to his calling, he found here 'ogmhnaoi ba corrai in Eirinn' ('the most exciting young women in Ireland'). These days the road runs prettily, emptily on through Colligan Glen to Dungarvan and the sea.

The place where this road merges with the main Waterford road is called The Pike, and here stands the statue to the glorious memory of the greyhound, Master McGrath. He was at his peak from 1868 to 1871, when he lost only once in 37 outings. Among his triumphs were several on English tracks against illustrious English competition. So, 'Three cheers for old Ireland, and Master McGrath!' goes the local song about him, a song whose air is traditional, but whose words tell as much of the human underdog as of the real dog.

The glimpses of Dungarvan Bay as the road descends give a welcome sense of openness. But to appreciate to the full the bay's sweep, a drive from Waterford along the coast road is necessary and well worthwhile. This road rides the tops of cliffs for thirty miles and offers one spectacular seascape after another as it winds around the coastline. There are a number of unassuming villages along the way, and one which is not quite on this road and not exactly unassuming either. But Dunmore East is worth making a slight detour to see, not only for its charming location but to observe the kinds of things that happen when an old, settled fishing village is invited to accommodate city types and new money.

The first stop on the East Waterford coast road proper must be Tramore, the only thoroughly developed seaside resort in the whole of the Southeast. There is a brash and breezy air of a workers' playground about the place, of hurdy-gurdies and cheap-and-cheerful tee-shirts and the smell of frying food. Children love it, and it seems not to do adults much harm either. There is also race week, as vivid a fixture in the calendar here as Galway races are in the West. There are noted stud farms in the Southeast, including one founded by the famous trainer Vincent O'Brien at Ballydoyle, near Cashel, but racecourses are not as plentiful in the Southeast as in other parts of the country, though that is not the only reason that race week is the climax of the Tramore holiday season.

Tramore's main attraction, however, is its strand. The town's name in Irish is An Trá Mór, meaning 'the big, or great, strand'. The name certainly fits the huge expanse of stoneless, shingle-free sand, great for walking, and with sloblands and sea-life that the naturalist will find rewarding. There are also some exhilarating clifftop walks. The tower-like structure looking out to sea across Tramore Bay is known as the Metal Man, from which ships may take a bearing on the treacherous coast. The walks produce numerous reminders of the rich prehistoric remains that abound in the area. But it is unclear if these remains inspired the most elaborate resort attraction in the town, Celtworld. This gives the visitor the chance to travel back to the days of Ireland's earliest settlers – the Fir Bolgs, or Belly Men; the Tuatha De Danaan, or the tribe of Danu; the Parthalonians; and, last but by no means least, the Celts. The legendary seven invasions of Ireland are revisited as one is transported from screen to screen to the accompaniment of atmospheric music and sensational optical effects. But no mention is made of the local neolithic people, the Decies, whose name is a synonym for the whole county south of the mountains.

Annestown, Bunmahon, Stradbally: these villages are kin to Dunmore East in looks and layout. 'Bunmahon must be pierced with shafts!' declared the patriot and ideologue Thomas Davis in the 1840s. And indeed it was, there being evidence of ancient copper workings here. A certain amount of mining was carried out but nothing much came of it except that the cliffs are somewhat undermined and there are signs warning against walking on them. At this point, the cliffs are 200 feet high. Each village has its own sandy cove which is more often than not deserted. The largest and most popular beach between Tramore and Dungarvan is at Clonea.

Dungarvan is the administrative capital of County Waterford, and its openness to the sea gives it a breezy, somewhat spacious feel. It consists of two communities: the main town and, on the Colligan estuary's eastern bank, Abbeyside. A solid market town, Dungarvan is the kind of place where one might expect to find an old-fashioned hardware store which sells nails by the pound and sacks of feedstuffs and maintains a display of plaster statues of Our Lady, Jesus and St Patrick. It is surprising to find that, heading out to rejoin the main road to the west, there are traffic lights and, on the by-pass, a rather large industrial estate.

Branching off to the left of the main road to Cork, just as it begins to climb west of Dungarvan, will lead to where the chain of coves and villages continues. It carries on into County Cork at Youghal and comes to a temporary stop at Ballycotton, east Cork's counterpart to Dunmore East. The road that

goes by the western edge of Dungarvan Bay is the one for Ring and Helvick and Ballinagaul. These communities constitute a *Gaeltacht*, an area where Irish is still the primary spoken language, though it tends to be spoken pretty quietly. In Ring, the centrepiece of the locality, there are more television aerials than thatched cottages, which is simply to say that it is a workaday, going concern, not given much to making an exhibition of itself. The language is housed and nourished in an Irish College dating from the early days of independent Ireland, when the acquisition and cherishing of Irish was the aggressively pursued educational and cultural priority. All around here, once again, there are splendid vistas of the sea, and the clifftop walks are secure and well mapped out and a particular joy to bird-watchers. Choughs – red-legged crows – find the area especially congenial.

Though the translation of Ballinagaul is 'town of the foreigner', the Celtic note remains pronounced along the remainder of the west Waterford coast. In particular, the village of Ardmore is a treasure-house of remains of early Christian Ireland. These are all associated with St Declan, whose name has been intimately linked with the area since

Tramore's Celtworld gives visitors a chance to explore Ireland's Celtic past.

the seventh century, making Ardmore the oldest parish in Ireland. A great number of places in Ireland are connected with powerful ancient clerics, but Ardmore is notable for not having its remains appropriated or rehabilitated by anybody, which makes it resemble such celebrated monastic sites as Glendalough and Clonmacnois, except that here the remains are mixed in with the everyday life of the village.

The extent of the remains, too, is noteworthy. Like many of his contemporaries, St Declan left a blessed well. But he also left a blessed stone. It is on the beach, and has a number of legends associated with it. One is that rheumatism can be cured by crawling under it. But this sounds like the kind of story knowing locals tell gullible travellers, since the cure could only be attempted by somebody who didn't suffer from rheumatism – somebody, that is, who was as good as cured of it. More elevated are the remains on the outskirts of the village. These consist of the cathedral and the round tower which is 95 feet high and among the best preserved in the country. Said to have been originally inspired by Italian campaniles, these towers functioned as watchtowers and as places of refuge. Their only aperture, which resembles a window, is at the top, and the entrance is 8 or 10 feet off the ground. When the enemy drew near, the monks scrambled up, then drew in after them, their ladders, though once an attack was launched they were terribly vulnerable to fire. The cathedral has some remarkable stone carvings of such subjects as the Fall of Man, Adam and Eve and the Judgment of Solomon.

The road that forks to the right at the bridge at Youghal leads up the estuary and into the Blackwater valley, which for natural beauty and historical associations is at least the equal of any river valley in the country. Further west, in north County Cork, the valley is synonymous with the Plantation of Munster, with extirpation and dispossession and the Elizabethan epic's righteous cruelty. But, between Youghal and Lismore in particular, it seems so virgin and serene – with only the Knockmealdowns in the distance to suggest a colour besides forest

green – that it is easy to imagine that this must be where Edmund Spenser, who knew the territory well, was thinking of when he wrote in *The Faerie Queen*:

> *Whilom, when Ireland flourishèd in fame*
> *Of wealths and goodness, far above the rest*
> *Of all that bear the British Islands name*
> *The Gods then used (for pleasure and for rest)*
> *Oft to resort thereto, when seemed them best.*

But appearances are deceptive. The landscape cannot be separated from the way in which it is inhabited. The valley may be a picturesque bower, but it also contains a string of substantial houses, all the way along, on either bank, each visible to its neighbour, each unobtrusively in command of a stretch of road and river. But while these houses share a common history, and are united by their cultural and social status, their view of where they stand can be somewhat mixed. One of the most impressive of them, Dromana – perched above the water's edge opposite the point where the road divides for Cappoquin and Lismore – is the home of the Villiers-Stuart family, remembered for its contribution to the securing, in 1829, of Catholic Emancipation. The gate to Dromana, which is on the Cappoquin road, dates from just about the same time, and has now been restored to its original exoticism. Inspired by the Brighton Pavilion brand of orientalism, it was erected as a wedding present, and remains the only piece of Hindu Gothic in the Southeast.

At Cappoquin the river makes its magnificent turn, and it is worth leaving it for a brief trip to the Cistercian monastery at Mount Mellary, a little way up the mountains from the village. Founded in 1832, when it was built by monks on a previously uninhabited site, it seems just the spot for a life of silent devotion. The bracing air and the emptiness are conducive to a contemplative moment, and there are splendid mountain views. Further explorations of the Knockmealdowns on foot may be undertaken hereabouts along the Munster Way.

It was the road from Cappoquin to Lismore that inspired Thackeray's comparison in his *Irish Sketch Book* (1843):

Nor in any country that I have visited have I seen a view more noble – it is too rich and peaceful to be what is called romantic, but lofty, large, and generous, if the term may be used; the river and banks as fine as the Rhine; the castle not as large, but as noble and picturesque as Warwick.

When the core of the castle was built by Prince, later King, John in 1185, Lismore had had some five hundred years of illustrious ecclesiastical history. The castle tower sits on the site of the monastery which gave Lismore its fame, and which was the centrepiece of a substantial seat of early medieval learning. There is a Book of Lismore, and a Lismore crozier, and King Henry II came here shortly after landing to explain himself to the bishop. The castle was given as a present to Sir Walter Raleigh, who then sold it to Richard Boyle. His son, Robert (1627–91), the physicist and author of Boyle's Law, was born here. In the 18th century Elizabeth Boyle married one of the Cavendishes, Dukes of Devonshire, in which family Lismore Castle and its extensive lands remain. Only the castle gardens are open to the public, though these contain some excellent specimens of rare and exotic plants, introduced by one of the 19th-century dukes.

Not quite as well sited as the castle, though equal to it in historical interest, is St Carthage's Church of Ireland Cathedral, named for the saint who first made Lismore's name and preserving the town's episcopal connections. Its appearance today comes from the same 19th-century building boom which increased the castle to its present size by adding the large and somewhat artificial-looking west wing. The tombs in the cathedral nave are very much older, and some of their stone ornamentation includes figures which have a suspiciously waggish air about them. The cathedral also contains an exceptional stained-glass window by Edward Burne-Jones, the noted 19th-century English Pre-Raphaelite painter.

It is not very surprising that Lismore was one of the first twelve places in the country to be named a National Heritage Centre. That

The oriental quirkiness of Dromana Gate, Cappoquin, County Waterford.

seems the least to which its history has entitled it. And with the former courthouse converted into a heritage centre, the local lending library restored to its original charm, and maps and signposts the order of the day, it certainly looks the part. Best of all, the village has been tidied up, with evidence of fresh paint and renovation, so that it no longer has the faded and forgotten look of some Irish villages. But if the weight of history is too burdensome, there are always the Knockmealdowns. Five miles north of Lismore on the Clogheen road is the celebrated viewing point called The Vee, the name deriving from the 90-degree hairpin bend on which the point rests.

The road rises in easy stages past a fast-moving mountain stream, the Ownashad, which means 'the river of jewels'. Before long, the skimpy fields give way to the stands of pine that are so familiar in the Southeast as to suggest that it must be an offence against the State to leave a mountain bald. There is a glacial lake on the left called Béal Loch, meaning 'mouth lake', which the locals say is bottomless. Another name for it is Petticoat Loose, deriving from a local legend about a young girl who was seduced and abandoned and who haunts the area, though some have sanitised the name by claiming it refers to the rhododendrons which, courtesy of Devonshire Estates, flounce all around the mountain by the lake.

From The Vee, the view takes in Butler country from Slievenamon on the west and, on the east side, the Galtees and the southern rim of the Golden Vale are seen. Straight ahead, as far as the Slieve Bloom mountains, lies the plain of Tipperary. On a fine day the Devil's Bit is visible. This is the inner kingdom of the Southeast in all its greenery and soft light. A little way back up the mountain, overlooking The Vee, is an odd-shaped structure which looks like a stone beehive. This is the grave of Major Samuel Grubb, whose dying wish was to be buried standing up with this view in front of him. It may not have been the most comfortable eternal repose, but what he was getting at is pretty clear.

MUSTS IN THE SOUTHEAST

* A glass of sloe gin made from the fruit of blackthorns planted by the Normans.
* Curracloe Strand, County Wexford.
* St Canice's Cathedral, Kilkenny.
* Altamont Gardens, near Carlow.
* A punt on the Barrow.
* The purchase of a piece of local craft work.
* A book by John Banville.
* A cruise on the Blackwater.
* A yahoo in Yola.
* An evening's dog racing in Clonmel.
* A trip to the Saltee Islands, especially in the bird migration season.
* The Cistercian Abbey, Mount Mellary.
* A pint of Smithwicks within smelling range of the brewery in Kilkenny.
* The East Waterford coast road between Tramore and Dungarvan.
* Inistiogue village.
* Celtworld, Tramore.
* The Rock of Cashel.
* An aria in Wexford in October.
* The round tower at Ardmore.
* Mitchelstown Caves.

Lismore Castle by night.

3 The Southwest: a Separate State of Mind

Sean Dunne

COUNTIES

CORK

KERRY

If certain aspects of history could be condensed into a single place in County Cork, St Gobnait's graveyard in Ballyvourney would be an ideal site. There, among the low hills of mid Cork, many different aspects of Ireland are contained within a small area. Pre-Christian standing stones can be seen in a field while the grave of St Gobnait lies within the walls of a graveyard that also contains two separate churches: one, now closed, Protestant; the other, now a ruin, Catholic.

There are two holy wells near the graveyard. One lies under a statue of Gobnait, a sixth- or seventh-century saint after whom many girls in this part of County Cork are still called. On a flat stone nearby a rusted crutch once took its place among an array of other objects – a broken comb, a small crucifix, coins, a hairpin – that had been left there by pilgrims who made their way around an ancient path and pleaded with the saint to meet their urgent petitions. The crutch, it was

believed, was left behind by a cripple who walked home after the saint had cured him.

The site, which is reached by a narrow road, is dominated by the grey statue of the saint. Yet, not far away, a pre-Christian fertility figure, carved in stone and known as a *sheelagh-na-gig*, is fixed to the wall of one of the ruined churches. The figure is of a woman whose hands rest on her exposed genitals.

The graveyard in which this mixture of pagan and Christian occurs has been called an Irish Valhalla. The famous people buried there include the composer Seán Ó Riada (1931–71) and the poet Seán Ó Riordain (1917–77), together with a number of local singers, storytellers and musicians.

Ó Riada, who was only 40 when he died in 1971, had taken Irish traditional music and injected it with a creative electricity which remade it as a vibrant, communal expression of life with all its troubles and joys. His funeral, led by a piper playing a lament,

The hidden valley of Gougane Barra, County Cork.

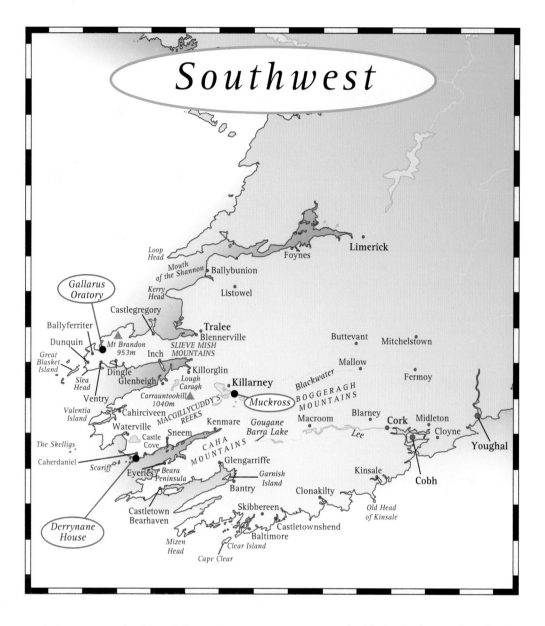

Southwest

Loop Head
Mouth of the Shannon
Kerry Head
Foynes
Limerick
Ballybunion
Listowel

Gallarus Oratory

Castlegregory

Ballyferriter
Dunquin
Great Blasket Island
Slea Head
Mt Brandon 953m
Dingle
Ventry
Tralee
Blennerville
SLIEVE MISH MOUNTAINS
Inch
Killorglin
Glenbeigh
Lough Caragh

Buttevant
Mitchelstown

Mallow

Fermoy

Cahirciveen
Valentia Island
Waterville
The Skelligs
Caherdaniel
Carrauntoohill 1040m
MACGILLYCUDDY'S REEKS
Sneem
Castle Cove
Kenmare
Killarney
Muckross
BOGGERAGH MOUNTAINS
Blackwater
Gougane Barra Lake
Macroom
Blarney
Cork
Midleton
Cloyne
Lee
Youghal

CAHA MOUNTAINS
Scariff
Eyeries
Beara Peninsula
Glengarriffe
Garnish Island
Bantry
Clonakilty
Kinsale
Cobh
Old Head of Kinsale

Derrynane House

Castletown Bearhaven
Mizen Head
Skibbereen
Baltimore
Clear Island
Castletownshend
Cape Clear

made its way past the River Sullane. Poets took turns to carry his coffin among the headstones and television cameras. His mellifluous Cork accent was heard again on the radio as old recordings of his talks were played.

In west Cork, Ó Riada had been driven by a sense of music and culture as something local and living. He founded a male voice choir which is now conducted by his son, Peadar, and which still sings in the local church every Sunday. In its songs, a dying tradition is sustained that at its best strikes some ancient, vital note. Some of the songs are centuries old, yet the events which gave rise to them are recounted with the freshness of gossip. As with the surrounding landscape, which can be read like a book by those expert in the story of its lineaments, there is a sense of history in everyday happenings recounted in these lyrics.

Part of that landscape includes Gougane Barra, a hidden valley which holds the source of County Cork's main river, the Lee. Gougane Barra was home to another saint, Finbarr, who was said to have lived there in a hermitage before he founded the city of Cork at the beginning of the seventh century. With its beautiful lake and mountains, Gougane Barra is a place which attracts crowds in summer. In winter it offers a rare solitude. It became famous as a result of two inhabitants – the Tailor, Tadhg Ó Buachalla, and his wife, Ansty – whose stories were written down by an English writer and inventor, Eric Cross (1905–80).

The book, a harmless and lively collection of yarns collected from a natural storyteller, caused consternation when it was published in 1942. Parts of it were read out in the Seanad (the Upper House of the Irish parliament), and, in what now seems an extraordinary example of the censorship mentality which dominated the country at that time, the relevant sections were then excised from the Seanad proceedings lest anyone be scandalised by reading them. In their house on the side of the hill near the lake, the old man and woman whose ordinary lives gave rise to the scandal were visited by protesting priests, one of whom made the old man burn a copy of the book.

At their grave in a small cemetery overlooking the lake at Gougane Barra, the sculptor Seamus Murphy (1910–75), who carved the statue of St Gobnait in Ballyvourney, cut a herringbone tweed pattern into the headstone and inscribed Shakespeare's memorable line as an epigraph for the Tailor: 'A star danced and under that I was born.'

As one travels west from Cork city, the landscape is as wondrous as Gougane Barra. It is a different terrain to that of north Cork which, while broken by mountains, is often lush and fruitful. West Cork can be rough and its very wildness – those dark mountains that lead to precipitous cliffs – is part of its attraction. The well-kept prairie fields of north Cork are counterpointed by the small, hungry acres that dot the mountainsides in the most remote parts of the Beara peninsula.

Despite the beauties of its landscape, many people have emigrated from west Cork in recent times. In 1841 the Victorian travel-writers, Mr and Mrs Hall, noted:

> It is impossible to describe the final parting. Shrieks and prayers, blessings and lamentations mingled in one great cry from those on the quay and those on shipboard until a band stationed in the forecastle struck up 'St Patrick's Day'. The communicating plank was withdrawn, and the steamer moved majestically forward on her way. Some, overcome with emotion, fell down upon the deck, others waved hats, handkerchiefs and hands to their friends and the band played louder.

Whilst such partings now take place in the anonymity of airports, there is no doubt that the intensity and sadness of the occasion can be just as strong, if not quite as dramatic.

The paradox of west Cork lies in the fact that while hundreds have emigrated – as they have emigrated from other parts of Ireland – in recent years, many others have come there to live. The area has become home to hippies and New Age seekers and a haven for wealthy Dutch, British and Germans. As a result, west Cork is the most cosmopolitan part of rural Ireland. The tastes of the newcomers have encouraged many cottage industries and some of the country's finest small-scale food producers. In the small village of Ballylickey, Val Manning presides over Manning's Emporium, a shop filled with locally made cheeses and sausages, organic vegetables and delicious types of bread. Restaurants reflect this richness. The best of them – Clifford's on the Mardyke in Cork city, for example, or Ballymaloe House near the village of Cloyne – have not had to look far for ingredients.

Skibbereen is one of the focal points for the many artists who have settled in west Cork and whose work is frequently on display at the West Cork Arts Centre in the town. Skibbereen is close to Lough Hyne, a unique sea-water lake whose life-forms are much studied by marine biologists. At evening, around its shores, there are few sounds besides the lapping of water over sea urchins and starfish, the cry of a curlew in a lapidary darkness that is broken only by the scatter of lights in houses on the surrounding hills.

The nearby coastal village of Castletownshend has been called the last outpost of the British Empire. To those who love it it is a haven of peace behind the high walls of enclosed demesnes. Those who hate it see it as what one writer described as 'an enclave of congealed Cromwellians'. It was in this village that Edith Somerville (1858–1949) and her cousin, Violet Martin (1862–1915), under the *nom de plume* of Somerville and Ross, wrote in a partnership that endured for their whole lives. The comic *Irish R.M.* stories were their most popular works but their most powerful novel was *The Real Charlotte*.

Edith Somerville was a brilliant, talented woman: artist, writer, designer, farmer, Master of the West Carbery hunt. She was the organist in St Barrahane's Church for 70 years. The floor at the east end of the church contains a mosaic which Edith designed and laid. The church also has some stained-glass windows, rich lozenges of colour, by the artist Harry Clarke. The organ on which Edith Somerville played can still be seen, while the house in which she lived, Drishane, remains intact. When, in 1946, she became too old to climb the stairs at Drishane, she moved to Tally-Ho Cottage in the village, where she died in 1949.

The often brooding, wild coast of west Cork is here and there lightened by small, brightly painted villages, like Allihies and Eyeries, on the Beara Peninsula. It also includes the former naval base of Kinsale, a town now distinguished by its narrow streets and the many restaurants they contain. Outside the town, signs point to the site of the Battle of Kinsale. This battle, fought on Christmas Eve in 1601, was a turning-point in Irish history; the defeat of the Irish on that day became a dark shadow in the national memory. It was the last effort by the old Gaelic aristocracy to oppose the British colonisation of Ireland.

Soon after the battle, work began on a star fort on a cliff outside the town. James Fort, with its bastioned walls, was later complemented by another star fort, Charles Fort. In a county rich with ruins of castle and fort, these two are particularly notable for their solid perdurance, formidable monuments as they are to the imperial certainties which built them.

Allihies was once the site of copper mines that are now disused, dangerous and haunting. In the early 19th century over a thousand people worked in the mines. Daphne du Maurier based her novel *Hungry Hill* in this part of County Cork. When the novel became a film in 1946, Hungry Hill – an alliterative place-name that must have seemed a godsend to a novelist with du Maurier's sense of drama – became famous

The coastal village of Castletownshend, County Cork.

Eyeries village on the Beara Peninsula, County Cork.

around the world. Allihies is popular with summer visitors who enjoy the beaches of the Beara peninsula and take a trip on the nearby Dursey cable car, the only one of its kind in Ireland, which connects a small, almost deserted island with the mainland. On the road between Allihies and the fishing town of Castletownbere, a Buddhist-inspired conference and retreat centre has been developed on the edge of a cliff at Dzogchen Beara.

Other parts of County Cork also contain the remains of closed mines. In her book *Discovering Cork*, Daphne D.C. Pochin Mould points out that the story of mining in west Cork can be traced to Bronze Age activity on Mount Gabriel, near the village of Schull. She quotes an expert who declared that 'the Mount Gabriel workings are the oldest radiocarbon-dated copper mines in northwest Europe'.

The coast of west Cork is studded with islands. The farthest from the mainland is Cape Clear, three miles out. Reached by ferry from the picturesque fishing village of Baltimore, Cape Clear is popular with bird-watchers who go there in spring and autumn to observe the spectacular fly-pasts of

migratory birds. The patron saint of the island, St Kieran, is believed to have celebrated the first mass in Ireland on a site near the harbour. Island folklore is still replete with tales of 'Soupers' – Catholics who became Protestants during the Great Famine in exchange for food.

During the years of that famine, in the recurrent shortages of the 1840s and 1850s, thousands of people died in County Cork. Towns and villages which are bright and attractive now were then the scene of bitter tragedy. The village of Schull was one such place. There is nothing hungry or deathly about the village now and it is a favourite and animated holiday place for the Dublin chattering classes whose doings and connivances are a source of gossip and cash to locals.

Famine graves, such as those outside the town of Skibbereen or at Carrigastyra near Macroom, are physical evocations of the misery otherwise only conceivable through the accounts of contemporary writers. One such, N.M. Cummins, wrote a vivid letter to the Duke of Wellington which helped raise £10 000 for famine relief, in the way that television reportage might do nowadays:

In the first (hovel), six famished and ghastly skeletons, to all appearance dead, were huddled in a corner on some filthy straw, their sole covering what seemed to be a ragged horse-cloth and their wretched legs hanging about, naked above the knees. I approached with horror and found by a low moaning they were alive; they were in fever – four children, a woman, and what once had been a man . . .

But the past in west Cork is not entirely a matter of lament and subjugation. If colonialism was sometimes responsible for a great deal of hurt and anger, it was also responsible for the great gardens on Garnish Island, near Glengarriffe, which attract many visitors to their sub-tropical lushness. The British Foreign Office sold the island to an MP, Annan Bryce, in 1910 and he employed an English architect, Harold Peto, to draw up a design for the gardens. The very names of the plants there can be a kind of poetry: Damaris, Princess Alice, Golden Horn Persimmon, Army Nurse, Marie Boisselot, Magnolia rubra grandiflora.

Many towns in County Cork have displayed a new design-consciousness in recent years, much of it encouraged by the innovative architect Billy Houlihan. Up to the 1960s, despite the fact that many of these towns had evolved over several centuries from Anglo-Norman and Tudor ground plans, their streets seemed frozen in a kind of post market-day stagnation. Now, in towns such as Bandon and Clonakilty, shopfronts and streets gleam with pride in their antiquity, a prettiness that is seemly and beguiling, lending a cosmopolitan, continental air to these far western outposts.

In the surrounding countryside, finger-posts point to sites of ambush from the Troubles, that period in the early 1920s when men like General Tom Barry, who had previously been a soldier in the British Army, became local legends in the guerrilla warfare that kept this countryside in insurrection.

It was in west Cork as well that the leader of the pro-Treaty forces, Michael Collins, was shot in an ambush in 1922. The subject of who actually fired the shot that killed him is still of interest to many, though to others it is the most boring question in Ireland. At Béal na mBláth, where Collins was shot, a large monument stands near the side of the road. Like St Gobnait's graveyard, Béal na mBláth is a place which knits together the different strands of Irish history into a single landscape. A small cross cut into a stone marks the spot where Collins died. A commemoration is held there in August every year. Afterwards, the road is deserted again and the breeze flutters through the leaves of the wreaths left to moulder in the weather.

As the Hollywood star Virginia Mayo discovered when she was in town for one of the early Cork Film Festivals, and described the city as 'a cemetery with lights', the people of Cork take considerable pride in everything that concerns themselves. As in any second city, a potential inferiority complex is kept at bay by an inordinate pride in the least achievements of the citizens and by a deft clipping of wings if anyone 'gets above their station'.

Locals once boasted that Cork city contains the longest and the tallest buildings in the Republic, the first designed to deal with madness and the second with bureaucracy. The longest building, formerly Our Lady's Hospital, was constructed to cater for the mentally ill. The tallest is the County Hall, to which, it is claimed, a few extra feet may have been added in order to outstrip the height of Dublin's Liberty Hall.

The sculpture at the base of the County Hall was made by the late Oisin Kelly. It shows two ordinary men pondering the height of the building. If they could speak, it would doubtless be in the distinctive Cork accent. A BBC television series on the English language made in the 1980s featured a short discussion of English as it is spoken in Cork – an area, it was claimed, where spoken English still carries Elizabethan overtones. It was deemed that subtitles were necessary literally to spell out what the men were saying.

The charm of Cork can be found in its narrow lanes or in its conversation rather than in any great series of architectural delights. Dominated by the river, which divides the city in two, it is a place of hills and terraces, and of suburbs that finger deep into the countryside. Its place-names run from the Italianate Montenotte and Tivoli to the Anglo-influenced Sunday's Well and Bishopstown.

The city's origins lie early in the seventh century, when St Finbarr founded a small monastic community close to where Gilabbey Street now stands. The word *Cork* comes from the Irish name *Corcach*, which means 'marsh' – the ground upon which the inner city was built, having had to be channelled and culverted and dyked to give building purchase in the sluggish estuary of the Lee.

The Vikings came to the city in the tenth century, and the Normans followed two centuries later. The English came in due course and, when they finally departed in 1922, left behind a courthouse, a barracks and post boxes engraved *Victoria Regina*, all of which are still in use. Traces of lost history are constantly discovered in the city when archaeological surveys are conducted in the hiatus between the destruction of old buildings and the construction of the new. The remains of old walls, the outline of houses, the ruins of a long-buried Dominican abbey, jewellery and household objects have all been discovered in this way, fragments of the history that is buried in strata beneath the busy streets. The public museum in Fitzgerald Park contains artefacts from many of these excavations.

On a human level, the city is really a series of villages linked by geographical appellation under the name of Cork: Blackrock, Ballintemple, Knocknaheeny, Gurranabraher are all areas unto themselves. The division of the city by the river into North and South is itself part of Cork's character. The main street, Patrick Street, winds between Patrick's Bridge and the Grand Parade. Its curved character seems appropriate for a small city and also reflects the fact that many of the streets were built over waterways that were gradually covered over in the course of the centuries. Even now the city can emit a sense of marshy dampness that, in summer, contrasts with the way sunlight falls on rising rows of Northside terraces, many of them constructed in the old red sandstone and limestone that are the basic materials of Cork architecture.

The names of old streets and terraces reflect the lost imperial connection: Wellesley Terrace; Wellington Road; Military Hill; Victoria Road. These places are just minutes away from the modern private and public housing estates that stretch for miles on both sides of the river and carry the names of very different Irish heroes and martyrs. The outskirts of the city also contain a number of industrial estates and factories. When Henry Ford opened a factory in Cork in 1919 for the construction of tractors and, later, cars, he declared: 'My ancestors came from near Cork and that city, with its wonderful harbour, has an abundance of fine industrial sites. Cork has for many years been a city of casual labour and extreme poverty. There are breweries and distilleries, but no real industry.'

The River Lee has been an essential factor in the economic development of Cork over the centuries. The second-century geographer Ptolemy wrote of a southern Irish river called the Dabrona, and some later writers, in what now seems fanciful speculation, considered this to be the Lee.

The writer Sean O'Faolain (1900–91) wrote of Cork city as a place which could trap the sensitive soul. He spent much of his life fleeing from its nets. He called it 'my four-letter city'. Nonetheless, shortly before his death he was granted – and accepted – the Freedom of the City. O'Faolain grew up in Half Moon Street, a narrow street near the city centre. His childhood home is just a few lanes away from the Coal Quay market. Old photographs of this area show shawled women haggling among clothes, cabbages, mounds of potatoes, chairs and tables. Nowadays there are fewer traders but the market is still held. It is at its busiest on Saturdays.

The city's main indoor market is known as the English Market and can be entered from the Grand Parade, Prince's Street, and Patrick Street. The English Market is also a warren of fishmongers, vegetable sellers and butchers. Under its roof one can buy olives and sesame seeds in one stall and then move along to another where, on marble slabs, drisheen (the local sausage) and tripe are set in rows. The largest fish stall is run by the O'Connell family and is a masterpiece of sculptural assembly: gutted plaice, quivering lobsters, mussels with seaweed draped across them, smoked or tropical fish, sides of salmon, boxes of oysters and scallops. For those who love food and cooking, the English Market is a delight.

Since the 1980s a large arts community has come into its own in Cork, centred in two areas: the Triskel Arts Centre in Tobin Street and the Crawford Art Gallery in Emmet Place. The latter has an excellent restaurant which offers one of the best lunchtime menus in the city. Other popular restaurants include Isaac's in McCurtain Street, the Arbutus Lodge in Montenotte and Clifford's in Dyke Parade. All are distinguished by their careful and inventive use of local produce. The Long Valley bar in Winthrop Street is a favourite lunch venue. There, sandwiches are an art form served by white-coated women to a background of music that ranges from martial melody to jazz. In the Quay Co-Op on Sullivan's Quay, vegetarians may graze to their heart's content.

In the 19th century Cork city saw another burst of artistic creativity. One of its most famous writers then was Francis Sylvester Mahony (1804–66), who wrote under the name of Father Prout. His best-known poem was 'The Bells of Shandon'. Mahony is now buried in St Anne's churchyard beneath the carillon he celebrated, which is perhaps the most famous landmark on the city's skyline. St Anne's is the property of the Church of Ireland, as is the finest church in Cork, St Fin Barre's Cathedral, which was designed by William Burgess and completed in 1880. Saints Peter and Paul Church in Paul Street, another fine building, was designed by Pugin though much of its external beauty is concealed by the buildings that surround it.

Shandon is famous for its bells but it is also a source of folklore. The story is told of a man who, when told that he had just become a father, and that his wife had given birth to yet another son and not to the daughter whose birth he desired, was told: 'If you want a girl, then the next time you're doing it, leave on your cap and face towards Shandon.' There is no record of what issue resulted from this very Irish form of sexual congress.

Cork city is a place of steps and hills, and the Shandon area in particular is a warren of narrow lanes and steep streets, and of small, tightly packed houses. Efforts have been

Market traders in the English Market, Cork City.

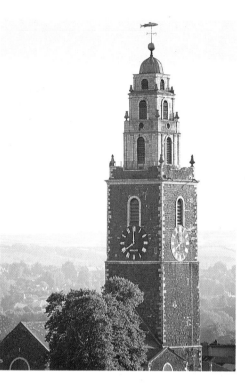

The bell tower of St Anne's Church, Shandon, Cork City.

eclectic mélange of buildings that range from cloisters to small skyscrapers. The Honan Chapel, a small Hiberno-Romanesque church built in 1916, is one of the jewels of the university. It contains stained-glass windows by Sarah Purser and Harry Clarke, along with features typical of the Celtic revival movement which dominated the crafts in Ireland in the early decades of this century. The Boole Library in the university is named after George Boole (1815–64), the first professor of mathematics at the college. His work in mathematical logic, and his use of symbols to express logical forms and processes, influenced many subsequent mathematicians and also played a part in the development of computers.

Cork is a city in which many features exist in the singular: The Library, The GPO, The Park, The Fountain, all of which can be visited in an hour's walk. And there is also The Paper, a name given to the *Cork Examiner*, as if there might well be no other newspaper in the world. The *Examiner* has chronicled the doings of its city for over one hundred and fifty years, mostly under the stewardship of the Crosbie family. A number of well-known writers have written for it, among them Frank O'Connor, the art critic Hilary Pyle, the poets Paul Durcan and Patrick Galvin, and the novelists Francis Stuart and Mary Leland. Its sister paper, the *Evening Echo*, a tabloid publication, is primarily a source of news, gossip and entertainment and its small-ad pages are a daily index of Cork life.

A number of busy festivals are held in Cork each year. The Jazz Festival and the Film Festival, both held in the autumn, are the most popular. The latter was initially a star-studded affair and attracted many film stars to the city. Their antics often caused great delight, as when Dawn Addams asked in a hotel for a bath filled with asses' milk. The manager refused and she promptly headed for another hotel where her request was met. The Film Festival is now a serious forum for new movies and it is a high point in the city's cultural calendar.

Two of Cork's Lord Mayors, Terence McSwiney and Thomas McCurtain, died

made in recent years to improve the look of the district but, thankfully, these efforts have been well controlled and Shandon has not yet succumbed to the gentility principle. The main buildings now include a large craft centre and the Firkin Crane, a circular building that was once a store for the city's large butter industry and is now used as an arts centre.

Yet if the Northside has character, it also has deprivation, and some of the worst poverty in Ireland has been experienced there. Locals argue that they are deprived of industries, government offices, hospitals and colleges. Most of these are found on the Southside of the river where the university, the Regional Technical College, and the regional hospital are all, as they say, within spitting distance of each other.

University College, Cork was founded in 1845. Queen Victoria visited it in that year and officially declared it open. A statue of the Queen stood in the grounds for many years but was taken down in more nationalist-minded times to be buried in a university garden and then exhumed, to some controversy, for the 150th anniversary celebrations. The university itself is an

The City Hall and
River Lee, Cork City.

tragically in the 1920s during the period
which, with some understatement, is known
as the Troubles. McSwiney died after 75 days
on hunger strike in Brixton Prison in London,
while McCurtain was shot in his city home. It
was at this time as well that the Black and
Tans, a British force notorious for its brutality
towards nationalists, ran amok through the
city streets after an IRA ambush, setting fire
to the City Hall and to many of the main
shops in Patrick Street.

The republican tradition was strong in the
city – giving it the nickname of 'Rebel Cork'
– but so too was the tradition of joining the
British Army. While the city contains
monuments and memorials to those who died
in the nationalist cause, it also contains a
memorial to those who died in World War I.
This memorial stands on the South Mall, a
wide street which is the financial and legal
heart of the city, its pavements lined with
solicitors' and estate agents' offices. The poet
Paul Durcan wrote about the South Mall in a
pithy couplet:

Pinstripes or no pinstripes,
By their backsides shall ye know them.

The city has a lively musical and sporting
tradition. In the late 19th century visiting
Italian opera companies could be assured that
Cork audiences would sing along with the
best-known choruses. More recently Cork was
the boyhood home of the great rock
musician, Rory Gallagher.

Cork has seen at least one sportsman who
was considered by everybody to be a genius.
Hurling is the sport most fervently supported
in Cork and Christy Ring was the greatest
hurler of all. Ring, who died in 1979, won
eight All-Ireland medals, a record at the time.
A bridge is named after him in the city and a
statue, which depicts him with a hurley in
hand and dressed for a game, can be seen at
Cloyne, his native village in east Cork.
Hurling is followed with such fanaticism that,
as major games approach, whether between
Cork and other counties or between local
teams like Glen Rovers, St Finbarr's or
Blackrock – best known as the Glen, the Barrs
and the Rockies – it sometimes seems as if
the whole of life, with the exception of the
forthcoming game, has been eliminated as
extraneous matter.

The city and county together make one of
only two places in Ireland – the other being
Armagh – where road-bowling takes place.
Bowling, which is pronounced 'bowelling' in
Cork, is played with metal bowls and is
fondly followed by gamblers. The sport's
most famous practitioner is Mick Barry. His
greatest claim to fame is that he became the
first man to loft a metal bowl over the high
viaduct on the Bandon road. In a provincial
city, it is people like Mick Barry and Christy
Ring who become heroes. The excellence and
individualism they display confirm a sense of
local importance.

HURLING

Hurling is effectively Ireland's national sport. Once the rules are understood, it is a riveting and engrossing game when played well. It is also incredibly fast. References to it can be found in ancient Irish manuscripts, where the hurling skills of heroes are frequently discussed. The hero Cuchulainn, for example, was as gifted on the hurling pitch as he was on the battle-field. As a youth, he is said to have beaten a team of 150 boys at Armagh single-handedly. He is also said to have used a hurley to drive a ball into the mouth of a savage hound.

A version of hurling known as camogie is played by women. The game also has affinities with the Scottish one of shinty. Hurling, like camogie, Gaelic football and handball, is now played under the auspices of the Gaelic Athletic Association (GAA) which was founded in 1884. The GAA is a national organisation with branches in every county, all of them run on an amateur basis. For many years, in a gesture known as The Ban, GAA members were not allowed to support other sports such as soccer or rugby. Likewise, GAA pitches cannot be used by practitioners of other sports. It is allowable, however, to use them as sites for rock concerts and other mass events.

Such attitudes towards other sports are a legacy of the GAA's associations with nationalism. Hurleys (the wooden implements, made from ash, with which the game of hurling is played) were used as mock rifles in military manoeuvres before the 1916 Rising. The game was frequently banned over the centuries as the English tried to wipe out indigenous culture. Yet the survival of hurling was never in doubt. Banning it gave it the allure of a desirable subversive activity. A statute passed in Kilkenny in 1366 declared that the land of Ireland should not be used for 'the game which men call hurlings, with great clubs at ball along the ground'. The statute had little effect.

A hurling match is played by two teams of 15 players each. Historically, references have been found to mammoth games with hundreds of players on each side who tried to drive the ball across large areas from one village to another. A small ball (a *sliotar*) is used and the aim of the game is to drive this ball between posts set at either end of the pitch. A goal is scored when the ball goes under the cross-bar; a point when it goes over. A goal is equal to three points.

Hurling is a game which demands courage, dexterity, and strength. Injuries occur but, more often than not, they are suffered by the timid or the awkward rather than by the skilled player. It is not a game for the weak but neither is it a game for the insensitive and the crude. Its most famous practitioners have displayed a grace and rhythm closer to music than to rougher sports.

For many centuries, hurling has been a sport which expressed the rivalries between neighbouring areas. Townlands, counties, parishes, streets, housing estates and villages often boast their own teams. The game is highly competitive at local level but it is at its most popular when played between fiercely competitive counties battling for the game's ultimate accolade: an All-Ireland championship title.

The game has been stronger in certain counties. Kilkenny, Tipperary and Cork, for example, are traditional hurling counties. Gaelic football has been stronger in others, including Kerry and Louth. Hurling has been stronger in the southern province of Munster and the Munster Final, the winners of which advance to the All-Ireland final, is a major sporting event which draws thousands of supporters. The atmosphere of the great Munster Finals is itself the stuff of legend.

Famous hurlers have included Christy Ring from Cork, John Keane from Waterford, the Rackards of Wexford, Tommy Doyle of Tipperary and Mick Mackey of Limerick.

The character of Cork is displayed as well in its slang and its argot. Some of the most common words include *flah* (for sexual intercourse); *mockeyah* (pretend, not serious); *dawfake* (to make up, to counterfeit). One characteristic of local speech is the tendency to reduce words, so the Barrack Street Band becomes the 'Barracka' and Patrick Street 'Panna'.

If you flew over the northern part of County Cork, you would see a landscape more fertile by far than the rough terrain of the county's western regions. The plenitude of lush fields is traversed by the Blackwater, a river of rich meads, dense woodlands and fine, prosperous towns like Mitchelstown, Mallow and Fermoy, with the ruins of castles and decayed big houses scattered over the countryside. Like other parts of Ireland, it is a landscape where the imperial past mixes with the democratic mêlée of 20th-century Ireland.

One such big house, once the heart of a demesne whose walls and gates can still be seen, is Bowens Court, the family home of the writer Elizabeth Bowen (1899–1973). One of her ancestors is said to have had a row with Cromwell who later apologised and told Colonel Bowen that he could have as much land as his hawk could fly over before it landed. In her book *Bowens Court*, Elizabeth Bowen wrote of that event:

> This story has been a little upset by what I have, later, learned about hawks and hawking. Apparently, a hawk rockets straight up through the air and hangs where it is until it drops on its prey. In which case, Cromwell was smart in his proposition, for Colonel Bowen would not have got much land.

Whatever the case, the Bowens held a large part of the land near Farahy for centuries. The great house, where candles were lit in the windows at Christmas, was sold by Elizabeth Bowen in 1959 and later demolished, but one can still walk the grounds and look, as she did, on the Ballyhoura hills. Elizabeth Bowen and her husband, Alan Cameron, are buried in the small graveyard at Farahy, the village at one of the gates of the estate.

North Cork is full of literary interest. A few miles from Bowens Court, near the town of Doneraile, the stump of a castle lies near a marsh. This is all that remains of Kilcolman Castle, once the home of the poet Edmund Spenser (1552–99). There, he worked on his most famous poem, *The Faerie Queen*, which evokes in subtle ways this local landscape he knew so well. Kilcolman is now a bleak and lonely place, all the more poignantly so for the knowledge that Spenser's son died in a fire there after the castle was attacked by local rebels.

Centuries later the town of Doneraile was home to another writer, Canon Sheehan (1852–1913). His work was praised by Tolstoy and his novels much loved by loyal Irish readers. Outside the town stands Doneraile Court, one-time home of the St Leger family of horse-racing fame. The house has an important connection with Freemasonry, for it was within its walls that a woman joined the Freemasons. Elizabeth Aldworth was hiding in the library of Doneraile Court when a Freemasons' meeting was in progress. She overheard the discussion and those who discovered her decided that the best thing to do was to enrol her in the Lodge. She was the only woman ever to join the Masons.

Mitchelstown, founded by the Kingston family and now one of the main towns in north Cork, was once dominated by a stupendous castle. This was destroyed in 1922 though its gardens are still worth a visit. The stones from the castle were taken to County Waterford and many were used in the building of a new church at the Cistercian Abbey of Mount Melleray. Thus, what had once been a symbol of Protestant power became part of a monastery which, in 1832, became the first monastery to be built in Ireland after the Catholic Emancipation Act of 1829. When the 18th-century traveller Arthur Young visited Mitchelstown, he described it as a 'den of vagabonds, thieves, rioters and Whiteboys' until Lord Kingsborough made it his residence. In the nearby Galtee mountains there is a wild magnificence in the wooded valleys that, in their day, would have sheltered many of these renegades between their forays to town.

The town of Fermoy, set on the River Blackwater and once known as 'the Irish

Aldershot', is a fisherman's delight. The town was initially designed by an 18th-century Scotsman, John Anderson, who founded a mail service that ran between Cork and Dublin. The Blackwater is one of Ireland's most beautiful rivers, its banks overlooked here and there by forests with shadows that fall across the waters and lead, in more romantic and even inebriated moments, to comparisons with the Rhine. The countryside between Fermoy and Lismore, in County Waterford, has much dense woodland out of which rear a number of fine houses in various states of repair, surveying what were once their pleasure grounds.

Another north Cork town, Buttevant, situated on the main road between Cork and Limerick, hosts the Cahirmee Horse Fair which every year draws hundreds of travellers into the town to haggle, exaggerate, argue and finally spit and slap palms together as a sale is sealed. It is even more famous, though, for the horse race held in the town in 1752. The course was set from Doneraile to Buttevant, starting beneath the steeple of one church and ending beneath the steeple of another. Thus was the sport of steeple-chasing born.

East Cork has associations of a different kind. There, a great estate at Fota Island contains a famous house, a wildlife park, a leisure area and an arboretum. Once the home of the Smith-Barry family, Fota House was renovated and open to the public throughout most of the 1980s, before it was closed again. In its gardens, a superb arboretum contains trees which include a banana plant, though the fruit has never ripened, and a handkerchief tree *Davidia involucrata*, from which off-white flowers, like handkerchiefs conjured on branches, grow late in the year. The oldest tree there is a cedar of Lebanon dating from the 1820s. The tallest is a giant fir which was 40 feet high in 1892 and eventually grew to 120 feet.

Fota is now also home to a wildlife park and many animals are bred there. They include cheetahs, giraffes and oryxes. Gibbons and spider monkeys scream and swing from trees above small lakes in the park. Peacocks can be heard there as well,

their loud cries a reminder of the days before security alarms were invented, when these elegant birds patrolled the grounds of large estates.

Fota is close to Cobh, a coastal town dominated by St Colman's Cathedral. The cathedral's spire is visible far out at sea and overlooks the naval base at Haulbowline. The world's oldest marine yacht club, the Royal Cork, initially known as the Water Club, was founded in Cobh in 1720 but is now based at Crosshaven. Once named Queenstown, in commemoration of a visit by Queen Victoria, the town was the last stop for thousands of emigrants who took the boat from there to America. Emigration is the focus of the Queenstown Project, a major heritage enterprise situated in the town's railway station. Like the northside of Cork city, Cobh is a steep and hilly place where some of the houses rise in elegant crescents while others, outside the pale of planning, sprawl in higgledy-piggledy formations.

The *Sirius*, the first steamship to cross the Atlantic, sailed from Cobh in 1838. And if the town was the first call for the *Sirius*, it was the last for one of the world's most famous ships: the *Titanic* visited Cobh in 1912 and many Irish emigrants were among those who drowned when the liner sank, its apparent invincibility breached by the jagged edge of an iceberg. After the *Lusitania* was sunk by a German torpedo in the waters off the Old Head of Kinsale in 1915, many of the bodies were taken ashore and buried in a mass grave at Cobh.

Cobh was once the home of a famous and colourful boxer, Jack Doyle. He was also something of a singer and it was said of him that he could sing like Jack Dempsey and box like John McCormack. His other achievements included marriage to Movita, a woman who later became the wife of Marlon Brando.

Doyle was also known for his love of alcohol. He would have enjoyed himself in Midleton, a town which holds the world's largest pot still at the Jameson Heritage Centre. The still can hold over 30 000 gallons of whiskey. Outside the town, roads lead to Cloyne and Ballymaloe House. In 1734 Cloyne became the home of George Berkeley,

THE RING OF KERRY

Like *Finnegans Wake* by James Joyce, the Ring of Kerry ends where it begins and begins where it ends. As a tourist route, the Ring is a perfect attraction since, within its circumference, it contains a number of different sites and also provides some extraordinary views. As a car or bus edges along a road near the drop of a cliff, one can look down on beaches or out on the ocean. On the same trip one can stop for a meal in a small town like Kenmare or for a drink in one of the villages along the way. In this way, the Ring of Kerry is a rich circumference of delights.

Killarney is as good a starting point as any other to tour the Ring, a trip of roughly one hundred miles around Iveragh, the largest of Kerry's three peninsulas. The journey can be made north through Killorglin or south through Kenmare; either way, one returns to where one began. Organised tours of the Ring are common but many prefer to take it at their own pace.

The village of Killorglin is the home of the Puck Fair, an annual festival usually held on 10, 11 and 12 August. Some tourist brochures confidently describe this fair as the world's oldest business event. The festival centres around the primitive scene of a captured goat suspended on a platform above the town. The goat, which is captured locally, becomes King Puck of the fair.

Other places on the Ring of Kerry include Cahirciveen, Sneem, Glenbeigh, Valentia Island, Caragh Lake and Caherdaniel. Derrynane House, close to Caherdaniel, was the home of Daniel O'Connell (1775–1847), the legendary 'Liberator' whose life is recalled in the museum there. Leaders have also been associated with Sneem (from the Irish *snaidhm*, meaning 'a knot') which is the burial place of the Irish president and scholar, Cearbhall Ó Dálaigh (1911–78). He combined an interest in culture with an integrity of purpose that led him to resign from office after a Minister for Defence called him 'a thundering disgrace'. In a country where it is said that phrases make history, that phrase made more history than most. The village was once home to Charles Graves (1846–1931), a

mathematician and Church of Ireland bishop who was the father of Alfred Percival Graves – author of many famous songs, including 'Father O'Flynn' (based on the exploits of a local parish priest, Father Michael Walsh) and 'The Jug of Punch' – and grandfather of the poet Robert Graves (1895–1985).

The Ring of Kerry is studded with ruins and archaeological sites, including Staigue Fort near Castlecove, a ring fort dating from around 1000 BC, with walls 13 feet thick at the base. Stairways are built inside the walls which rise to 18 feet in height. The walls of Staigue Fort are masterpieces of local construction using uncut stone and the same basic techniques as built the drystone walls which quilt the whole west of Ireland.

The most famous archaeological site in County Kerry lies 12 miles off the coast. These are the Skelligs, two tall rocks known as Skellig Michael, or the Great Skellig, and Little Skellig. The Skelligs are now the subject of a heritage centre on Valentia Island, an island from which the first cable link across the Atlantic to America was made in 1858. The Skelligs are home to the largest gannetry in Europe. With the Blasket Islands and Puffin Island, they also hold the world's largest colonies of storm petrel along with kittiwakes, fulmar and shearwater.

The Great Skellig was once a home for monks whose monastery, 600 feet above the sea, can still be seen. It was built around AD 600 and monks lived there for six centuries. The beehive huts where they stayed, reached at the top of

Caragh Lake and Macgillycuddy's Reeks, County Kerry.

hundreds of steps, exemplify much that was typical of the Irish monastic tradition: a love of isolation, a fondness for the natural world, and an ascetic sense that thrived on hardship. While the men who lived on Skellig had a strong sense of the mystical, they had to be physically tough, too, to live in this bleak and wondrous place, where a rigorous spirituality was maintained at a decent distance from comfort. The attraction of the Skelligs has known a negative side: too many careless visitors came to the island and walked among the ruins so that they were seriously threatened. Some insensitive visitors – the spiritual equivalent of football hooligans – vandalised the site by taking stones away from the original walls. The heritage centre on the mainland has eased this traffic considerably and much of what one needs to know about the Skelligs, short of actually going there, can be learned at a safe remove.

While the Skelligs are reached by boat, Valentia Island is joined to the mainland by a bridge. Valentia slate was once quarried near the village on the island. Kerry's most famous Gaelic footballer of recent times, Mick O'Connell, is a native of Valentia Island. To see him play at his best, you knew that you were witnessing sport brought to perfection with a symmetry and skill that seemed at times beyond the human. The unassuming intensity of his personality was legendary. The story is told that, when his fellow players stayed in Dublin to celebrate yet another All-Ireland victory, he took the train back to Kerry, cycled from Cahirciveen and then rowed out to the island with no sound in his ears but the noise of water dripping from the oars. He had helped Kerry to achieve another win and that was all there was to it.

Another famous contemporary footballer and trainer, Mick O'Dwyer, is associated with Waterville, another stop on the Ring of Kerry. The village is close to Church Island in whose oratory St Finlan is said to have prayed in the sixth century. The cemetery on Church Island is well worth examining for the quality of the lettering incised in the old gravestones that lean in the grass. Also close to Waterville is the Pass of Coomakista, where the road rises to 700 feet and affords a spectacular view, as do the Conor Pass and the Coomanspig Pass near Portmagee, which climbs to nearly 1100 feet.

Depending on the direction in which one started, the town of Kenmare is the last or first town on the Ring of Kerry after it starts or before it ends in Killarney. The town can be traced back to 1670 and, in 1775, the Marquis of Lansdowne planned its ordered shape. Like scores of Irish towns, Kenmare was once linked to the railway system, but no train has run from the town since the last day of 1959.

The first suspension bridge in Ireland was built at Kenmare in 1838. The town was also the home of Mary Frances Cusack, a Poor Clare sister known as the Nun of Kenmare. A writer and independent-minded controversialist, she was involved with local political rows and left the Kenmare convent in 1881. An aura of piety surrounds her memory and this has served to cloak her genuine radicalism, a radicalism she shared with members of other religious orders in Ireland in the 19th century.

While a tour of the Ring of Kerry can leave one tired, it can also leave a kind of exhilaration. At the end of a day, one can look back on an inordinate number of sights and experiences. The landscape will have changed with the light and will have ranged from the coastal to the agricultural. Sheep may have blocked the road at one point and a long beach may have been glimpsed from another. One may have learned a little about figures out of history, like Daniel O'Connell or the Nun of Kenmare, but the dominant impression is always left by the landscape and the sea. The Ring of Kerry is surely one of the most spectacular routes in Europe.

The tall rocks of Skellig Michael, the most famous archaeological site in County Kerry.

The clock tower in the main street, Youghal, County Cork.

who was appointed bishop there. He is famous as a philosopher – his best-known work being *The Principles of Human Knowledge*, published in 1710 – yet he had many other interests, among them the foundation of a college in Bermuda 'for the Christian civilisation of America'. In his years at Cloyne Berkeley developed his interest in tar-water, a subject upon which he wrote a book which was published in 1744. He said of tar-water that it was 'of a nature so mild and benign . . . as to warm without heating, to cheer but not inebriate'. For most people in County Cork, Cloyne is more famous as the birthplace of the hurler Christy Ring.

Unpalatable substances such as tar-water will not be found on the tables at Ballymaloe House – probably Ireland's most famous restaurant – just a few miles outside Cloyne. Run by Myrtle Allen, Ballymaloe began as a restaurant and has since spawned a number of books, television series, food products and a cookery school.

Youghal (pronounced 'yawl') is the largest town in east Cork. Its main street is dominated by a clock tower erected in 1771. Youghal is an old town and fragments of its ancient walls can still be seen. It was once a busy harbour town visited by many ships, but this business declined late in the 19th century. Its most famous historical boast is that Sir Walter Raleigh once lived there, and that he introduced the potato to Ireland in the garden of his home. The certainty with which this boast is made is in inverse proportion to the amount of evidence which backs it up. Raleigh introduced tobacco to Europe as well, which caused more harm than the versatile spud. Myrtle Grove, said to have been his Youghal house and set close to the lovely St Mary's Collegiate Church and to 17th-century alms houses, is open to the public.

Youghal was the stamping-ground of the journalist and writer, Claud Cockburn (1904–81), who lived in his later years at nearby Ardmore on the Waterford coast. Often in serious need of money, Cockburn was of necessity a prolific writer, adopting a number of pseudonyms. James Helvick was one such name, and under it he wrote the novel *Beat the Devil*, later made into a film starring James Cagney. Patrick Cork was another, a name which manages to combine a national saint with an entire county. Long before the 20th century had even reached the three-quarters stage, Graham Greene said that, with

G.K. Chesterton, Cockburn was one of the greatest journalists of the century. The publications with which he was associated included *Private Eye* and the London *Times*, along with his 1930s' newssheet *The Week*. When he worked at *The Times*, he won a competition for the dullest headline of the week. His headline read: 'Small earthquake in Chile. Not many dead.' Needless to say, he got on famously in Ireland.

There must have been a time when the lakes of Killarney seemed to have been set on the earth to facilitate Victorian engravers and artists. Forests, lakes and mountains stretch into the distance and clouds loom over them. You can readily imagine a Victorian painter perched near a rock, sketching quickly to capture the scene before the light changes.

Nowadays, in scenes somewhat redolent of centuries past, horse-drawn jaunting-cars, with tourists perched on either side in what often seems a hearty form of ballast, move along the wide avenues near Muckross House or on the roads outside Killarney town, forcing a slower pace upon the hundreds of tour buses that visit the town in summer and have no choice but to chug slowly behind them. Ironically, in one of the last places in Ireland where a horse can be king of the road, the town is also home to a transport museum.

Killarney contains more bed-and-breakfast establishments, guesthouses and hotels per square mile than any other place in Ireland. The names of such establishments are a study in themselves. Some come from the surnames of dead popes or from other aspects of Catholicism – Roncalli House, for example, or the Grotto. The provenance of others can be guessed at: Mystical Rose, Perpetua, Casa Casila Farm.

While it has always had its admirers, Killarney came into its own in the 19th century. Victorian travel-writers sharpened their metaphors and found their talent challenged by Killarney's sights. In 1843 William Makepeace Thackeray saw the mountains 'clothed in purple like kings in mourning'. Earlier, in 1780, the traveller, writer and agriculturalist Arthur Young said Killarney was 'superior to all comparison'. Such writers described the lonely islands and deserted ruins of castles. At their most intense, they seemed unable to describe the place at all and instead found themselves humbled before it – a rare event where writers are concerned. One such writer, Lady Chatterton, was overwhelmed by what she saw. Her book *Rambles In The South of Ireland* appeared in 1839:

> It is a region of enchantment – a hundred descriptions of it have been written – thousands of sketches have been made, but no description that I have read, or sketch that I have seen, made me familiar with Killarney. The Upper Lake, and the Lower Lake, Muckross, and Innisfallen, must be seen to be understood. It is the colouring – the gleam of sunshine – the cloud – the tone – the effect – what in short cannot be conveyed by the pen without the cant of art, and is beyond the power of the pencil – that give a magic to the scenery of Killarney. . .

Evening on the Lakes of Killarney, County Kerry.

It is worth noting that the densely forested appearance of Killarney was once typical of many places in Ireland. Whether as havens in which to hide or as a source of timber for ships or casks, the forests were an integral and unavoidable feature of the landscape. The demands of industry and trade, together with changes in climate, were large factors in the destruction of old woodland. In this sense, the forests around Killarney are at once an aspect of the present and a picture of the past.

Those who wish to explore the lakes and the surrounding demesne could usefully start at Muckross House and Killarney National Park, just over one and a half miles from the town itself. Within one extensive area visitors can trace the growth of old oaks, catch sight of deer, study fauna and flora, explore old buildings, walk for miles, or watch a bookbinder at work in Muckross House, a large pile built in the Elizabethan style in the 19th century.

Whilst the gardens around the house are much admired for their profusion of rhododendron, ecologists are worried by the growth of this imported scourge which thrives in the Killarney climate and threatens to smother the native vegetation. A contemporary writer, Kevin Corcoran, whose book *Kerry Walks* is a handy guide to the county, has written of it:

As an introduced species, the rhododendron grows unchecked, unable to fit in with the ecological balance of the native forest. It now threatens the entire forest system, as it smothers all ground life beneath its thick tangle of branches and impenetrable shade. The final death will come when, through the absence of seed regeneration, no more oaks grow to replace the present generation of adult trees. Frustratingly we must accept that we have set in motion the death sentence of this unique heirloom.

Muckross House is another unique heirloom, but one whose future seems assured. Designed by William Burns and built between 1839 and 1843, the house has hosted many famous visitors and it still has about it the air of a lived-in, comfortable house. Queen Victoria went there and the carpet upon which she walked can still be seen. The house was once given as a wedding present to the daughter of an American, Bowes-Bourn. After her early death, the house was handed over to the state by her husband and father, and the grounds became known as the Bourn-Vincent Memorial Park.

Muckross Abbey is within walking distance of the house. In quiet times it can be a silent place of stone steps, arches and gravestones; of Shakespeare's 'bare ruin'd choirs where late the sweet birds sang'. Once a friary, it was built in 1448 and maintained by the Franciscans until Cromwellian soldiers drove them out in 1652.

A limestone monument at Muckross Abbey marks the memory of some Kerry poets, one of whom, Aogán Ó Rathaille (c. 1675–1729), is among the finest of all Gaelic poets. His work reflects the frustration of a man whose

A jaunting car at Killarney, County Kerry.

world was dying as the old, aristocratic Gaelic order gave way to the new world of boors and planters. Many writers have translated his poems, including Frank O'Connor who caught the note of pathos and fierce pride that marks much of Ó Rathaille's work:

And I can never cease weeping these useless tears;
I am a man oppressed, afflicted and undone
Who where he wanders mourning no companion hears
Only some waterfall that has no cause to mourn.

Muckross is also home to a pedigree herd of Kerry cattle, an animal which, like the Kerry Blue dog, is one of the few to take its name from an Irish county.

The atmosphere of Killarney is often best appreciated by breaking away from the well-used routes. There is no shortage of worthwhile sights. Torc Waterfall, which is 59 feet high, is one such place. Most visitors climb part of the path beside it and stop at the railings or the bridge where the roar of the falls can be heard and the rush of its waters witnessed. Those who are fit should keep climbing beyond these points, for it is then, when the solitude of the landscape blends with quiet, that Killarney can be appreciated at its most pristine and primeval. Many walkers now follow the route of the Kerry Way. Maps of this walk are easily acquired.

One of Killarney's most famous sights is the Meeting of the Waters, where water from the Upper Lake joins the water of Muckross Lake and Lough Leane.

On Innisfallen Island, the ruins of an ancient monastery are visible. An important Irish manuscript, the *Annals of Innisfallen*, was written on the island in the 13th century. The manuscript is now in the British Museum. The island is also said to have been the home of a saint whose anglicised name is St Finlan the Leper. As an aside, it is worth noting that the Irish word for leper is *lobhar* (pronounced 'lover'). This word was part of a common appellation given to roads and lanes near hospitals, where patients with contagious diseases could stroll in quiet quarantine. It has, however, been frequently anglicised as 'lover', and as a result many places in Ireland

known, say, as Lover's Walk or Lover's Road take their names from leprosy, and not from romance as many dewy-eyed couples suppose.

Such couples can also be found, with more reason, at Ladies' View near Killarney, one of the many points from which the panorama of the lakes can be surveyed. Some have suggested that the place takes its name from its popularity with Queen Victoria's ladies-in-waiting. Many visitors also like to visit Kate Kearney's Cottage, a former coaching inn near the Gap of Dunloe, once notorious as a smugglers' den and drovers' dive, now much sanitised.

Likewise, the town of Killarney has improved greatly in recent years and lanes which were once neglected and sleazy have now become attractive and bright. Small shops abound in the town and many of them sell tasteful items – local crafts, for example – that belie the area's image as a haven for 'Oirishry'.

The town's main church is St Mary's Cathedral, a 19th-century limestone building which was designed by the ubiquitous Pugin. As an edifice, it is worth contrasting with the fine modern church at Fossa, outside the town, where the work of contemporary Irish artists lends atmosphere to a modern centre of worship. A large window in the Fossa church looks out on a lush Kerry landscape that must surely be one of the most stunning views visible from any church in Ireland.

Killarney's many hotels make the town popular with the organisers of major events and conferences. These include the South of Ireland Bridge Congress, which is held in May, and the All-Ireland Ladies' Basketball Championships, which takes place in April.

The town is also a useful base for mountaineers and hill-walkers. The mountains of Kerry include the highest in Ireland, Carrauntoohill, which, towering to 3414 feet, has earned its title as 'the roof of Ireland'. Carrauntoohill is in the MacGillycuddy Reeks range and is topped by a cairn and cross. The place-names in the mountains of Kerry are as intriguing as those in the lowlands: the Devil's Ladder, for example, or the Hag's Glen.

The now deserted Blasket Islands, County Kerry.

Dun an Oir on the Dingle Peninsular, scene of a bloody massacre of Spanish and Italian forces in 1580.

churches, cottages and other buildings, the peninsula wears history like a coat.

Dingle is the most westerly town in Europe. An easy-going place where people of many nationalities meet at the height of summer, it has a number of fine restaurants that offer fare to please all palates. Steve MacDonogh, the author of the best available guide to the area, has estimated that the town has over fifty pubs:

> There are large modern pubs and pubs so small that five's a crowd; one that's a travel agency; another that sells wellingtons and leather belts and another that sells everything from beds and bicycles to creosote and fertiliser.

Dingle also has the Café Liteartha, the most interesting bookshop in Kerry, where the business of browsing among books can be combined with the equally serious business of drinking tea and eating. The shop is a particularly fine storehouse of books about Ireland.

Inevitably, the extraordinary landscape of the Dingle peninsula has played its part in movies, most famously in David Lean's *Ryan's Daughter* (1969) where the coastal scenery of west Kerry seemed to become a character in itself. More recently the area featured in *Far and Away* (1992), starring Tom Cruise.

As with most places in Ireland, in the landscape of Kerry stories lurk behind place-names and fields tell yarns. Near Killarney, for example, there are two cairn-topped mountains known as the Paps. In folklore, these are said to be the breasts of Dana, the goddess of the Tuatha De Danaan, the same legendary race which once engaged in a battle with another group known as the Milesians near the Slieve Mish mountains. Scotia, the wife of the Milesian leader and the daughter of a pharaoh, was killed during the fighting. She was buried in Scotia's Glen close to Tralee.

In the Dingle peninsula, mythology combines with history and poetry. It has always been a potent force for poets, and the foremost modern poet writing in Irish, Nuala Ní Dhomhnaill (1952–), has drawn deeply from the history and lore of the peninsula.

If Killarney represents one image of Ireland, the Dingle peninsula presents another. For many Irish people, the peninsula is home to a kind of primal dream. It holds the most westerly point in Ireland, Clogher Head. Excellent beaches at Inch, Castlegregory and elsewhere are as much a part of the area's attraction as its rough fields and deserted islands. It is a place which can stay in the memory in different ways – as, say, a summer day spent on a warm beach or the recollection of the way watery light falls across a bog at evening. It is a peninsula of spectacular views and high roads, of harbours, cliffs, villages and strands. With a mass of ruined or preserved hermitages,

She has shown that such lore contains its own kind of truth that the rational world often rejects. Ventry (Fionn Trá) Harbour is one such source of folklore. A famous battle is said to have been fought here after the Irish hero, Fionn Mac Cumhail, ran away with the wife and daughter of the King of France. Armies arrived in ships led by the King of the World, no less, to get the women back. The battle raged for a year and a day as the Fianna, Fionn's army, fought in the harbour.

Another, less mythological slaughter took place at Dun an Oir, the Golden Fort, in 1580, terminating the so-called 'Desmond Wars' – a Vatican-financed rebellion against English power in Ireland. A force of Italians and Spaniards held the fort against bombardment by English battalions, which included the poet Edmund Spenser in their ranks. When the papal forces surrendered, they were massacred to a man.

Farther along the peninsula, a small township of beehive huts, or *clochans*, can be seen. Like those on the Skelligs, these were homes to monks. The same monks built Gallarus Oratory. Described as the perfect piece of early Irish building, its corbelled roof, made entirely of keyed stone, is as strong today as when it was first built. Seamus Heaney has written beautifully of what it is like to visit Gallarus:

Inside, in the dark of the stone, it feels as if you are sustaining a great pressure, bowing under like the generations of monks who must have bowed down in meditation and reparation on that floor. I felt the weight of Christianity in all its rebuking aspects, its calls to self-denial and self-abnegation, its humbling of the proud flesh and insolent spirit. But coming out of the cold heart of the stone, into the sunlight and the dazzle of grass and sea, I felt a lift in my heart, a surge towards happiness that must have been experienced over and over again by those monks as they crossed that same threshold centuries ago.

A couple of miles away is the 12th-century Hiberno-Romanesque church of Kilmakedar, whose east window is said to be the 'eye of the needle' through which it is easier to pass than for a rich man to get into Heaven. Visitors are not encouraged to try Heaven on for size by wedging themselves through it.

Around the village of Ballyferriter, the heart of the Dingle *Gaeltacht* includes the village of Dunquin, the great rise of Mount Eagle, the curve of Slea Head and, out from the shore, the Blasket Islands. In the harbour at Dunquin, upturned curraghs rest, relics of the days when these traditional light boats caulked with tar were used extensively on this wild coast. When carried along by men who walk under them, they seem like the bodies of insects supported by trousered legs.

The Irish language is still the daily means of communication for many people in this area. The language itself arouses ambiguous feelings in many Irish people who regret that it is dying but cannot be bothered to learn it because of its negative associations. These include the way it was once taught in many schools when it seemed as if it wasn't so much taught as shoved like a distasteful food down pupils' throats. There is also a great deal of official claptrap surrounding it. Politicians and others in public life fix phrases of Irish like a tail on the end of speeches they make in English, and this lip-service aptly sums up official attitudes. It is part of the official state apparatus but its decline as a living language continues. Since the 1980s the situation has improved a little and there is now coming to be a new fear-free enthusiasm for Irish, especially in urban areas. If census reports are anything to go by, there is enormous goodwill towards the language. Like land and environment, language now has its own ecology and the Dingle peninsula has always been important for those who would wish to see the Irish language preserved.

Standing at Slea Head, one can look at the Blasket Islands, themselves one of the most potent symbols of a threatened Gaelic culture. The Blasket cluster includes seven islands in all, the most important being the Great Blasket, Innisvickilaun, Inis Tuaisceart and Tiaracht. Innisvickilaun, or Inis Mhicealáin, is the island home of the former Taoiseach or Prime Minister, Charles J. Haughey (1925–), the most controversial and colourful politician in modern Ireland. The frequent sight of his helicopter commuting between the mainland and the island provided a theme

for countless conversations and endless speculation. The island is also connected with a most poignant Irish air called 'Port na bPúcai' which local folklore says is a fairy lament. One of the best books on the Blasket islands, Muiris MacConghail's *The Blaskets: A Kerry Island Library*, quotes Tomás O Dála, a former inhabitant of the island, as he talks about the song:

> *The fairy woman came to the outside of the house and she was singing, saying the tune and there was someone inside who had an ear for music: he had the tune by morning. The woman had vanished. There were words to it:*

> *I'm a woman from the fairy host, who came over the wave.*
> *I was carried off by night far a while over sea*
> *I'm in their kingdom, under control of fairy women*
> *And I shall not be in this world after the cock crows*
> *Then I will go into the lios [fairy fort]*
> *It is not a pleasure for me but there must I go,*
> *And all in this world must I leave.*

The Blasket Islands became most famous as a result of a remarkable series of books written by people who lived there. The culture and history of the islands is commemorated in an interpretative centre at Dunquin. The island books include *An tOileánach* (The Islandman) by Tomás O Criomhthain (1856–1937), *Peig* by Peig Sayers (1873–1958) and *Fiche Bliain Ag Fás* (Twenty Years A-growing) by Muiris Ó Suilleabháin (1904–50). There have been others but these are the most important, and of them all *An tOileánach* is the finest. Each is an autobiography. While a kind of reverential sclerosis often clings to

the memory of the Blasket Islanders, it is important to remember that when these books were written they were the work of ordinary people telling their own stories. The islanders were greatly encouraged by foreign philologists and scholars like Robin Flower, Carl Marstrander and George Thompson.

While island life is easily romanticised, life on the Blaskets was tough, as the interpretative centre at Dunquin shows. Emigration and poverty took their toll on the islanders and in 1952 it was announced that the government was to transfer the islanders to the mainland. All but one family were gone by the end of 1953 and, at Christmas that year, those who watched from the mainland could see only one light shining on the island. The following year there was no light at all. The Blaskets are a symbol of a lost culture and while they can now be viewed with a collective nostalgia, they had become too difficult a home for those who lived there. Against a temperamental sea and an often indifferent state apparatus, the islanders eventually left, but the books which their culture created keep their world alive. The vivid and vigorous language of those books is a model for writers and storytellers.

Heading back from the Dingle peninsula, one comes to the town of Tralee and to the northernmost of Kerry's peninsulas, the Iveragh. Less rugged than the western peninsula, it has a different story to tell from the time when the great Anglo-Norman families of Fitzgerald and Fitzmaurice held sway for centuries over its beaches, caves, moors and bogs, rivers, hills and undulating fields.

Tralee is the home of Siamsa Tire, the national folk theatre. The town, which originally developed around a 13th-century castle, contains a number of 18th-century remains and some fine 19th-century buildings that are still intact, among them the courthouse designed by Richard Morrison and St John's Church.

Other sights in north Kerry include the windmill at Blennerville and the strand at Ballybunion, the latter a seaside resort which has a bucket-and-spade association for thousands of natives. It was from Ballybunion that a voice was transmitted by

EMIGRATION

Exile has been a feature of Irish life for centuries. For the old Irish monks, exile was 'the white martyrdom' and, in one of his poems, the sixth-century St Colmcille (who was also known as St Columba), grasped its poignant starkness:

> *There's a sea-blue eye that stares*
> *At Ireland drawing away.*
> *It will never look again*
> *At the women of Ireland, or its men.*
> (translated by Sean Dunne)

To an extent, it is inevitable that some enisled men and women would tire of their insular situation and move elsewhere. Yet emigration in Ireland grew to be something more. It became a way of life for millions of people, who left home in a tragic diaspora that continues to this day.

In the years before the series of famines that afflicted the country for six years from 1845, many people emigrated as a matter of course. After the famine, however, the numbers increased dramatically. It has been estimated that two and a half million people emigrated from Ireland between 1846 and 1856. Millions of others emigrated in later decades. This led to a major reduction in the population and simply became an accepted part of life in Ireland.

The emigrants left ports like Queenstown (now known as Cobh) in County Cork and went mostly to America, Canada, Australia, Newfoundland (which in Irish is known as *Talamh an Eisc* – 'the Land of Fish') and England. Both men and women emigrated. Many found work, mostly as unskilled labourers, and paid for the eventual passage of another family member. Many famous Americans, such as John F. Kennedy, Ronald Reagan and Henry Ford, were the descendants of such Irish emigrants.

Emigration created a literature and folklore of its own. The party held the night before an emigrant left home was known as the American wake. Emigration also became a theme for writers of popular ballads and sentimental poems. Lady Dufferin's poem 'The Irish Emigrant' was one of the most famous and it reflects the innocent dream of those who thought that other lands were, if not quite paved with gold, at least full of economic hope:

> *I'm bidding you a long farewell*
> *My Mary, kind and true!*
> *But I'll not forget you, darling,*
> *In the land I'm going to.*
> *They say there's bread and work for all,*
> *And the sun always shines there;*
> *But I'll not forget old Ireland*
> *Were it fifty times as fair.*

Emigration continued to be just as much a feature of southern Irish life after Independence in 1922. One estimate puts the number of emigrants between 1926 and 1986 at over 790 000. The numbers reflected poverty and economic uncertainty. They also reflect the Irish state's inability to provide work for thousands of its own people. During a brief period of industrial expansion and economic optimism, the numbers decreased in the late 1960s and early 1970s but then they started to climb again. Emigration had been mainly a rural phenomenon but, by the 1980s, emigrants were of both rural and urban backgrounds.

The effects were obvious in many parts of the country, where it was no longer possible, say, to field full hurling or football teams, or where the numbers of children in many country schools dropped dramatically. While the physical impact of emigration is easy to ascertain, it is more difficult to measure the psychological effect left on a community by the fact that so many of its young, energetic people have left. To put it mildly, it has been what one commentator, Gearoid Ó Tuathaigh, called an 'extraordinary demographic and social phenomenon'. Whether at the edge of harbours or on the balconies of airports, generations of Irish people have watched their friends and relatives leave for other lands that have been enriched by those very emigrants. Ireland has suffered from this diaspora, however, and the idea of emigration almost seems a natural part of the national consciousness. It has never ceased, however, to be hurtful. The poignancy of that ancient poem by St Colmcille has not been diminished for the people of modern Ireland.

telephone from Europe to the USA for the first time. It happened in 1912 and the speaker was W.T. Ditcham, a Marconi employee.

A massive faction fight was enacted on the beach at Ballybunion in 1834 and it is said that over 3000 people took part. Twenty were killed. Nowadays Ballybunion hosts an event each summer which gives rise to more gaiety but nearly as many sore heads: the Ballybunion International Bachelor Festival.

Listowel is a splendid, planned town which these days hosts both horse races and an annual literature festival. The ruined Norman castle which lies at its centre was besieged in 1600 during the O'Neill war and, when it was finally captured by Sir Charles Wilmot, he ordered that all those who had held out there should be killed. North Kerry contains many other ruins and sights that mark out its history, including Lislaughtin Abbey at Ballylongford, which was attacked and devastated during the Elizabethan era, and Carrigafoyle Castle, destroyed by Cromwellians in 1649.

The literary heritage of the area is extensive. The town's most accomplished writers are John B. Keane and Brian MacMahon. Keane is far and away the most popular playwright in modern Ireland. His best-known play is *The Field*, which became a movie starring Richard Harris. The play deals with land, murder and community secrecy and is based on a true story that Mr Keane may have heard in the pub he and his wife Mary ran for many years. The story hints at a secret, private world behind the world of public appearance. Such a world was made manifest in what became known as the Kerry Babies case, when a public inquiry was held into the death in 1984 of a baby born to Joanne Hayes, a young woman from Abbeydorney. Another baby had been found washed up on a strand and she was held to be responsible for its death. As it happened, she wasn't; but the resultant events became a notorious indicator of attitudes to women and morality in Ireland.

Kerry and its people were for many years the butt of thousands of jokes that characterised them as the epitome of stupidity and cuteness. In Kerry this is seen as a sign of inferiority among outsiders who feel threatened by Kerry prowess on the football field and in other areas.

From the factories on the edges of its towns to the hundreds of archaeological sites which visitors can see, the county is a microcosm of the whole country, reflecting the social changes that have taken place over thousands of years and the cultural complexity which history has shaped. It is a county where the folk memory can be strong and the turn of phrase can be terse and sharp.

John B. Keane, besides being a famous playwright and publican, is also one of the county's great raconteurs and storytellers. He has written approvingly of Tom Daly, a former Kerry footballer whose relatives asked him to make a will before he died. The will was a concise masterpiece: 'I, Tom Daly,' it said, 'being of sound mind, drank every halfpenny I had before I died.'

MUSTS IN THE SOUTHWEST

* The English Market in Cork City.
* A meal – even a small one – at Ballymaloe House.
* The Crawford Art Gallery.
* Fota arboretum and wildlife park.
* An evening walk along the stand at Youghal or Allihies.
* Gougane Barra.
* An impermeable raincoat and a stout pair of boots.
* The Ceim Hill Museum near Union Hall.
* St Fin Barre's Cathedral.
* A walk in the streets and lanes around Shandon Steeple.
* Howling support at a hurling match.
* The Honan Chapel in University College, Cork.
* The Blasket Islands.
* A solitary sojourn in a beehive hut.
* A reading of Tomas Ó Criomhthain's *The Islandman*.
* Puck Fair.
* A music session in Dingle or Ballyferriter.
* Gallarus Oratory.
* Listowel Writers' Week.
* A list of place-names and their origins.
* Muckross House and Muckross Abbey.

4 The West

Michael Finlan with Bernard Loughlin

COUNTIES

CLARE

GALWAY

MAYO

SLIGO

In the west of Ireland, where nowadays wild-looking, desolate mountains loom over vast extents of blanket bog, there were once rich woodlands standing deep in their own must and mast. This is a landscape which has been changed out of all recognition by the hand and tools of man. As you look at how it is now, you must try to imagine also how it was, and what has made it as it now appears. For this region, more than any other in Ireland, hides many half-remembered and long-forgotten stories under its beautiful skin.

At the Ceide Fields in County Mayo twenty years of painstaking archaeological excavation have uncovered part of this mystery in the form of an extensive New Stone Age settlement that flourished here around 3000 BC. Around the architecturally daring pyramid of the interpretative centre built recently at the centre of this site – one of the least controversial of these tourist complexes in Ireland – the stone walls of

ancient fields and the remains of houses in complex village street patterns reveal an Irish Pompeii, overwhelmed not by volcanic ash but by the inexorably creeping bog that built up once the tree cover was cleared and the ever sodden Irish climate relapsed into one of its wet phases.

Bog is the dominant landscape feature of the west of Ireland. From the great tracts of it that well around the Shannon like a spongy ectoplasm being spewed by the river, to the raised bogs scattered across the face of the Connaught uplands like moles growing out of their blue-grey complexions, the browns and blacks of the turf make the cerulean moodiness of the ever changing skies even more intense.

As the revelations at the Ceide Fields make clear, the west of Ireland was once much more fertile than it is now. The first inhabitants slashed and burned the forests to make land for tillage and husbandry. For a few generations this land was richly

The Old Lighthouse, Clare Island, County Mayo.

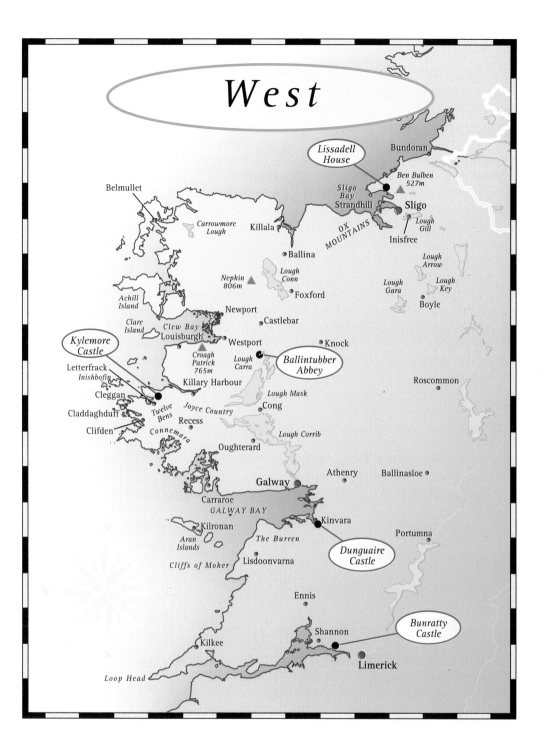

productive, thus possibly explaining prehistoric buildings such as Dun Aengus on the Aran Islands, which must have been created by the collective labour of well-organised societies with considerable resources of manpower and skill. Over the millennia of man's interference with the landscape, the erosion of soil from the hill slopes and the gradual acidification of the lowlands through lack of drainage may have reduced the arable land area by as much as a hundredfold, driving the human population to ever greater extremes of inventiveness to be able to survive on what remained. By the time Oliver Cromwell came to wreak the Lord's will on Ireland in the 17th century the relict human population in Connaught would have been so small that he could well have imagined the whole province to be a God-sent open-air reservation where the native Irish could be segregated and confined after he ran them off their fertile lands in the midlands and east. 'To hell or to Connaught' was the diktat under which he herded them in droves across the Shannon, and this in spite of one of his lieutenants having reported from a recce in the same Connaught that 'there's not enough water to drown a man, not enough timber to hang him and not enough earth to bury him'. The thousands of unwilling migrants in this enforced internal diaspora of necessity accommodated themselves to the inhospitable terrain.

Under the ancient Gaelic system of land tenure laid down by the Brehon laws, the holdings grew steadily smaller as successive generations divided and sub-divided them. For a few of these generations, from the 17th century onwards, the land yielded sufficient crops of the versatile and nourishing potato to give an adequate subsistence. Yet, as we now know, the almost total dependence of the Irish people on the potato made them tragically vulnerable when blight, a mould encouraged by a run of wet, muggy summers, ravaged the crop in the 1840s. This region suffered more than any other in Ireland from the effects of the Great Famine. Its people died or emigrated in their hundreds of thousands. The bureaucratic appellation given to these areas at the time, the 'congested districts', almost suggests that this was a tragedy waiting to happen, God or Nature's way of clearing out this regrettable infestation of humanity. The Board for Congested Districts did try to alleviate the worst effects of the Famine through a system of reliefs designed to create employment. The constructions which resulted from this Victorian form of dole are known as famine roads or famine piers to this day. At the highest point on the road from Louisburgh to Leenane, near the romantically named Delphi on Doo Lough, there is a metal plaque attesting to the benevolence of the Commissioners for Congested Districts. Nowadays it is hard to see any economic

rationale for these roads leading seemingly from nowhere to nowhere else, or the little rocky jetties that give only the barest shelter to the shallowest of craft, but at the time they offered a form of Poor Law Relief that saved at least some of the native population from joining the throngs on the emigrant trails to the ports of the south and east coasts.

The west is certainly not a congested place today. You can travel for many miles and see no other inhabitants than hardy mountain sheep, rangy cattle, scavenging birds, startled hares, and hear only the sound of the wind over the heather and smell the salt ocean, never too far away, that sends great flotillas of clouds arching and rolling and scudding over this Empty Quarter in which encampments of nomads following their herds would not be unexpected. Outside the major towns human settlement remains quirky and scattered. More often than not you wonder how and why people live where they do, in tiny houses surrounded by a few crooked trees at the end of roads that look as if they have been gouged out of the mountainsides by a giant finger idly scoring a mark in the soft brown turf. At crossroads in the middle of seeming nowhere men march along the rough roads with cattle switches in their hands, peering off into the distance for their straying charges. Women wrapped tightly round with housecoats, their legs clad to the knees with grey woollen socks thrust into clobbered rubber boots, stride purposefully to wells with a bucket on each arm. Children stand in little knots at halting places known only to themselves, waiting for school buses to take them to places of learning built where a few roads meet. In these parts the people are robust, self-sufficient, uncomplaining, getting by on the bit of cattle-rearing, the odd bout of seasonal labour, the farmers' dole, or remittances from America, England or, increasingly, continental Europe. What new houses there are tend to be modest, modern replicas of the traditional three-roomed cottages that have mostly fallen into disrepair. Only on the outskirts of the major towns do you see the more pretentious *haciendas* that signify money from trade or the liberal professions.

With all its harshness, this is a land of strong, characterful women. The sea queen and pirate Grace O'Malley (Grannuaile in Irish), who famously supped as an equal with the first Queen Elizabeth, had her lairs along the coast. St Patrick, the man who could be said to have broken this female hegemony once and for all when he ushered in the era of the patriarchal church, is said to have prayed and fasted for forty days and nights on Croagh Patrick overlooking Granuaille's redoubt in Clew Bay.

In County Clare, on the other side of Galway Bay, you come right back to the beginning of things. The strong sense of the past that always lies just under the surface in the west bursts through in the Burren in massive terraced slabs of naked limestone, formed hundreds of millions of years ago from crushed and compacted seashells in prehistoric oceans. At first sight the Burren seems a planet from which all life has been banished. Only stunted vestiges of the forests that flourished here after the last Ice Age are now discernible among the fascinating array of wild flowers and shrubs that cling for dear life to the grykes, or crevices, in the Burren's weather-pitted surface. Yet, for all its geological nakedness, with its millennia of numinous history engraved in its stone, the timeless Burren is a good place from which to observe the emerging modern Ireland. From the top of the plateau you can watch transatlantic jets coming in to land at Shannon Airport, one of the motors which has powered Ireland's belated industrial revolution. This is also where one of the great environmental battles of the 1990s was waged, around Mullaghmore mountain, when the proposal to build an interpretative centre for the Burren region was opposed by a broad coalition of people concerned that the extra traffic it might bring to these backroads and the tramp of human feet over the limestone might damage irreversibly this precious wilderness.

This conflict between the conservationists and the modernisers could be said to have begun when Seán Lemass (1899–1971), who succeeded Eamon de Valera after the latter's final term as Taoiseach, set about establishing an industrial base in Ireland in the 1960s. The Whittaker Plan attracted substantial business investment from overseas and helped to transform Ireland's hitherto mainly agricultural economy into one based on a mixture of food processing, components manufacture and, latterly, high-tech industries such as computing and pharmaceuticals. These efforts were so successful that in the early 1970s, for the first time since the Famine, emigration slowed to a trickle and some of the Irish abroad even began returning home.

A new town called Shannon – the first new town in the country – grew up around the airport. Eight thousand people live there today. The electronics and information technology companies that have gathered there have developed close associations with the new University of Limerick, which incorporates the Plassey Technology Park, making the whole area a sort of silicon valley of hi-tech endeavour. Part of Shannon's early success was the inspired idea of setting up the world's first tax-free airport, a status that was later extended to the industrial estate. Yet the greatest changes in Ireland were wreaked not so much by the luxury goods for which this was a first commercial outpost but by the celebrities who moved through the airport in the early days when refuelling stopovers were almost mandatory. They brought a whiff of *la dolce vita* with them and made their brief contacts with the old sod into social occasions. It was here that a barman invented Gaelic coffee by floating whipped cream on top of black coffee laced with Irish whiskey, a drink that recalled Guinness, yet seemed exotic, and came to feature on bar and restaurant menus throughout the world. With the coming of jets, Shannon lost much of its refuelling business and ceased to be a way-station for travelling VIPs.

The southern part of Clare, in contrast to the stony ramparts of the Burren, is relatively flat, studded with many lakes, and affords rich pastureland that runs right to the Shannon estuary. A few miles east of the county capital, Ennis, stands Craggaunowen Castle where an open-air museum contains a *crannog*, or artificial island, in the middle of a lake, on which has been built a timber and straw dwelling such as was common thousands of years ago. A fifth-century ring fort has also been erected. Inside the glass-roofed main building is housed the leather and timber boat, *The Brendan*, built by the adventurer Tim Severin. This is an exact copy of the vessel in which St Brendan the Navigator is supposed to have sailed to America in the sixth century. Severin crossed the Atlantic in it in 1976, thus demonstrating that the voyage recorded by St Brendan in his journals could indeed have been made in such a craft.

If the rigours of monastic life and the prospect of a diet of oatcakes and water do not appeal, it is possible to emulate the gormandising feats of the lords and ladies of the castle at the medieval banquets that are held in the great stone-floored dining hall of Bunratty Castle, originally built in the 15th century and now restored with splendid medieval furnishing. The banquets consist of authentic dishes of the past, hearty, toothsome and plentiful fodder to be washed down with goblets of mead. Traditional musicians and dancers combine genteel singing and harp-playing with spirited jigs and reels for the entertainment of the guests,

two of whom will have the dubious honour of being made lord and lady of the rout for the evening.

Beside the castle a more recent form of nostalgia is evoked in Bunratty Folk Park, where an Irish village of the 20s or 30s has been reconstructed. Among the interesting museum displays there are fully functional shops where you can buy replicas of the goods of that long gone era, though not, unfortunately, at the prices that prevailed then. In summer they hold *ceilís*, traditional Irish dances, in one of the farmhouses and serve bowls of Irish stew and soda bread to sustain the energy of the dancing couples. One of Ireland's most famous pubs, Durty Nelly's, which has four separate bars spread through a labyrinth of low rooms, is located next door.

By contrast to southern Clare, the more rugged landscape of County Galway is criss-crossed with thousands of stone walls hand-built over centuries, whose uneven patterns mark out a patchwork of fields where potatoes and other subsistence crops were once planted and domestic animals now graze. Vestiges of the old Gaelic culture survive here, mostly vividly the parts of Connemara where Irish is still spoken. At the entrance to Connemara, the largest *Gaeltacht* in Ireland, sits the city of Galway, a creation of chiselled limestone that has parleyed its colourful mercantile past into a present full of *joie de vivre* built on art, academe and business acumen.

Sometimes it seems that there are two distinct Galways: the tract of nearly four thousand square miles between the Shannon and the Atlantic which is County Galway (the second largest county in Ireland), and Galway City (fifth biggest in the Republic), itself virtually a city-statelet for most of its 500 or so years of official history. The city and the county have an easy and fluent relationship with one another, but they remain separate, like a well-matched couple who occupy the same space but each go about their own business within it. Geologically, too, there are two Galways. A fault system, which runs roughly from Galway City fifty miles westwards towards Clifden on the coast,

Bunratty Castle, County Clare, now restored to its medieval splendour.

divides the granites and quartzites and rarer marbles of the rugged Connemara region to the west and south from the richer limestone pasturelands in east Galway.

Linguistically, almost following the geology, there are again two Galways. In Connemara and on the three offshore Aran Islands in Galway Bay, rich, well-rooted Irish is still the mother tongue of the majority of the population. The rest of the region and the city itself, though generally bilingual, use an English heavily inflected with the rhythms and expressions borrowed from Irish that inspired J.M. Synge's (1871–1909) theatrical patois, a language that hovers somewhere between the real and the imaginary, full of the passion of a peasant life of which he saw the last flowering, that remained closely in touch with the earth and the elements yet had a deep spiritual belief in other worlds not necessarily approved by the official Church of the day.

In social and cultural terms there is a single Galway. The citizens of city and county – from the Aran islanders thirty miles out to sea to the courteous inhabitants of Portumna by the Shannon – are united by a powerful bond of pride at being Galwegians, a pride that is affirmed by seeing and using the city of Galway as their capital, and Dublin as merely a place for occasional visits, All Ireland Finals and affairs of state in which Galway politicians have always had an influence out of all proportion to the county's demographic size.

And it is necessary to lay down this factual bedrock before stating that there are a thousand Galways to be discovered by those who come to stroll through the streets of the City of the Tribes, or wander the shores of Galway Bay, or lose themselves deep in their tangle of hinterlands. From the lowlands flooded by the mighty Corrib River to the highlands and islands of Connemara; from the purpled eternity of boglands around the Twelve Bens Mountains to the jewel-greened, stonewalled, hunter-and-doglands in the south, there is all the bracing vitality that is captured in the words of the fabled song 'The Galway Races'. At a deeper level there is something surreal born of the triumph of the indomitable, bright side of the Irish spirit that underpins the charm and appeal of all the Galways. In harsh economic terms, for example, the area is designated as particularly disadvantaged by all official European Commission statistics, yet, year after year, in the teeth of worldwide economic recessions, the wagering at the same Galway Races, a week-long extravaganza, easily exceeds the records set the year before.

During the annual Galway Arts Festival the streets are infested with the madcap creations of the inventive street theatre group called Macnas. The name is Irish for the joy and madness of a calf released from its wintering shed onto the green pastures of spring, and neatly captures the spirit of their caperings which are quite self-consciously pagan, and a release from all the pious suppressions of the Catholic past. The most famous Macnas creation is a giant smiling Gulliver who towered over the chimneys of the narrow streets of the city on his first outing and has since brushed wonder over the faces of young and old alike in other Lilliputs from Dublin to Seville. Another creation of theirs features a troop of grotesque Fir Bolg figures who shake hands with amazed visitors, kiss children and cavort and dervish to the music of drums and pipes wild enough to rouse all the dead and all the devils of hell. Tellingly, a local rock band called the Saw Doctors, with a similar genesis to Macnas, became famous through playing a mixture of rock and roll and country and western, a genre bred in this polyglot city where anything, within generous reason, goes. Macnas themselves have played as a support act on a world tour with U2, Ireland's most famous pop group.

Yet for all the cosmopolitan atmosphere of the Arts Festival that brings performers and audiences from all over the world, to stand on Eyre Square, the one-time fair green of the ancient city, is to be almost literally walled in by history. It is one of the ironies in which Galway specialises that you can sit drinking coffee in a café in the Eyre Centre shopping complex, protected from the weather by the glass roof, listening to the best of 20th-century shopping mall muzak, while

The Twelve Bens rising out of the boglands of Connemara, County Galway.

contemplating masonry some 600 or 700 years old in the restored section of the old city wall that is the complex's centrepiece. The wall dates from the 13th century when the Norman De Burgo family fortified the town they had seized from the Irish O'Halloran clan and began to develop a port and trading centre. In 1484 the town was granted a charter by Richard III of England. A strong continental trade was developed, with Spain in particular, by a number of powerful Norman families, of whom the Lynches became the most influential.

The streetscape in the ancient heart of the City is still dominated by the carved stone façades of the merchants' houses of the 17th and 18th centuries, many of them splendidly preserved and still occupied today. The Spanish Arch of 1584 is named after the Spanish traders whose ships would at one time have filled the port at the mouth of the River Corrib and contributed so handsomely to the wealth of the same merchants. The idiosyncratic Galway City Museum beside the Spanish Arch records all this history in a fascinating jumble of random objects and hand-written explanatory notices. The map drawn by the historian John Speed in 1610

The 16th-century Spanish Arch, Galway City.

reveals a well-planned city of Hanseatic proportions where every house had its own garden, with public spaces designed for easy intercourse and trading among the citizens and the captains of the sailing vessels that crowded the brisk and busy harbour.

All civic power in this polity at the very western edge of English influence was kept in the hands of 14 families, who came to be known pejoratively as 'the tribes of Galway'. When the De Burgos family became hibernicised and renounced their allegiance to England, changing their name to Burke – a surname still very common in these parts – they were ostracised by their fellow burghers, who, in 1518, resolved that 'at Christmas, Easter, no feast else, any of the Burkes, Mac Williams, Kellys, nor any sept else without licence of the Mayor and council, on pain to forfeit £5, that neither O nor Mac shall strut or swagger through the streets of Galway'.

Norman and English Galway's fiercest enemies, though, remained the old Irish clan chieftains to the west, notably the O'Flahertys. Over the gate facing Connemara, in 1549, appeared the inscription 'From the fury of the O'Flaherties, Good Lord deliver us.' The prayer worked against the vengeful O'Flahertys, who never captured Galway, but not against the omnipresent Cromwell, whose army, led by Charles Coote, besieged Galway for nine months in 1652 and took their revenge for the long wait when they finally reduced the city to surrender. By the end of the 17th century, after the old Irish order had backed the losing Jacobite forces against William of Orange, Galway had entered a commercial and social decline that would last for two centuries.

Important landmarks in the city's renaissance were the establishment of Queen's College in 1849 and the opening of a rail link to Dublin in the late 1800s. The student body of University College Galway, one of the constituent colleges of the National University of Ireland, now numbers nearly five thousand. Its faculty buildings, spread along a beautiful site on the banks of the River Corrib, are a mixture of Oxbridge Gothic and the unashamedly modern. The economic and intellectual influence of the university has created an almost Left Bank bohemianism in the old quarter of the city, where pubs like Tig Neachtain and The Quays are homes from homes to philosophers, misfits, brooders, writers, musicians, carpet-baggers, hippies and heads of all persuasions. There are many fine bookshops to be found in this same area, of which the most famous is Kenny's, a friendly, family-run establishment on many floors and annexes that also has its own art gallery. The collection of signed photographs on the walls of Kenny's, of well-known authors who have done signings, readings or simply called in there, is a pantheon of modern Irish letters.

Eyre Square, whose green bears the name of President John F. Kennedy (a visitor to Galway in 1963), was named in its entirety after a family which included Proud John Eyre: so proud, it is said, that when his steed shed a silver shoe, he would not stoop to pick it up. The statue of the elfin little man with the notebook commemorates Pádraic Ó Conaire (1883–1928), the Irish language short story writer whose Connemara tales helped spearhead the Irish literary revival at the beginning of the century. The great cannon guarding the busy square were presented to the Connaught Rangers regiment of the British Army just after the Crimean War. The Rangers, many of whose soldiers were Galwegians, joined the Irish War of Independence in 1920 by staging a mutiny in India.

Lynch's Castle, the ancestral home of the Lynch family, now a bank, is the main landmark in Shop Street, a street whose name is a nice evocation of how Galway has always been viewed by visitors from its hinterland. A gorier landmark nearby is the piece of wall, Gothic doorway and relief sculpture of a skull and crossbones, called Lynch's Memorial in memory of a mayor of Galway called James Lynch Fitzpatrick. It is said of him – most likely apocryphally – that he hanged his own son since no hangman could be found to carry out the execution for his son's murdering of a Spanish sailor in a brawl in 1493. This is said to be the origin of the term 'Lynch Law'.

Close by is the Collegiate Church of St Nicholas of Myra with its soaring spire and classical lines. Whether through association with that Levantine saint or because Columbus is said to have prayed there before his fateful voyage, this church is held in high esteem by seafarers, of whom there have always been many in this most maritime of Irish cities. Many of the memorials within the church were put there in gratitude by sailors and their families. On Saturday mornings in the streets outside there is a country market of great vitality where the many native and foreign potters, weavers, organic gardeners, bee-keepers, and other artisans who have settled in the region, vend their wares from colourful stalls.

Across the river from the Spanish Arch, separated from the city proper by the often turbulent brown waters of the Corrib, straggles the Claddagh. This ancient fishing village, now much modernised, retained its separate identity outside the walled city for many centuries. The people of the Claddagh still elect their own king and maintain a powerful local culture expressed by the wearing of the hands-and-heart Claddagh Ring. At one time these gold bands were worn by women all over the west coast and they would have formed part of their dowries. If the ring was worn on the right hand with the heart towards the fingernail it showed that the girl was open to offers of marriage. If worn on the left hand with the heart towards the palm it signified that she was already betrothed.

Galway harbour has always been a difficult one for boats because of its ripping tides and the cross-currents caused by the Corrib's seasonal surges. So open is the port to

Galway Bay that sometimes the centre of the city feels as if it is lying in the teeth of Atlantic gales, giving it a bracing, bustling airiness. Nowadays, after hundreds of years of canalising the river and fortifying the sea defences, its main docks are mostly accessible through locks, and in their basins you see fishing smacks and tramp steamers lying side by side. When the winds calm – as they often do even in this most westerly place – swans float gently on the Corrib, common terns and arctic terns back from their long migrations to the south hawk and scream over the small fry the river carries in its beer-brown waters and salmon in their season flash and leap in the pools under the Salmon Weir Bridge.

Part of Galway's cultural resurgence in the last few decades has come from the trail-blazing theatrical tradition it has fanned into life from a few embers left glowing from earlier times. The Taibhdhearc Theatre is the national theatre in the Irish language, with a programme that places a special emphasis on traditional music and bilingual presentations. The Druid Theatre in Chapel Lane, a few hundred yards away, has established an international reputation in recent years, especially with its revivals of classic Irish plays such as *The Playboy of the Western World* by J.M. Synge, *The Wood of the Whispering* by M.J. Molloy, *Famine* by Tom Murphy and others which have a special connection with the west of Ireland. Druid has also conscientiously nurtured new writing and has always been willing to experiment both with its actors and its audience, each as loyal as the other to this brave and brilliant little cockpit of a theatre that has gone out from the west of Ireland to capture the hearts of the world in valiant touring schedules that take the players from Shercock to Edinburgh, from the Aran Islands to Sydney and from Kiltimagh to Toronto. Other new theatre companies come and go in Galway (Punchbag being the most venerable after Druid), and other cultural ventures, from publishers to potters, find their little niches among the valerian and the buddleia that root in the ruins of the old warehouses and sheds that cluster round the port. Over the last fifteen years or so, these pioneers have

cleared the way for the boutiques, record shops, antiquaries, health food stores, trendy offices and all manner of other trades that have settled in the old quarter, whose fine buildings are being restored with quite staggering speed.

Beyond its ancient heart, though, Galway is something of an urban sprawl of housing estates and shopping developments which give the city's suburbs an almost American air. However, the sea is never far away and Galwegians take full advantage of it at resorts like Salthill, where night clubs, hotels, bars, restaurants, amusement centres and a watersports-cum-leisure complex entertain townsfolk and out-of-towners alike. With its two miles of breezy promenade looking out over the bay to the hills of Clare in the south, Salthill is still the most popular resort on the west coast.

West of Salthill, through Barna and onwards towards Spiddal, along the shore of the bay, and further west still towards Carraroe, the traveller is venturing into a more primordial world. Brown boglands, quartz-flecked rocks, steely, wind-ruffled lakes and blue-green seas combine to make pageants of landscape that have inspired Irish painters including Paul Henry (1876–1958), Maurice Mac Gonigal (1900–79), Jack B. Yeats (1871–1957) and Sean Keating (1889–1977), whose works can be seen in the National Gallery in Dublin and in other collections around the country. This is Joyce country, where the Twelve Pins tower over the one-time fiefdoms of the Joyces and the O'Flahertys, whose hardy descendants still carry on the ancient struggle to gouge a living from this grudging soil. The type of the sturdy peasant waging this battle with the elements was much mythologised in the writings and paintings of the turn-of-the-century artists when they discovered what they took to be a redoubt of the old virtues. This was the west of Ireland to which W.B. Yeats summarily dispatched J.M. Synge to explore for material when he first met him palely malingering in Paris.

Today Connemara is a well-developed tourist region, with all the modern amenities – bilingual roadsigns, information offices, seafood restaurants and comfortable hotels, some of them of the first quality, like Renvyle House, one-time summer home of Oliver St John Gogarty (1878–1959), the Buck Mulligan of Joyce's *Ulysses* – but it yet preserves the integrity of a place apart where the heritage of the language and culture has deep roots. The Folding Landscape maps and guides to Connemara and the Aran Islands that have been drawn and compiled by Tim Robinson, an English writer who came to this region first of all as a painter, are repositories of the lore that has accumulated around the very stones of these places. Yet there are ironies here, as everywhere in modern Ireland, seeming clashes of culture that are in fact the same process of assimilation that has gone on for thousands of years. In a pub, for example, a traditional *sean nós*, or unaccompanied singer will render a song in Irish, the old language filling all the space, while someone in the background may be quietly doing business, also perhaps in Irish, or maybe even in Spanish, French or German, over a mobile telephone. There are still the thatched roofs, featured in Paul Henry paintings, of the lonely homesteads at the head of the glen, but not that many. There are still men with donkeys working on the bogs, though turf-cutting machines and tractors are progressively taking over. The fleet of curraghs is as numerous as ever, though these days their swept, svelte prows are as likely to be propelled through the waves by outboard motors as by the strokes of men on the peculiar narrow-bladed oars that gave them great power and mobility in the Atlantic swell in years gone by. The distinctive Galway Bay hookers, craft that bear striking resemblances to north African sailing ships and even to Arab dhows, were once the draughthorse boats of the bay, ferrying cargoes of turf from the mainland to the Aran Islands and to the turfless Burren area of County Clare on the southern coast. Nowadays many of them have been restored as pleasure boats by enthusiasts who turn them out in their best rig and tackle for the regattas that sprinkle the sea with sails in the summer months.

In this 'last parish before America' – a claim made by many regions along the western seaboard – robust ingenuity has created enduring life on a rugged and dangerous coast and an impossibly poor agricultural terrain, as celebrated in such classic works as J.M. Synge's *Riders To The Sea* (about the noble resignation of a mother losing her last son to the sea which both gives and takes away) and the sweeping romances of Galway City writer Walter Macken.

The Connemara pony, the best children's pony in the equine world, thrives on thin pastures where other horses would starve. Indeed, the breed loses many of its essential characteristics when bred and fed on too fertile pastures. Thatched roofs, where they survive today, are still lashed to the stone walls and gables of the houses by ropes weighted down with rocks. Intricate patterns are created among the stone walls of the fields by stacks of turf and ricks of hay. Seaweed harvested from the sea, as kelp, is left to dry and desalinate along the strands before it goes to fertilise the potato gardens, as the fields here are still called. These are carved symmetrically into long ridges to keep the tubers up out of the wet, and the gardeners take an ancestral pride in being able to do this by eye, which is not nearly so easy as they make it seem when you watch them at work in a steady, sure rhythm that has been handed down from father to son through many generations.

The thousands of students of the Irish language who flit and twitter along the boreens in the summer like so many gaily coloured revenant birds stay as guests in local homes while they study at the Irish colleges. This two-way exchange benefits both the local economy and the national culture, which still needs to go to drink at these wellsprings from time to time, as well as at the gushing soda fountains of Coca-Cola and MTV, from which we imbibe with equal ease and pleasure.

Other areas especially worth seeing include the fishing port of Rossaveal, one of the biggest in the country, the bridges and islands of Lettermore and Lettermullen, a sheltered archipelago that hosts curragh-

THE ARAN ISLANDS

It is a logical progression from that face of Galway represented by Connemara to that of the Aran Islands, only six minutes away from the new airport at Rossaveal. Or one can choose the traditional sea route either from Rossaveal port itself or on the slower scheduled services from Galway port. Any sea or air road that leads to the legendary isles of Inishmore ('Large Island'), Inishmann ('Middle Island'), or Inishere ('Eastern Island') is a magic road. The mighty forts erected in pre-Christian times, the mossed remains of ancient churches and monastic settlements from the time when Aran was a seminary for the early church, the active presence even of the traditional costumes of the hardy islanders, all conspire to create a very special world bounded by stone and sea. Inishmore's crowning glory is Dun Aonghus, one of the finest prehistoric monuments in Western Europe, a fort of concentric enclosures on top of a striking cliff. The view from Dun Aonghus is one of the finest in Ireland.

All around the port of Kilronan, the island capital, are the ruins of countless churches, notably those of Cill Chorna, St Ciaran's Monastery, Temphall An Cheathair Alainn ('Church of the Four Comely Saints'), and the Seven Churches (though there are the ruins of only two) near Eoghnacht village. Nearby is Leaba An Spiorad Naoimh ('Bed of the Holy Spirit'), an ancient site of prayer and penance. Other points of interest on the island include the Black Fort near Killeany, Arkin Castle, a relic of the Cromwellian garrison, and, the holiest spot on the island, Teallach Eanna, said to be the burial place of no fewer than 120 saints.

Inishmann, like Inishmore, is laden with the ancient relics of saints and warriors. It is also the island which most strongly preserves the old customs of a proud and friendly people, an island with special warmth. Cathaoir Synge ('Synge's Chair') is a sheltered spot at the cliffside, near Dun Beag, where the famous playwright spent the many hours during his island sojourns which led to the production of such magnificent works as *The Playboy of the Western World*. Inishere, close to the Clare coast, is the liveliest and merriest of three merry islands. Its Pattern Day is held on 14 June each year. Its monastic ruins include the tiny church on St Gobnait, reputedly the only woman allowed to live on the three islands during one ascetic period.

Sins are graded in Ireland. It would be a mortal sin to spend less than a full day on any of the three islands of Aran; a venial sin not to stay overnight.

The Aran Islands, County Galway, site of one of the finest prehistoric monuments in Europe.

racing festivals in summer, and the unique coral strand at Carraroe, the small town which is the capital of the south Connemara *Gaeltacht*. There is excellent game fishing at Screebe, as at many places along this coast, where small boats complete with bait and tackle can be hired by the hour or the day. And when you have absorbed all the flux and flightiness of the Connemara landscape, and imagined how tenuous life has always been here, and brooded perhaps a little on the iniquities of the past, you can go to visit the thatched cottage at Rosmuc where the patriot Padraic Pearse (1879–1916) dreamed of an Ireland surely much different to the one which issued from his revolution, an Ireland not perhaps as content as he might have imagined with the old verities of blood and sacrifice, but an Ireland that has continued to grow and mature around not so much the bedrock of the monolithic past as upon the slippery movements of its multi-faceted present.

Further north is the charming lobster-fishing centre of Carna, surrounded by fine beaches. On St Macdara's Island, out in the Atlantic, the corbel-roofed church named after the patron saint of local fishermen has been restored to its original splendour. To this day local sailors never pass the island by without dipping their sails in tribute to their saint. The most spectacular Connemara hooker races – which are not what they might sound to American ears – are held at Carna each July for three days.

Clifden, the capital of English-speaking north Connemara, nestling behind the mountains, centre for the annual Connemara Pony Show, and one of the best pieces of urban planning in the region, was established in 1812 by local landlord John D'Arcy. It is remarkable, too, for the equal prominence given to its Protestant and Catholic churches, whose spires amicably and strikingly share the same skyline. Close by, at Derrygimlagh Bog, is a cairn commemorating the first transatlantic flight, when aviators Alcock and Brown landed here on 15 June 1919 after a 16-hour flight from St John's in Newfoundland. The cairn also marks the site of the first transatlantic radio station,

established in the same era by the Marconi company, which transmitted to London the news of the aviators' safe crash-landing in the bog.

Ballynahinch, about eight miles from Clifden on the Recess road, is another noted salmon angling centre, where the salmon fishery was once so important that the agent who looked after it for the local landlord was able to build a mansion in his own right, as can be seen on the road out of Roundstone. The home of Richard 'Humanity Dick' Martin MP (1754–1834), who inspired protective legislation for animals in these islands, is now a luxury hotel well worth visiting to see its gardens that run down to the banks of the river. Recess village is the source of the prized green Connemara marble that is made into ashtrays, keyrings, candlesticks and a hundred other gewgaws for sale in the local tourist shops, as well as being used for more sober purposes in buildings all over Ireland.

Kylemore Abbey – now a girls' boarding school run by Benedictine nuns whose order came here from Ypres after the First World War – was originally built as a kind of Irish Taj Mahal by a Mancunian industrialist called Mitchell Henry and his wife who fell in love with this site overlooking Loch Na Coille Moire (the 'lake of the big wood') when they came here on their honeymoon in the 1860s. The chapel in the grounds is a miniaturised replica of Norwich Cathedral, all the more remarkable for being in this sheltered enclave of rhododendron, birch, ash and oak in the midst of the bleakness of the Connemara moors.

Letterfrack, a charming village which was founded by Quakers, and became briefly notorious in the 50s and 60s for its tough boys' reformatory, is now the centre for the Connemara National Park that covers some 5000 acres in a great sweep that includes four of the Twelve Bens, including the tallest one, Benbaun, that rises to 2395 feet. Along with the national parks in Donegal and Kerry, the Connemara park is trying to breed and preserve the native strain of Irish red deer.

Inishbofin in Clew Bay, served by the mainland port of Cleggan, was once the stronghold of the sea queen Grace O'Malley, and was later used by the Cromwellians as a kind of concentration camp for captured priests and nuns. Unlike many of the other islands off the Irish coast, the people of Inishbofin are English-speaking and have always been so, descendants as they are of the Cromwellian settlers. The boat leaves from Cleggan more or less as it lists, and as the weather permits. The only caveat about going there, as to any other Irish island, where the licensing laws are more honoured in the breach than in the observance, is that you should check the forecast before you go for fear that you might get stranded there indefinitely, with strong drink as the only consolation for the enforced enislement.

To stay on the mainland, though, is to be drawn to walk or cycle or drive or otherwise progress any way and in any direction you like through the Twelve Bens, that appear and disappear from myriad perspectives not so much like mountains as petrified ancestors. All roads in this beautiful area seem to lead to the fjord-like inlet of Killary Harbour near Leenane. This long arm of the Atlantic, scene of one of Paul Henry's most famous paintings, is so deep and so capacious that the entire British fleet once lay here at anchor, with berths to spare. These days shellfish rafts and salmon cages are all that float in the ripping tides that scour up it

twice a day bringing food and clean water from the ocean. It was here in Leenane itself, a quaint town that makes an almost inevitable stop along the way, that the film of *The Field*, directed by Jim Sheridan from the novel by John B. Keane, was shot in 1990.

In contrast to the brown rocky glory of Connemara and the islands, a trip through the village of Oranmore on the city's eastern flank leads to yet another kind of Galway. Here the gourmet and huntsperson – if they are not indeed one and the same – rub shoulders in such noted pubs and restaurants as Paddy Burke's in Clarinbridge or Moran's of Kilcolgan Weir, the headquarters each autumn for a fabled international Oyster Festival where prowess, among the barmen and waiters, is measured in the hundreds of oysters they can open in an hour, and, in the participants, by the number of the succulent bivalves they can swallow, accompanied by brown bread and washed down traditionally by Guinness, though champagne will do at a pinch.

At Craughwell Ireland's most famous foxhound pack, the Galway Blazers, chases fox as vermin-victim, in this most venerable of English borrowings into Irish life, over a countryside of stone walls and scattered villages that could not be more unlike the England of the shires of which the red, yellow

Kylemore Abbey and Loch Na Coille Moire (the 'lake of the big wood'), County Galway.

and black outfits, not to say the accents of the huntspersons, would put you in mind. Like all the Irish hunts, the Galway Blazers have had their fair share of characters. One of its most ebullient for many years was Lady Oranmore who, when told by a concerned journalist that her horse was sweating badly after a hard day in the field, said, 'And so would you be, young man, if you'd spent the day between my legs.'

Further south at Kinvara, near the Clare border, a Festival of Boats is held every year where the pennants fluttering from Dunguaire Castle complement the sails of the yachts that fill the bay. Dunguaire is another of the castles that host medieval banquets and entertainments, which in this case draw heavily on the works of W.B. Yeats, Lady Gregory and the Blind Poet Rafferty, all of whom had strong associations with this area. Thoor Ballylee, for years the tower-house home of W.B. Yeats, where he wrote poems such as 'The Winding Stair' and 'To Ireland in a Time of Revolution', has been well restored, even down to persuading a stare, or starling, to nest again in a crevice in the wall. On a quiet day when there are not too many people about you can sit in the same casement his Nobel-laureated eminence once occupied and see and hear the shallow, swarming river run over the gravel outside the window, as he once did.

> *An ancient bridge, and a more ancient tower,*
> *A farmhouse that is sheltered by its wall,*
> *An acre of stony ground,*
> *Where the symbolic rose can break in flower.*
> *Old ragged elms, old thorns innumerable,*
> *The sound of the rain or sound*
> *Of every wind that blows;*
> *The stilted water-hen*
> *Crossing stream again*
> *Scared by the splashing of a dozen cows;*
> *A winding stair, a chamber arched with stone,*
> *A grey stone fireplace with an open hearth,*
> *A candle and a written page.*
> Meditations in Time of Civil War

Thoor Ballylee is only a mile or so from the ruins of Coole Park, home of Yeats' great friend and mentor Lady Gregory. All trace of the house is now gone, after it fell into disrepair and was sold for scrap in the 1940s,

but you can still walk in the gardens and grounds as they did, count the swans on the lake to see if there might be nine and fifty, and try to decipher the names on the famous Autograph Tree, where such artists as George Bernard Shaw, Sean O'Casey and Augustus John did what all fond and foolish young romantics have always done to the bark of trees.

A short distance off this main route, but well worth the diversion, is Athenry, 'the ford of the kings', a town fortified by the Normans around the great castle built by Meiller de Bermingham in 1240. Through a combination of historical and economic factors – though mostly the fact that it was not bombed or pillaged by Cromwell or any of the other marauders – the town still lives largely inside its magnificently preserved walls, whose impressive range of ramparts and towers around the castle, its 15th-century market cross and some fine buildings from later epochs give a little medieval respite from the otherwise fairly pervasive modernism of its hinterland.

At Aughrim, a few houses gathered around a ford just past the market town of Loughrea on the road to Ballinasloe, the power of the native Irish chieftains supporting King James was finally crushed by the forces of King William in 1691. Thousands were slaughtered in the resulting massacre. Even to this day farmers' ploughshares turn up musket balls, broken swords, cannonballs, the rusting debris of history, which helps to give a macabre twist to the even-handed account of the battle which is given in the heritage centre in the village.

As Galway runs eastward to merge with the lands that border the Shannon, its music still echoes around villages like Woodford, one of the most richly endowed centres for Irish music in the whole county, and echoes around the walls of places like Derryhiveney Castle, on the outskirts of Portumna, which dates from 1653 and is believed to be one of the last true castles – as opposed to fortified tower houses – ever built in Ireland.

Everywhere you go in Galway you are aware of the travelling people camped by the roadsides, or pulled into halting sites provided by the county council on the edges of towns, selling scrap or carpets, or tinkering with old cars. In Ballinasloe, the capital of east Galway, on the first Monday of each October, the Horse Fair, the largest surviving traditional horse fair in Ireland, is the time and place appointed for their hosting and mustering in all their clannish intimacy and ferocity, as if the O'Flahertys and the Joyces who were so much feared by the English of the town had come back to haunt them. On that day Ballinasloe thunders to the sound of thousands of hooves moving towards its fair green, a ten-acre field that has been preserved sacrosanct from development at the very heart of the town though there have been threats recently to its integrity. The fair dates back for centuries. Here, during the last century, the purchasing officers of the Czar of Russia and the Emperor of France came to buy the superb Galway hunter-type horses for their cavalry. Many other armies also used the Ballinasloe horses for their mounted regiments. But it is to the travelling people of Ireland, now as then, that Ballinasloe belongs for this week of festival and celebration. The town surrenders its streets to herds of horses and hordes of visitors in one of the great Irish bacchanalian orgies that, for all its rather louche reputation for faction-fighting and drunken excess, remains withal friendly, tolerant, jovial, a kind of Irish *Bierfest*, where what fighting there is is generally only between the best of friends.

The 12th-century Romanesque doorway of the monastery of Clonfert, County Galway.

Even this far inland, St Brendan the Navigator turns up again, for at nearby Clonfert he founded a monastery in 563. In spite of having been burnt five times between this date and the 12th century, by the good fortune of being taken into Protestant care at a later date much of the 12th-century cathedral has been preserved, including the superb western doorway that is one of the jewels of Irish Romanesque architecture. It is well worth the journey down twisting country lanes to find the whimsy and grotesquerie of the carved figures on the rounded pillars, that seem to be propping the whole weight of the church. The medieval sensibility, for all our staring and speculating through door and window jambs, remains as dark and

mysterious as the interior of the church itself.

Each May and June the village of Oughterard, 12 miles west of Galway City, becomes the angling capital of Ireland as trout rise greedily to the mayfly during the 'dapping' season, when fishermen drift in boats dangling these gorgeous insects from long rods in the hope of enticing trout to rise to them. Lough Mask and Lough Corrib are the Great Lakes of Ireland where fishing passions are so strong that they have even – and this in recent times – unsettled a government which tried to restrict access to these broad waters by introducing a highly unpopular rod licence. This led to a campaign whose tattered posters and banners still flutter from trees and fences in the area proclaiming the people's tenacious adherence to their immemorial rights. In the end it was the government of the day which backed down, in a classical Irish compromise that at the time had all the portentousness of a new Treaty of Versailles.

Something of the same indomitable spirit is to be found in the mystical Burren of County Clare. Here the very soul of Ireland seems to be exposed to view. The giant sentinel rocks, the so-called erratics, that were stationed here by the melting and retreating glaciers fifteen thousand years ago, are as real and vital a presence as the farmer on the hillside, himself probably a descendant of the people first mentioned in an 11th-century collection of stories called *Boireann in Corcrumruad* – 'the stony place belonging to the people of Mruad'. Nowhere else in Europe is there such a diversity of plants growing together as on this ice-scraped and wind-scoured seeming desert. Some are alpine, in other words not normally found below 3000 or so feet of altitude, and therefore most out of place within reach of the salt spray; others are Lusitanian – found otherwise only along the Atlantic coast of Portugal – or Mediterranean, while still others are arctic plants which have adapted to these conditions.

Trundling slowly and inexorably down from the north the glaciers did not just leave their sentinel rocks behind. Out of their melting bellies, before they fell over the Cliffs of Moher to die groaning in the Atlantic, the

seeds of flora from the arctic lands dropped into the grykes in the limestone pavements. In the post-glacial period these arctic flowers and plants, together with the native ones that had remained dormant, sprang forth again to co-exist, as nowhere else, in the thin soils of the Burren. The continued survival of these botanical wonders from between the last two Ice Ages is attributed to the moist Atlantic winds warmed by the Gulf Stream that blow over the Burren, the heat storage qualities of the limestone and the light reflected from the ocean onto the rock face, that no doubt all helped to shelter the flora from the worst of the ice's ravages. Along the limestone roads today, gallimaufries of plants in red and purple and blue, lime-lovers and lime-haters, ericaceous and alkaline alike, consort and disport themselves together in a botanical garden born out of geological and climatic coincidence.

After the glaciers came forests of pine, hazel, yew, oak, ash and elm, the native trees of Ireland. Stunted clumps of hazel survive to this day, clinging to the ancient gutters. Man then arrived here, four or five thousand years ago, to clear the pavements again and impose his mark upon these tracts that became rockier and poorer the more man interfered with their delicate symbiosis.

The farmer walking across the clints today does so against a background of the relics of his human past. Dolmens, the tombstones of the once mighty, stand against the stony skylines. The pavements hold scores of gallery graves too, more rudimentary dolmens for less mighty men, and the striking ruins of no fewer than five hundred stone forts dating from the start of the Celtic Age. Inside some of these gravesites archaeologists have found urns, containing cremated human remains, laid out in what are obviously ritualistic patterns. The most striking of these monuments is the dolmen at Poulnabrone, which is topped by an enormous capstone propped up by two jagged flags. When it was excavated, the remains of between sixteen and twenty-two adults and six children – including a new-born baby – were found in the chamber. Monuments like this are also assumed to have had a symbolic role in the

lives of the community. They may well have contained the remains of revered ancestors who served as intermediaries with the gods or spirits who were believed to control the natural world. These people also left behind in the dark pools and caves more intimate tokens of their passing. On the edge of an ancient battlefield, a thousand years before Christ, some desperate warrior, probably to hide his status, folded his gold gorget neatly in half and hid it in a fissure. In 1932 a young farmer called Patrick Nolan, herding goats one day, with time on his hands, poked it out of its hiding place with a stick. The Glenisheen Collar, as it is now called, is one of the finest surviving works of the Bronze Age goldsmiths of Ireland. Old daggers, swords and spears have also been discovered here, showing that ownership of what now looks like a kind of desert must once have been keenly contested.

There is a paradox here. This stony world that looks as if it could not support a herd of goats, let alone herds of cattle, has withal some of the most prized grazing acreage in Ireland. In and around the bare pavements, the sweet grasses never stop growing. Cattle can graze here all the year around, a unique circumstance in Ireland.

The naturalist, W.H. Hudson, best expressed the link between this mystical region and those fortunate enough to live there: 'The nature of the soil we live on, the absence of running water, of hills, rocks, woods, open spaces; every feature of the landscape, the vegetative and animal life – everything in fact that we see, hear, smell, and feel – enters not into the body only, but the soul, and helps to shape and colour it.'

The Burren is criss-crossed with old roads first tramped by these early peoples. One leads to the triple-ramparted fort of Cahercommaun. Another runs to the great settlement of Cahermacnaghten where, in the heyday of the Celtic race's hegemony here, the O'Davoren family ran a great law school which imparted the rudiments and subtleties of the Brehon Laws, which governed everything from land tenure to the cutting of trees. Other roads lead to the striking ruins of the great monastic settlements of Corcromroe

Spring flowers peeping
through the
'pavements' on the
Burren, County Clare.

Abbey, Kilfenora and Dysert O'Dea, whose high crosses are among the most distinguished in the country. Kilmacduagh on the eastern edge of the region, near the village of Corofin, is an especially impressive memorial to the holy men of its age, with its leaning round tower, a church dating from the 12th century and hundreds of intricate stone carvings scattered through its graveyard.

Over the ages, running water burrowing through the soft limestone of the Burren has created miles of dark caves and underground passages that offer a speleological playground to cavers and pot-holers. The less venturesome can savour a brief, less risky taste of underground life by visiting the Ailwee Caves, near the village of Ballyvaughan. This is one of the largest cave systems in Ireland, oozing with stalagmites and stalactites, nowadays spectacularly lit up by arc lamps for the wonder of the modern visitors who descend into this colourless world in their bright, brash chain-store anoraks and t-shirts. Other caves, like those near the fishing and music-making village of Doolin, can only be entered through openings exposed by the sea at low tide. Another one,

at Poll an Ionian, near Lisdoonvarna, possesses the longest free-hanging stalactite in Europe, over twenty feet in length. The old cave at Kilcorney is fabled in folklore as the haunt of a herd of wild horses, said to emerge periodically to ravage the plains of Ireland. New caves are still regularly discovered, such as that on Knockaun Mountain, at Poll na gCeim, where a narrow entrance leads to one of the deepest, longest and most difficult systems in Ireland, the exploration of which is strictly reserved to the experts of the Underworld.

The race known as the Fir Bolgs are thought to be the first to have lived in the Burren in prehistoric times. Later came the Dalcassians, a name that Clare people are still proud to call themselves. The Dalcassians resisted the invading Norsemen and produced one of the most charismatic and influential warriors in Irish history in Brian Boru. As High King of Ireland he defeated the Norse at the Battle of Clontarf outside Dublin in 1014, only to be slain by one of the enemy while offering up thanksgiving prayers in his tent.

The O'Briens of Thomond ruled Clare in the Middle Ages and successfully resisted the Norman armies until these had dispersed and settled in more hospitable parts of the island. The remarkable survival instincts of the Irish in those times are vividly exemplified in the redoubtable Maura Rua (or Red Mary) Mac Mahon who lived with her husband Conor O'Brien in Leameneh Castle, the ruin of which still stands. When her husband was put to the sword by the Cromwellians, she would not allow his body to be brought into the castle. 'We want no dead men around here,' she explained. Within a few days of her first husband's demise she married a live Cromwellian soldier, thus ensuring that her son Donagh O'Brien would inherit her property. She and her Cromwellian consort, one John Cooper, lived contentedly into a prosperous old age.

The sway of the O'Briens eventually declined but the county retained a rebellious and volatile streak, perhaps inspired by some of this romantic history. It became known as the Banner County when it rallied to the cause of 'the Liberator' Daniel O'Connell, electing him a member of Parliament in 1828, thus enabling him to bring about Catholic Emancipation the following year. Clare also staunchly supported Charles Stewart Parnell, even at the most critical period of his political life when his liaison with a married woman, Kitty O'Shea, was disclosed. Still later, in 1917, the county elected Eamon de Valera, one of the leaders of the Easter Rising in 1916, to the British Parliament, and subsequently to the First Dáil. De Valera eventually became Taoiseach and, in his final years, President of Ireland.

The Cliffs of Moher, on the edge of the Burren near Lisdoonvarna, not only offer a spectacular view of kittiwakes, puffins, razorbills, fulmars, guillemots and other cliff-nesting birds at ease with the buffeting winds blowing straight up the sheer drops, but also reveal a cross-section of the geology of the stony lands that march here to their proud submergence in the ocean, like ranks of broad-chested soldiers determined to meet their ends bravely in their eternal trial of strength with the Atlantic. Here the alternating layers of shales and flagstones which make up the Burren are exposed for all to see.

Among the more mysterious and hieratic permanent residents of the Burren wildlands are its herds of wild goats, that can frequently be glimpsed against the skyline on the highest crags. Goatskin is the essential element of the Irish *bodhrán*, a deep-throated drum beaten either with the fingers or with dried bones in time to the jigs, reels and

The Cliffs of Moher, County Clare, showing their characteristic alternating strata of shale and flagstone.

hornpipes which form the treasure house of Irish traditional music. No county in Ireland has so much music in store as County Clare. What with the Willie Clancy Summer School in Milltown Malbay, *fleadh cheoils* in every town and village, and places like Doolin that have become shrines on the pilgrimage route that young people from all over the world in search of the 'native woodnote wild' have sacralised over the last twenty years or so, it sometimes seems that the air that rushes over the Cliffs of Moher comes from a thousand flutes, *uilleann* pipes, sound boxes of fiddles and human lungs that have between them an inexhaustible repertoire of tunes and songs.

Lisdoonvarna is Ireland's most famous spa town. For eleven months of the year it dispenses sulphurous waters and rest cures to its devotees. Then, each September, when the rest of Ireland is settling down for the relative quiet of autumn, the town explodes with life as it is transformed into the matchmaking capital of Ireland. Bachelors and spinsters, many of them from Munster's farming community in particular, come in the hope of finding spouses there. The merrymaking and the crack continue all through September, with dancing at the Spa House in the early morning continuing at other sites, including Ballinalacken Castle on the outskirts of the town, throughout the day and far into the night. Lisdoonvarna is also periodically the location for the Merriman Summer School, the longest established of these peculiarly Irish institutions which combine rigorous lectures, debates and readings with more mundane entertainments. Of the Merriman it is said that, where other summer schools have drinks between lectures, they have lectures between drinks. These summer schools – with one almost every weekend from May until September, on subjects that range from emigration to lesbianism – are great ways to get to know different parts of the country and whatever it may be that is exercising the public conscience of Ireland at the time, for, in the summer, when the real Dáil is in recess, these improvised parliaments are often serious forums in their own rights.

Venturing further away from the Burren, deep into the lands of the Dalcassians, one of the connections that binds the whole of Clare, from the tip of Loop Head at the mouth of the Shannon to Killaloe in the east, is that in many old farmhouses the floors are formed of flagstones from the Burren regions, which make a kind of stepping-stone passage into the secret world of talk around chimney nooks that keeps Clare bound to itself. In the old days, when house dancing was a popular recreation, there were special flagstones with iron pots buried underneath so that they would ring musically when struck by the heavy boots of dancers stamping out the fiery Clare sets, a form of dancing that is undergoing a revival all over Ireland. The modern bungalows also, from Whitegate on the shores of Lough Derg to the fishing village of Quilty on the Atlantic coast, often have external wall facings or patios made of the same flags. Roofs used to be made of them too, though these were so thick and heavy that the beam structure more often than not sagged under them, creating twisted, fantastic roofshapes that are intriguing to contemplate from a safe distance, but would be a bit worrying to live under.

In the county town of Ennis, dominated at its centre by the statue of O'Connell the Liberator, and, near its Courthouse, by the de Valera memorial, is Ennis Abbey, founded by the O'Briens in the 13th century and restored by them in the 14th. A quaint relic of the little, narrow-gauge railway which served this area until the 1960s is the engine of the old West Clare Railway preserved on a plinth near the railway station. This was the West Clare Railway made famous or infamous by the Percy French song 'Are you right there Michael?' The song continued to wonder 'Do you think that we'll get there before tonight?', a question still asked of some of the even less dependable modern conveyances that have replaced the trains.

Further east, just outside Ennis, lies the hamlet of Spancil Hill, the site each summer of a memorable horse fair also immortalised by a well-known ballad in that inexhaustible Irish genre of songs of exile and yearning. In nearby Feakle lived both the bawdy Clare poet Brian Merriman, he of the eponymous summer school, and the noted Clare witch

Biddy Early. Merriman, whose major work, 'The Midnight Court', features the womenfolk of Ireland ridiculing the vitality and virility of the menfolk, was in fact born much nearer the Burren, in the market town of Ennistymon. And Biddy Early, whose source of power was a bottle containing her potion, spent more time there, during her wandering lifetime, than she did in the east of the county. Her famous bottle is believed to lie in one of the West Clare lakes. Her cottage at Feakle is a kind of interpretative centre for witchcraft, which shows how this arcane art was always respected in Ireland, and how Christianity, for all its trying, never quite succeeded in extinguishing the older forms of belief.

Shannon Airport, a few minutes down the road from Ennis via Clarecastle and Newmarket-on-Fergus, is the arrival point today for the many thousands of descendants of those who left Clare during and after the Famine, who now often return with the specific mission of discovering their family tree. A heritage centre in the town of Corofin provides a wealth of detail on population movements following the Famine and is invaluable to visitors of Clare descent in search of their roots. Others return to be buried in the land of their ancestors. Flanking the Shannon estuary at Kildysart lies the area of Ballynacally, where there is a district whose proper postal address is Paradise. Only a few years ago the remains of an emigrant, being brought by helicopter from Shannon to his native Aran Islands, slipped from the slings beneath the aircraft and fell straight into Paradise, without having to pass through any Purgatory or Limbo.

The scenic drive back north, along the jagged coastline of West Clare, brings one through towns and villages synonymous with the 'crack' for which Clare is renowned throughout Ireland. Kilkee is a lively summer resort for the people of the region, boasting a fine beach and championship golf courses. Doonbeg is yet another link in the chain of Clare villages where Irish music and general merrymaking are an endemic part of the local culture. Spanish Point, which takes its name from the wrecking of Spanish Armada

galleons here in 1588, features in many of the songs of longing for return from exile that have been written and sung about this area.

The town of Ennistymon, with its breathtaking falls on the Inagh river, has actually converted an ancient Protestant church into a music centre where nowadays the old pulpit rings to the musical sermons of fiddlers instead of the fulminations of clerics. Here, stronger than ever, as one edges back towards the stonelands again, the beat of the *bodhráns* pulses deep in the heart of this most musical of landscapes.

The other road brings you to Kilfenora village, which has yet another heritage centre, heritage being one of the growth industries in this most industriously nostalgic land. Behind it the Burren begins again, the crags and flags leading back to the wonderland of gentians, orchids, ladies' bedstraw, mountain avens and more mysteries than all the botanical science which has been expended there will ever solve.

The names of the different areas of the Burren ring with their own music and magic. Corkscrew Hill, near Ballyvaughan, Gleninagh, once the base for a great fishing fleet of curraghs, Rathborney, Caherballykinbaraga, Noughaval, Poulawack, Caherconnell Fort, Gleninsheen, Finavara, Oghtmama, Parknabinnia and Cahercommaun Fort conjure up this wondrous world of stone, the very source of the indomitable spirit of County Clare.

Further north, in the equally resilient county of Mayo, the holy mountain of Croagh Patrick towers over the west coast, its coned head in the frequent clouds, its quartzite toes in the waters of Clew Bay. The tramp of millions of pilgrims over the centuries – many of them in bare feet for the traditional climb on the Sunday before the old feast of Lughnasa on 1 August – has exposed the fragments of quartz so that the path up the Reek, when viewed from a distance, often glitters in the sun like the road to heaven. Originally associated with the pagan god Crom, the mountain was christianised when St Patrick spent the 40 days of Lent here around AD 441. It was from the top of the sheer slopes on the south side of the mountain that he rang his mighty bell to chase the reptiles out of Ireland, all except the natterjack toad, which still survives in pockets of suitable terrain in Mayo and Kerry. The plain iron bell said to belong to the patron saint is preserved in the National Museum in a gorgeous gold- and jewel-encrusted reliquary that was chased for it in Armagh in the 12th century. Scientific sceptics who seek to refute this myth of why there are no snakes in Ireland – by talking of how the land bridge between this island and the continent of Europe was inundated by the sea before the reptiles made it back after their retreat south during the Ice Age – may end up getting a belt of the crozier themselves for their temerity.

The Atlantic Ocean and the glaciers of the past have gouged the great fjord of Killary Harbour and the foaming bays of Clew and Blacksod and Killala into the very heart of Mayo. The island of Achill, now bridged to the mainland, was ripped away from its natural hinterland by the powerful forces of time and tide that still sweep and scour along this coast. The drumlins which are now the myriad islands of Clew Bay were drowned in an epoch which, by times, in the right light –

such as the vision that is revealed from the summit of Croagh Patrick at dawn on the day of the great pilgrimage – seems to have been only a moment ago. An eternity of soft bogland blankets the long reaches of the Mullet to the north. The great lakes of Lough Conn and Lough Mask and Lough Carra spread themselves majestically in the valleys between the Nephin Beg Mountains, the Sheeffrys, the Maamturks and the formidable Ox Mountains that loom to the north.

Mayo is a county with a history as rich in texture, and as compelling, as its geography. In the seventh century, long after the time when the pre-Celtic people, the Tuatha De Danann ('the people of Goddess Dana'), fought and won a great battle on the plain of Moytura with the Formorians, a group of about thirty English monks quarrelled bitterly with their Irish counterparts in a monastery on Inishbofin, off the Galway coast. The English monks left the island and came to what is now the almost deserted hamlet of Mayo in the east of the county. Their settlement here became famous, even in faraway England, as Maigh Eo na Sacsan ('the plain of the English yew trees'). Today it is difficult enough to identify even the ruins of the ancient monastery which gave the

The island of Inishbofin, County Galway.

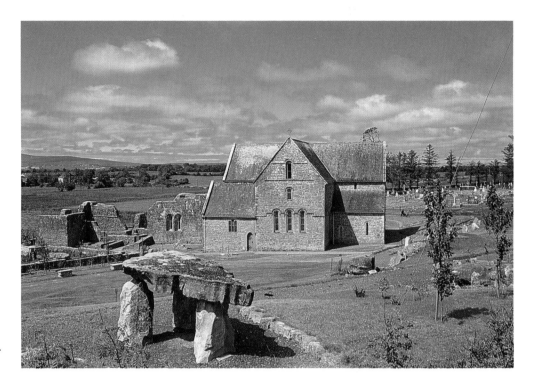

Mass has been celebrated at Ballintubber Abbey, County Mayo, for over 700 years.

county its name. But the appellation of Mayo was already so established in the popular mind by 1570, when Sir Henry Sidney was naming the new 'shire', that he had no hesitation in adopting it as its title.

Mayo never truly surrendered its heart and soul to any of the great political and economic forces that ground at it throughout the centuries. The English never fully controlled the Irishmen of Mayo. Nor its women. When Queen Elizabeth I promised Grace O'Malley security of her Mayo lands if she became a vassal of the Crown, the Mayo warlady replied, 'Is it not presumptuous of your Majesty to say you would confer this honour on me? I am Queen in my own right in my own place.' Her place was Clare Island, off the Mayo coast near Louisburgh. Her fierce bones lie buried there, at the end of lanes flaming with fuchsia, defying sea blight even as once, in life, she defied the redoubtable Elizabeth. Grannuaile's castle still glares proudly out across the seas she surrendered to none in her lifetime. It is a quirk of history that her own son, Theobald Burke of the Ships, fought on the English side at the Battle of Kinsale which confirmed English domination of the greater part of

Ireland in the 17th century.

The spirit of the sea queen lived on through the subsequent centuries. In 1798, when General Humbert and 1100 veteran French troops landed at Killala Bay, near Ballina, the plain people of Mayo and the west flocked to join him, even though they were ill-trained and badly armed, albeit making up somewhat for their lack of preparedness by the ardour of their resentment of the English. Humbert declared a 'Republic of Connacht' with a Mayo man, John Moore, as president. Such a crushing defeat was inflicted upon the English forces under General Lake at Castlebar that the battle is still recalled as the Races of Castlebar. Later, however, Humbert was defeated at Ballinamuck in Longford. He and his French soldiers were treated as prisoners of war by the English but the Irish were slaughtered in large numbers.

But the spirit of the rebellion, and all that came afterwards, is still remembered in Mayo's largest town of Ballina. When Humbert captured Ballina after a long skirmish as darkness fell, the locals of Ballina came out to light straw torches to guide the French troops. That road, even today, is called Bohernasup ('the Road of the Straw').

The Humbert Monument in the centre of Ballina also remembers the name of the local man Patrick Walsh who, sent in to Ballina ahead of the French to prepare the way for them, was captured and hanged by the English.

The history of Mayo, written today in the ruins of forts and castles and once-great abbeys, has always been one of resistance. At Ballintubber Abbey, in the south of the county, mass has been celebrated continuously for more than 700 years, a record in the English-speaking world. This has been sustained despite the fact that the abbey, established by Cathal Crobhderg O'Connor in 1216, was suppressed by King Henry VIII in 1542 and despoiled by the Cromwellians in 1653. Even during enforcement of the harsh penal laws directed against the Catholic Church in the 18th century, worship somehow continued here uninterrupted. However, the Catholic tradition was not maintained without cost. In the nearby cemetery is the grave of a man called Seán na Sagart ('Sean of the Priests'), who was notorious as a licensed priest-hunter in the Penal era when priests practised at peril of their lives.

Following the road of resistance, the pathway of the Mayo spirit, rather than any physical track, brings one to the village of Straide, near the town of Foxford on the road to Castlebar. Here Michael Davitt, founder of the Irish Land League, was born in 1846 and buried in 1906. Because of mass popular support for the efforts made by Davitt and Charles Stewart Parnell towards emancipation, lands were purchased by the government from the still powerful landlords and divided amongst the people, the first major victory for the Mayo spirit. The long struggle of civil resistance in the Land League era gave a very special Mayo word to the English language. During the agitation the people of the Ballinrobe area refused to work for, or even to speak to, the land agent for Lord Erne, Captain Boycott. In spite of workers from the Protestant north being brought in by Boycott to break the strike, the power of passive silence won through and a powerful word was born.

And the road of resistance and self-reliance that passes through Straide eventually reaches Foxford itself. The remarkable nun, Agnes Morrogh Bernard, Mother Arsenious of the Irish Sisters of Charity, came to Foxford at a time when its impoverished citizens were emigrating in large numbers. As an antidote she harnessed the River Moy in 1892 to power the aptly named Providence Woollen Mills. The firm which made the Foxford blanket world famous was shortly employing over one thousand workers.

This same road leads to the village of Knock, within only a few miles of the now virtually forgotten hamlet of Mayo. Here again it was the power of belief which transformed an otherwise backward village and gave its people hope. On 21 August 1879 fifteen of Knock's inhabitants claimed they had seen the Blessed Virgin and other figures miraculously appear at the gable end of the little church. The verity of the apparition was ratified by a Church Commission of Inquiry and, since then, Knock has become one of Europe's leading Marian shrines, with over a million pilgrims a year. It was visited by Pope John Paul II in 1979. However, even the contribution of the Pope, who came to give his imprimatur to the work already done, is locally rated secondary to that of the remarkable parish priest, Monsignor James Horan. Against the resistance of the government of the day – indeed against all the odds and a widespread scepticism within the Pale – the redoubtable Monsignor Horan managed to create an international airport at Knock to serve the shrine, the county and the whole of the economically depressed west. He died soon after the airport opened to traffic but the prosperous village, which gets a good living from catering to the pilgrim trade, and the imposing basilica which rises heavenwards at its heart, are his enduring monuments.

But if one leaves the forked roads of Mayo's history behind to follow, more logically, the contours of its striking geography, the old battlefields disappear. In gentle Castlebar, for example, a plaque on the edge of the Mall recalls the birthplace of the superb La Scala singer Margaret Burke

Sheridan (1889–1958), whose voice, said one critic, was 'dipped deeply in Heaven's honey'. Best remembered amongst the other colourful characters who once swaggered through these streets is the handsome and reckless 18th-century duellist George Robert Fitzgerald. Fitzgerald challenged so many opponents and was so successful in his duels that he put the fear of God into the local Establishment, from whom so many of his victims were drawn. It was contrived that he would be arrested after a duel with a man named McDonnell and, following a trial which was a sensation in its time, he was hanged at Castlebar in 1786.

North of Castlebar, clinging to its hill above the river, is the small town of Newport. It was to this area that J.M. Synge ascribed the 'gallus deed' of his world-famed *Playboy of the Western World*, a play about Christy Mahon who wins the heart of Pegeen Mike after he kills his da. It was, in fact, on nearby Achill Island that Synge first heard the story upon which *The Playboy* is based. It seems that a local man called Lynchehaun did not kill his father, as in the action of the play, but was involved in a rape charge in which the young woman was of the landlord class. The Achill opinion was that the alleged rape was in fact a seduction but Lynchehaun was tried and convicted. However, he escaped from prison and went to the United States. Here he later lectured frequently on his escape and became a sort of early tabloid sensation, a real playboy indeed, still a term in general use in Ireland to describe rakish fellows who get notions of themselves.

Achill Island itself is a magical place. Reached through the village of Mulrany, drenched in rhododendrons and fuchsia, the island, said the travel writer Edward Newman, 'is more like a foreign land than any I have visited'. Heather is the purple king of the Achill landscape, covering the bogs and rocks and spilling over the very lips of the tall cliffs towards the Atlantic. There are glorious beaches everywhere around Atlantic Drive, which also has breathtaking views of Ashleam Bay. No longer, though, even on this island, will one see a quaint custom of the past. When a girl was courted by two lovers and could not make up her mind between them, the matter was resolved by a foot race between the two. The island girl married the winner. Many of the races of the lovers were held on Keel Strand, another prefiguration of the donkey race in *The Playboy* that Christy wins to confirm his hold on Pegeen Mike. Synge obviously created his story from a lot

Knock, County Mayo, attracts over one million pilgrims a year.

of bits and pieces of local tradition that he picked up on his extensive walking tours of the region.

As he walked he probably met the summer herders of the Mayo cows, who lived in little clusters of 'booley' huts on the high pastures. These now deserted settlements, along with the scattered bones of famine villages and the ribcages of their potato fields, are part of the skeleton of Mayo's past that can be glimpsed through the flesh of heather and ling that has clothed it since. At the foot of Slievemore mountain near Doogort can be found another ghost of that vanished time in the Colony, established by Protestant missionaries in 1834 as a sort of workhouse-cum-school for local children who were willing to renounce their faith in return for education, food and other meagre creature comforts, rewards hard to resist in the lean times of the couple of decades which followed.

One of the unique features of Achill Island is the fierce pride of the islanders in their long tradition of maintaining warpipe marching bands. There are three top-class pipe bands on Achill. From a place of high emigration, the pipers and drummers of the bands are scattered all over the world today but on St Patrick's Day, having travelled home from abroad, the bands are reformed for a skirling morning of music which stirs the blood of the islanders and visitors alike.

The town of Westport is an unusual Irish town in that it was precisely and carefully planned. As in Birr, County Offaly, and some of the other landlord towns, the edicts and regulations of its original planners have been followed ever since in matters to do with shop signs, window shapes, door openings and so on. It was designed to be an adjunct to Westport House on the outskirts and was laid out in a triangular shape with a canal running along one side, the market square or octagon on another, and a tree-lined mall along the Carrowbeg river to complete the ensemble of pleasant civic airiness. Once a centre for the linen and cotton trades that were encouraged by the Marquesses of Sligo, its earlier prosperity has left some fine Georgian buildings and a lovely art nouveau Protestant church from the 1880s. In July

every year the tens of thousands of pilgrims who climb Croagh Patrick flood the streets of the town, making a Chaucerian scene: bronzed pilgrims with their staffs striding through the crowds of hucksters and vendors who hawk their wares from barrows and doorways all along the elegant streets that, slightly sniffily, manage to stay aloof from the throng.

Westport House, home of Lord Altamont, Marquess of Sligo, is the architectural glory of the area. The family are descended from, amongst others, Grace O'Malley – as indeed may be every second person in the region, to judge from the number of O'Malley signs over shops and pubs in Westport. The house itself is built on the site of an O'Malley castle, whose dungeons can still be made out among the foundations. Along with a beautiful main hall designed by Richard Cassell and a dining room that shows the hand of James Wyatt, there is a wealth of engravings, family portraits, paintings by Rubens, among others, and the sort of knick-knacks and bibelots that such a distinguished family gathers up over the generations. Famous visitors of the past have included Thomas de Quincey, the author of *Confessions of an English Opium Eater*, and William Makepeace Thackeray.

Westport House, County Sligo, ancestral home of Lord Altamont, Marquess of Sligo.

South of Westport, just inside the Mayo border, is the serene and truly lovely village of Cong. Cong has many histories, including the story of the famous Cross of Cong, crafted of gilt and bronze-sheathed oak in the 12th century to enshrine a portion of the True Cross, which after many vicissitudes, including losing its precious relic, is now housed as one of the chief treasures in the National Museum. Cong's beauty became famous worldwide forty years ago when the classic Irish film *The Quiet Man*, starring John Wayne, Maureen O'Hara and Barry Fitzgerald, was largely shot here. The village also boasts one of the great Irish follies, the Cong Canal, by which 18th-century engineers planned to link Lough Mask and Lough Corrib. The work went speedily and was completed in 1850. When the locks were ceremoniously opened, however, the waters disappeared into the porous limestone bed of the canal and there was no way it could be filled. It is the one canal in Ireland through which no boat has ever sailed.

The 13th-century Cong Abbey, whose ruins nestle in the heart of the village, was built by Turlough O'Connor (the High King of Ireland who also commissioned the Cross of Cong) to replace an earlier abbey dedicated to St

Feichim that had been destroyed by the Vikings. Outside the village, linked by a riverside walkway to the abbey, stands Ashford Castle, now a world-famous hotel, that was built in the last century as a private mansion by a member of the Guinness brewing family. Among its famous guests has been President Ronald Reagan who stayed there when he came to Ireland in search of his family roots in Ballyporeen, County Tipperary – though it was probably more the cinematic associations of Cong that attracted the 'Gipper' than any nostalgia for his ancestors.

Only a few miles away from Cong is the landlocked village of Tourmakeady. Nestled comfortably against the western shore of Lough Mask, Tourmakeady is the centre of one of Mayo's few surviving Irish-speaking areas. On the shore of silent Lough Carra, Moore Hall is today only a shell of its past glory after it was burned down in the Troubles of 1922. One of this gifted family, the writer George Moore (1852–1933), immortalised the lovely lake in his novel of the same name and was a leading figure in the Literary Renaissance as one of the founders of the National Theatre, The Abbey, whose early days he recalled in his memoirs

The beautiful main hall of Westport House, County Mayo.

Hail and Farewell. As already noted, the returned wine merchant, John Moore, was declared President of the Republic of Connaught in 1798 by General Humbert. Another Moore, George Henry, later represented Mayo in the British Houses of Parliament and was one of the leaders of the Tenants' Rights Movement which sought a fairer deal from the landlords.

A sweep to the north of the county, by Lough Cullin and Lough Conn, reveals a different Mayo. The angling village of Pontoon was the home of a larger-than-life Mayo character of the 19th century called Gallagher, noted for his daring and sense of fun. On one occasion Gallagher escaped from his own trial on the judge's horse. He later returned it with a note complimenting the judge on the quality of his bloodstock. However, inevitably, he and his aide, a man called Walsh, were arrested, tried, and sentenced to death. On the appointed day they hugged warmly as they mounted the gallows. Walsh's execution went as planned but the rope suspending Gallagher broke. He leisurely sampled a glass of wine and exchanged quips with the crowd while the second rope was being readied. This rope did not break.

Bogs dominate the north of County Mayo, filling the horizons with their luminous brown-purple glow, spreading seemingly endlessly through the windswept desolation of the Erris Peninsula and the Mullet Peninsula. Here, in yet another of the 'last parishes before America', the town of Belmullet has a street called American Street running straight to the edge of the ocean, in the Irish tradition of calling streets in towns after the place they lead to. There is space and peace in the Mullet Peninsula yet, with the remains of forts and of churches in areas like Cross and Fallmore and Inishglora like friendly ghosts gathered around the scatter of villages and hamlets where the present-day population lives, there is never quite the confirmation of the human abandonment that always remains, somehow, just imminent.

It is little wonder that many of the old Irish sagas refer to the Mullet. In one of the most bewitching of all stories, 'The Children of Lir', the gentle children were turned into swans by their jealous stepmother and spent three centuries in the seas and lakes of the Mullet, waiting, without ageing, for redemption. Even today it is impossible not to think of the mythical Children of Lir when wild swans fly overhead against an infinity of weather-blasted sea and sky.

Back in the cathedral town of Ballina, lapped by the Moy, a frequent sight in season is of men exercising their ancestral rights to harvest the silver of their own natural resources by netting salmon out of the Moy. For those not favoured with such a lucrative birthright it is necessary to book and pay – sometimes years in advance – to fish famed stretches such as the Ridge Pool, a kind of angler's Valhalla where catches are the next best thing to guaranteed.

Now that all the great battles are over, the sun of an evening gilds the face of the Moy and the graven face of the French general, high on his pedestal, who was one of the forces that shaped the modern Mayo. The spire of St Muiredach's Cathedral, sharply pointing towards heaven, is a version in cut stone of the holy mountain of Croagh Patrick, which has been worn down to its bones by the abiding passion and faith of a proud people who have resisted past temptations to compromise the principles that have preserved the integrity of their beautiful land, as one hopes they still will, whatever the modern temptations might be. On Achill Island in the summer of 1992, when a freak storm tore away the hillside above the village of Dooagh, the rushing river yielded several nuggets of real gold. Geologists claim that there is a rich gold seam in this region, running from the holy mountain of Croagh Patrick through the Louisburgh region all the way to Achill. The local people, holding the mountain in veneration, will not let mining operations begin. Their attitude is that the old land itself is more sacred than gold.

To the north and west of the Ox Mountains that march the Mayo border with Sligo lies a country of myth and magic whose singing place names are threaded through the poetry of W.B. Yeats like another kind of gold. Sligo's rich tapestry of legends and folklore helped to inspire his genius so it is fitting that the Nobel prizewinner who gave Sligo its voice now lies buried in Drumcliff churchyard, just north of Sligo city, in a plain grave for which he wrote his own epitaph: 'Cast a cold eye/On life, on death./Horseman pass by.' Nowadays many thousands of visitors come here by every form of motorised conveyance imaginable – very few of them on horseback – and stand for a moment away from the hurly-burly of modern life to contemplate his terse and salutary message from beyond the grave, within a curlew call of the eternal landmarks of the country of the mind he invented out of the physicality of the Lake Isle of Innisfree, Dooney Rock, whispering Hazelwood, the cairned glory of Knocknarea and the sheer scarps of noble Ben Bulben.

There is a beautiful spot on the Sligo coastline, near the village of Skreen, nearer still to the deserted village of Aughris, where the eroded cliffs swallow up the incoming waves and then boom them through caverns to produce a mysterious sound called locally the Coragh dTonn, taken to be a lament for the souls of dead of centuries gone by. At Glencar, near the border with County Leitrim, a waterfall tumbles down from the clouds into a silver pool, making another kind of music as it falls. Sligo, sculpted by the glaciers of the Ice Ages, mossed over by verdant rains from the Atlantic, full of the ghosts of a long and complex past, is truly, as W.B. Yeats called it, the 'Land of Heart's Desire'.

There has always been a great respect for learning here too, at least if one is to believe the story of the battle waged at Cooldrumman, near Drumcliff, in AD 461 between the monks of St Columba and the monks of St Finian over the copyright of a psalter. It is said that 2000 clerics died in the battle, in which Columba was victorious but was so ridden with guilt after it that he exiled himself, or perhaps was exiled, to Scotland, where he expiated his sin by preaching to the heathens.

Sligo is a county of all the arts. It is also known as Coleman Country after a doyen of the musical world which overlaps and

intertwines with that of Yeats, who wrote of the Fiddler of Dooney that, when he played his jigs and reels, they made folk 'dance like the waves of the sea'. The great Irish fiddler Michael Coleman, born in Sligo, emigrating later to the United States, was as eminent in his field as Yeats in his. Coleman, whose records of Irish fiddle music were amongst the first to be made, did much to popularise Irish music internationally. He is venerated to this day in a county well-endowed with Irish musicians, especially fiddlers and flute players. These Sligo musicians have always had a style of their own, a fast and furious romping 'drive', which makes them singular, worthy inheritors of the Fiddler of Dooney who met his cousin the priest on the road and thought: 'He read in his book of prayer/I read in my book of songs/I bought at the Sligo Fair': music here has always been a close spiritual cousin of religion.

The hills and valleys of Sligo recite their own long poem of history to those who know how to read it. The landscape is richly endowed with the funerary remains of the races the archaeologists name after the types of graves they left behind: the Court Tomb, Passage Tomb, Portal and Wedge Tomb peoples who built their ritual places on prominent sites to which they hauled stones from sometimes many miles away. Sligo must have been relatively heavily populated then. The county today holds nearly twenty per cent of the 320 court tombs in all Ireland and nearly thirty per cent of the 350 passage tombs. At Carrowmore, along the southern flank of Knocknarea, there is a veritable necropolis of such graves. This is said to be the second biggest Stone Age cemetery in Europe after Carnac in Brittany and covers nearly a square mile. It may originally have been even more extensive but farming and quarrying have eaten into the site over the years, considerably reducing its extent, and even what remained was only saved from a recent plan to make a municipal dump there by a strenuous local protest campaign.

Knocknarea, towering over the road between Sligo and the resort of Strandhill, is gilded with the legends the Celts created to explain these works with which their ancestors had strewn the countryside. The flat-domed limestone mountain is capped by Queen Maeve's cairn, though it is almost certain that the warrior queen of Connacht is not in fact buried there, for the cairn has been dated to 3000 BC, somewhat before her time. Another legend has it that a later King of Connacht, Eoghan Bell, mortally wounded at the Battle of Sligo in AD 537, ordered that he be buried upright, his scarlet spear in his hand. 'Place my face to the North', he said, 'and my grave on the north side of that hill by which the Northerners pass when flying before the army of Connacht.' Yeats used Knocknarea as the setting for his poem 'The Wanderings of Oisin'.

Ben Bulben, under which the great poet is buried, is the setting for the climax of probably the greatest Irish eternal triangle love story of all. The Ulster hero Fionn MacCumhaill sent his friend Diarmuid to the King of Ireland to ask for the hand in marriage of his daughter Grainne. But Grainne fell in love with the handsome Diarmuid instead. Together they evaded the anger of the unforgiving Fionn for seven years. But the day came when Diarmuid, wounded to the point of death by a wild boar on the slopes of Ben Bulben, could only be saved by a drink of water from the magic, cupped palms of Fionn. Twice Fionn allowed the water to leak through his fingers. Urged on angrily by Diarmuid's former Fianna comrades, he eventually hurried to the dying warrior with a drink. But it was too late. And, when Grainne saw Fionn returning with Diarmuid's faithful hound, she fell unconscious, her children and servants weeping around her.

Monastic Christianity arrived in the fifth and sixth centuries. Among the establishments founded then was the monastery on Inishmurray, a windswept island lying out in the maw of the Atlantic at the western end of Donegal Bay. The monks surrounded the buildings with a prodigiously thick and high dry-stone wall, or *cashel*, that still encloses the remains of three churches, including Teampull na bhFear ('the Men's Church') and a number of beehive huts which withstood the ravages of the Vikings who destroyed everything else when they raided in 807. Outside the cashel is Teampull na mBan ('the Women's Church'). It was believed that if a woman were buried in the men's place, or a man in the women's, the corpses would be transferred in the night to their rightful places, a form of sexual segregation in religion that persisted in Ireland until quite recently when men would sit on one side of the church and women on the other, and woe betide anyone who might defy the established order of things. Until 1948 there was a pilgrimage to perform the Stations of the Cross around the 200-acre island, though some of the pilgrims may have gone there for the darker purpose of bringing down misfortune on their enemies' heads by invoking the power of Inishmurray's famous 'cursing stones'.

By the 12th century Celtic power in Ireland and in Sligo was at its zenith, shortly to be toppled by the dynastic dispute between the local king, Rory O'Conor, and the King of Leinster, Diarmuid MacMurrough, that broke out into open warfare in 1166. Every road in Sligo and every by-road twisting around the flank of a hill leads to a battleground of that long-ago era, which eventually saw the power of the Celts broken at the Battle of Kinsale. After that the lands of the old chieftains passed into the hands of Elizabethan and, later, Cromwellian soldiers. The surnames of some of the Englishmen who came to till the former lands of the monasteries – Ormsby, Gore, Booth, Cooper, Perceval, Pollexfen – were those from which the gifted Yeats brothers would later descend.

The county had to swallow the bitter flames and ravages of the 1641 Rebellion, when the city of Sligo was burned to the ground. In the later struggle between King William and King James the Green Fort at Sligo, near the present-day Sligo Hospital, was one of the last Jacobite strongholds to fall. Also swallowed up in these hills, in their times and seasons, were the fleeing Fenians and fugitives from the other Irish risings against English domination that came as regularly as clock knells in 1798, 1803 and 1867. In the Easter Rising of 1916 a flamboyant Sligo woman, Countess Constance Markieviecz of

the Gore-Booth family of Lissadell House, played a signal role that would surely have dismayed the determined English planters she had on both sides of her family tree. The beautiful Sligo countess, who obtained her title through marriage to the Polish Count Casimir Dunin de Markieviecz in 1900, became the voice of the poor people of Ireland in two parliaments during her brief and passionate lifetime. As a leader of the Easter Rising in 1916, who fought bravely to hold St Stephen's Green in Dublin (where a bust of her now stands), she was sentenced to death. The sentence was commuted to life imprisonment but she was released the following year. She was elected to the British House of Commons in 1918, the first woman to be elected there, but never took her seat. Later she was Labour Secretary in the Dáil Cabinet and was elected to Dáil Eireann, the new Irish Parliament, in 1923. She died in a hospital in a slum area of Dublin 1927, to be followed to her grave by thousands of the poor amongst whom she had laboured. She and her sister, the poet Eva Gore-Booth, were the two girls 'both beautiful, one a gazelle' eulogised by Yeats in his poem about Lissadell. This beautiful house, now fallen on hard times and in great need of repair, surrounded by state forests rather insensitively planted almost to its very doors, lies just north of Sligo city and can be visited by arrangement in the summer months.

The rugged Sligo coast just north of Lissadell showed its teeth to the storm-tossed galleons of the Spanish Armada in 1588. Three of the great warships were wrecked and lost in Streedagh Bay. One of the few survivors, a Captain Cuellar, who later wrote of his adventures, said that most of the Spaniards who reached the shore were killed by the natives or just left there to die. Local tradition has it that more than a thousand Spanish sailors lay dead on the strand after the wrecking. They were buried six deep.

Only a century ago Sligo was port of call to more than five hundred trading ships each year. Sligo-registered ships, largely owned by descendants of Cromwellian planters, traded with Mediterranean, Canadian and Black Sea ports. The largest operators were the

Middleton and Pollexfen families, who ran a large sailing fleet until the 1850s. Later they turned to steamers and jointly formed the Sligo Steam Navigation Company in 1865, when the town had another brief period of prosperity. But, with changing circumstances affecting trade, and the harbour, never easy of access, beginning to silt up again, the company had only one small schooner on the seas by 1890 and the port went into a terminal decline. 'Memory Harbour', painted by Jack B. Yeats at Rosses Point when the shipping lanes were still busy, shows sailing ships, hardy sailors with wild brown faces, thatched cabins by the piers and bawdy-looking alehouses. 'Sligo was my school', said Jack B. Yeats 'and the sky above it.' The painter was the Eye that remembered the Sligo of his time, and his brother the Voice that spoke the 'ballads and stories, ranns and rhymes' of the old hills. Wandering through the sand dunes of Rosses Point on their summer holidays, they could see the magic shapes of the ships of their grandfather, one of the Pollexfen family.

The poet himself wrote in his autobiography: 'I had still the ambition, formed in Sligo in my teens, of living in imitation of Thoreau on Innishfree, a little island in Lough Gill. When walking through Fleet Street very homesick I heard a little tinkle of water and saw a fountain in a shop window which balanced a little ball upon its jet, and began to remember lake water. From the sudden remembrance came the poem "Innishfree", my first lyric with anything in its rhythm of my own music.' Today a two-hour trip, with Sligo City as starting point, takes one through the heart of all the lore-locked places which have been given tongue by his genius. To take the drive around Lough Gill is to pass the Holy Well at Tobernalt, the fiddler's Dooney, Slish Wood, past Cashelore stone fort to the best view of Innishfree, near the entrance of the Bonnet River, uninhabited – as is proper, somehow – but with its bee-loud glade of dreams still floating somewhere above it in the other world of misty Platonic idealism with which this whole countryside seems to be cloaked, Innishfree is the insular embodiment of poetic romanticism.

125

On the return journey the sculpture trail in Hazelwood is clearly signposted. Here, a few years ago, as an arts project initiated by a group of local people, wooden figures were crafted and then set in the heart of the hazel and beech forests. Horses, charioteers, great wheels, are glimpsed through the living forest, like a fragment of a legend entirely in keeping with a woodscape and a hillscape where the actual past, and what may never have been except in dreams, both gently flicker in the chiaroscuro of the imagination.

Outside the timewarp and wordwarp of Yeats country there is, today, a new and progressive Sligo, which yet remains one of the most picturesque and best preserved cities in Ireland. Thanks to Yeats, and to the annual Yeats Summer School, which brings students from as far away as Japan and Australia, it is now well known internationally. It is a place for which its citizens have a great fondness, often expressed in almost poetic terms even by those who are not poets. A former mayor, John Fallon, who fought in the World War I trenches, once said: 'I would waken up every morning in the mud and filth, with death all round me, and I kept myself sane by remembering the doors and the doorsteps of the streets of the town. And the smell of its baking bread.'

While not much remains in Sligo of its medieval past – the Norman castle, built by Maurice Fitzgerald in 1245 to guard the frontier on the Garravogue river between Connaught and Ulster, having long since disappeared – Sligo Abbey, parts of which date from 1252, makes another kind of bridge between the earliest settlement and the 18th- and 19th-century buildings which Yeats described as having 'a kind of dignity in their utilitarianism'. Many beautiful old shopfronts have been retained and Sligo is particularly well endowed with fine pubs, of which Hargadon's is one of the most atmospheric, with hardly a straight line to be found among the crazily leaning shelves, the lolling snugs and the bar top scrubbed back to the knots of its original trees.

The Sligo Art Gallery has an interesting collection of works by John Yeats (1839–1922), father of the formidably gifted brothers, who was himself a leading member of the pre-Raphaelite artistic movement and a very talented portraitist. Twenty-seven major works by his son, Jack B. Yeats, used to hang rather out of the way and ignored in an upstairs room of the County Library, for which you would have to get the key from the librarian, but now that his paintings are selling for hundreds of thousands of pounds at auction, there are plans to create a new gallery especially to house them. There are also works here by Paul Henry, Evie Hone, George Russell and other artists of the early part of the 20th century, as well as travelling exhibitions by contemporary painters and sculptors. The Yeats Memorial Museum, a room in the Sligo County Museum, documents the career of the great poet, including the citation for his Nobel Prize for Literature. The Model Arts Centre in an old school on the Donegal road has a lively programme of readings, lectures, art shows and theatre performances which are well publicised in the *Sligo Champion* and in the national press.

Strandhill, under Knocknarea, is the playground resort for the city. Its now empty cannon point their silent muzzles over long, golden strands. Nearby, closer to the city, is Coney Island, its dunes riddled with rabbits. One can drive to Coney Island and back, between the tides, following a line of markers. It is said that this little island gave its name to the American island of the same name: Sligo seamen, seeing the American island, then nameless yet also well populated with rabbits, are said to have named it after their homeland.

In Tobercurry, down towards the Mayo border to the south, one of the finest of the Irish amateur drama festivals is held annually. The town of Ballymote, nearer the Curlew Mountains to the east, is famed for music and for greyhounds as proud and brave and fleet as the wolfhounds of the dead Diarmuid. Here, in 1391, the *Book of Ballymote* was commissioned by the Mc Donaghs of Ballymote Castle. As well as giving genealogies for all the families of consequence in the area, the book provides a key to the ogham alphabet, that has permitted

The golden sands of Strandhill, County Sligo.

the deciphering of many of these cross-hatched inscriptions on monuments throughout the country. The *Book of Ballymote* is now in safe-keeping in the library of the Royal Irish Academy in Dublin.

Modernity always intrudes in Sligo, in both benign and malign ways. The village of Easky, on the coast at the southern lip of Sligo Bay – its very name an anagram of sea and sky – is a place where surfers from all over the world come to ride the long, shimmering waves that sound the Coragh dTonn lament inside the hollowed cliffs of Aughris. At Mullaghmore, towards the border with Donegal, the castle of Classiebawn, one-time summer home of Lord Louis Mountbatten (murdered here in 1979 when the IRA blew up his boat), looks ravishingly beautiful and innocent in the setting sun, stark and stern on its treeless headland.

Sligo is a march county. To the west it embraces and bestrides the sea, not as wild perhaps as Mayo for having the mountains of Donegal to shelter it from the north, but storm-tossed in its own way, with headlands and beaches being steadily eroded by the great tempests of winter. To the east it merges with the roughness and unkemptness of Leitrim and Cavan, and to the south bleeds off into the plains of Roscommon and Longford. Somehow it shares characteristics with all these places, distilling them into something distinctive of its own, a heady liquor of sea, mountain, history and myth, from which the otherwise abstemious W.B.

Yeats drank deep, to pour it out again in the glistening river of verse and plays and prose that has bathed this landscape in a tremulous, aqueous light that, once seen, is unforgettable.

MUSTS IN THE WEST

* A Spring day on the Burren.
* Seafood, a seaweed bath, a sea journey, sea shells, seashore, sea breeze, sea salt.
* The Galway City Museum at the Spanish Arch, especially if you engage the curator in talk.
* A play at the Druid Theatre, Chapel Lane, Galway.
* A long browse in Kenny's Bookshop, Galway.
* A Folding Landscapes map or guide, from all good bookshops.
* A day out on a hired boat on Lough Mask, Lough Corrib or Lough Conn.
* Learning a few words of Irish in Connemara.
* Buying a jumper from the Aran Islands knitting co-operative.
* A taste of *poitín*.
* A session of traditional Irish music in Clare.
* A feed of *boxty*, a traditional potato dish made with spring onions in a kind of pancake that enfolds meat, fish or other delectables.
* Oysters in Clarinbridge, whether it is festival time or not – though always watching for the months with the 'r' in them.
* Country and western music, Irish style.
* A Gaelic football or hurling match.
* A book of Yeats's poems.

5 The North: Old Ulster and the Other Ulster

Bernard Loughlin

COUNTIES

ANTRIM

DOWN

ARMAGH

MONAGHAN

CAVAN

FERMANAGH

DONEGAL

DERRY

TYRONE

Many of Ireland's most famous beauty spots are to be found in the northern part of the island. Renowned enough in song, story and guidebook to merit capital letters and definite articles, the Mountains of Mourne, the Ards Peninsula, the Antrim Coast Road, the Giant's Causeway and the Hills of Donegal ring the Ulster coast from the Irish Sea to the Atlantic. Inland, too, are some of the cardinal places of Irish history, where battles and hostings and covenants have changed the destiny of the whole island.

To understand Ireland you need to understand Ulster. To understand Ulster you need to see it as a whole, not just as the part that is often metonymically referred to as Ulster, which is really Northern Ireland, a political rather than a provincial entity. The ancient province of Ulster, one of the four provinces of Ireland, comprises the six counties of Northern Ireland, Antrim, Down, Armagh, Fermanagh, Tyrone and Derry, along with three counties of the Republic of Ireland, Monaghan, Cavan and Donegal. These days the three are divided from the six by the border that was created by the Government of Ireland Act of 1922, but all nine counties continue to share many characteristics and traditions that are recognisably of Ulster, from turns of phrase to ways of making bread.

Geographically this area has always been separated from the rest of Ireland by the chain of little hills called drumlins and their attendant lakes that straddle more or less the whole length of the present political border. Two thousand years or so ago massive earthwork ditches were built at the more pregnable points along this natural line of defence. The myth is that the Black Pig of Ulster got into a rage and ploughed a deep furrow with its snout as it roared off into the east, which is why in some sections it is called the Black Pig's Dyke or the Black Pig's Race. The less colourful truth is that these great mounds, with their moats and sharpened stakes, marked some kind of tribal boundary, an Irish version of Hadrian's Wall, that separated the peoples of the north from those of the south.

The herdspeople who built these defences also created epic tales about dynastic rivalry and cattle raids, that were eventually collected as the Ulster Cycle. These mythifiers of two thousand years ago would have been descendants of even earlier settlers who had penetrated inland up the wide sea loughs of Carlingford, the Swilly and the Foyle. At Mountsandel, at the mouth of the River Bann near Coleraine, are the remains of a settlement dating from 7000 BC, the earliest yet discovered in Ireland. These hunter-gatherer-fisherfolk would have found a rich living on this river that drains the immensity of Lough Neagh, the largest inland body of water in the British Isles. At Toomebridge, just where the lower Bann leaves Lough Neagh, the biggest eel fishery in Europe still operates using hazel wood traps – or *skeaghs*, as they are called locally – a technique which has not changed in hundreds of years, and is probably a refinement of methods used by the first inhabitants of these bountiful shores.

Somewhat later, and somewhat apocryphally, a more warlike wave of settlers arrived, led by the founder of the O'Neill dynasty, who famously chopped off his left hand and threw it ashore as the boat came in to land in order to be the first to stake his claim to the territory. History honours him still in the emblem of the Red Hand of Ulster that is to be seen on everything from flags to tea towels in this most regalia-bedecked part of the British realm.

From the modern point of view, the most marked change in human loyalties came with the Elizabethan and Tudor plantations of Ulster from the 16th century onwards. Here, it was the deliberate policy of successive English monarchs to secure a bridgehead in

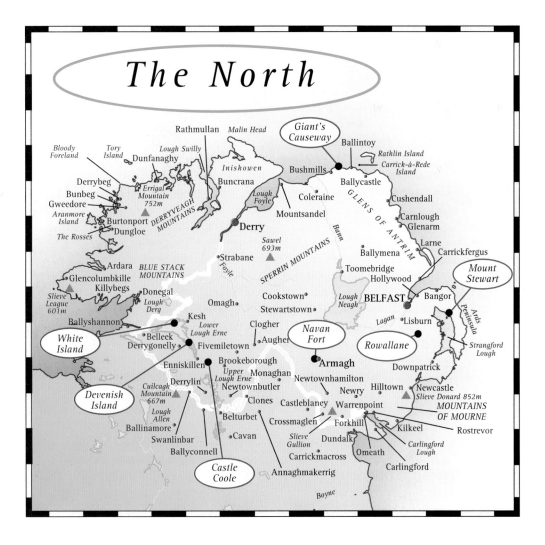

The North

Ireland by confiscating land from the natives, who were Catholic, to grant to settlers from Scotland and northern England, who were Protestant. It is this piece of social engineering for political ends which gives Ulster its unique character and, unfortunately, its unique problems.

The layout of many northern towns goes back to these Tudor and later models. They are generally built around a principal square, called the diamond, from which all the main streets radiate. The oldest church, now usually of the Church of Ireland, the established Irish Protestant church, faces onto the diamond, with the courthouse and market house often on opposite sides, or at least nearby, giving the ensemble a strong civic character. The escutcheons that grace these

buildings, proclaiming *Honi Soit Qui Mal Y Pense* and *Dieu Est Mon Droit*, and the other monuments that stand in the diamonds – Celtic high crosses, memorials of the Crimean, Boer and other wars, and testimonials from the grateful tenants to their landlords – are picture books in stone of the history of the towns and their localities.

In Northern Ireland history in the sense of battles and dates and personages is everywhere apparent, and nowhere more so than in the capital, Belfast. The wall paintings that adorn many of the gable walls in the working-class districts – depicting King William crossing the Boyne in 1690 and other signal events from the Protestant heritage, or the romanticised freedom fighters and figures from Celtic mythology of the Catholic version

– show two very different ways of looking at a shared past.

Nowadays Belfast is in every way an industrial city fallen on hard times. From being a small river crossing in the 17th century – with a port and harbour that ran right up the Farset to where High Street and Donegall Place now meet in the very centre of the town a mile or more from the present quays – Belfast expanded exponentially in the 19th century around the linen mills which processed the flax that arrived there from the countryside. The predominant landmark of downtown Belfast is still the City Hall in Donegall Square that vaunts the prestige and prosperity of the linen barons whose money built it. As a bastion of the loyalty they professed to the British Crown, it stands in the middle of a park well stocked with memorials to the glory of the Empire. The one to Queen Victoria herself is certainly the largest and most florid of its kind still extant in Ireland. Another to the Marquess of Dufferin and Ava – in his time Viceroy of India, Governor of Canada, ruler in the Queen's name of many outposts of Empire – stands just in front of a Garden of Remembrance dedicated to the many Ulstermen who died in the world wars of this century. There is also a memorial to the victims of the foundering of the *Titanic* in 1912, when it was struck by an iceberg on its maiden voyage. This largest and most luxurious of the ocean liners of its day was built in Belfast in the shipyards of Harland & Wolff, at that time the biggest shipmaker in the world.

Under the City Hall's baroque dome the ceilings and stained-glass windows show a pageant of the founding of the city by Sir Arthur Chichester in 1603. Scenes of heroic labour at shipbuilding, spinning, weaving and ropemaking (the city's founding industries) throw their gorgeous lustre down on marble floors and walls that have rung in their time to all kinds of dispute and defiance. It was here in 1912 that Sir Edward Carson and his followers signed the Solemn Act and Covenant in their own blood, the first move in the secession of Ulster from the Home Rule that was eventually granted to the rest of

Ireland. For a few years after the Anglo-Irish Agreement of 1985, bitterly resented by Unionists as another attempt to sell them down the river, the 300-foot-long Portland stone façade of the City Hall sported a large banner proclaiming 'Belfast Says No', that at Christmas time became 'Belfast Says No-el'.

Also on Donegall Square, among all the banks and insurance companies that stand stern sentinel over Belfast's canny savings, is the Linenhall Library. Founded in 1788 as the Belfast Society for Promoting Knowledge in the old White Linen Hall that stood on the present site of the City Hall, it is now tucked discreetly upstairs in a fine stone and brick building that was originally a linen warehouse designed by Charles Lanyon in 1864. As one of the oldest libraries in Ireland it is especially well endowed with historical texts and books printed in Belfast. Over the last twenty-five years it has also been conscientiously gathering every scrap of political documentation that has emerged from all sides in the Northern Ireland conflict, to make the most comprehensive archive possible of this phase of Irish history.

The streets around Donegall Place, High Street and the grandly titled Royal Avenue are linked by narrow alleys, called 'entries' in Belfast parlance. Up one of these – once narrow and noisome, now somewhat incongruously piazzaified with municipal seating for the local winos – lies Kelly's Cellars of Bank Street. Sandwiched between the mercantile relic of the Bank Buildings, now Penney's chainstore, and the Florentine palazzo of the Allied Irish Bank, this fine old pub was once a meeting place for the United Irishmen, whose strongholds were in the Presbyterian heartlands of Ulster. It is said that the northern command met here to plot the 1798 Rebellion. After its failure, Henry Joy Mc Cracken, one of their most romantic leaders, is supposed to have hidden under the counter before he was captured and hanged from the belfry of the old Market House, of which no trace remains.

It is in this downtown area that most of Belfast's outstanding buildings are to be found: the Ulster Bank in Waring Street, St George's Church of Ireland in Victoria Street, the First Presbyterian Church in Rosemary Street and, most ornate of this rather austere bunch, St Anne's Cathedral in Donegall Street. This Romanesque basilica was erected between 1899 and 1927, and is still not quite finished. Just as in the City Hall one can find the shields of all the provinces of Ireland,

here in the Chapel of the Holy Spirit there are stones on the floor from every county in Ireland. The fine mosaics on the wall depict the arrival in AD 492 of St Patrick at Saul in what is now County Down.

Freemasonry flourishes in Northern Ireland alongside other Protestant secret societies

The interior of the City Hall dome, Belfast.

such as the Orange Order, the Black Preceptory and the Apprentice Boys. You come across the meeting places of these sects all over Ulster, from tin shacks up country lanes to solid buildings with neo-classical facades like the Orange Hall in Clifton Street, where, on the apex of its roof, King William on his rearing charger looks ready to do battle with the Papish hordes all over again. On the Twelfth of July every year these halls become the vesting places for the army of 100 000 Orangemen who march to *Fields* all over Northern Ireland to plight their loyalty to Queen and Country. Each lodge member takes great pride in his turnout and the dark suits, orange sashes and bowler hats evoke a sort of foreman's respectability that has long since become archaic elsewhere. The enormous silken banners that precede each lodge are carried by six men, two in the middle, two in front and two behind, and are a moving cartoon of the events of the Protestant history and heritage they pledge to defend. The marching season, as it is called, lasts for months on end, warming up to the big one on the Twelfth of July and petering out after the Apprentice Boys' parade around the walls of Derry on 12 August.

Among those who accompany the marches are evangelical sandwich-men bedecked front and rear with biblical texts. Belfast is the capital of revivalist preaching and its exponents can be found everywhere. Freelancers berate bus queues or imprecate the passing traffic but the more respectable ones confine their sermonising to the hundreds of little chapels that dot the city and the dozens of tents that shelter Gospel Crusades during the summer months.

Belfast, though, does not lack more worldly entertainments. Great Victoria Street harbours two gems of Victorian architecture, a pub and a theatre, that cater for all the senses. In the Crown Bar, where gas lights are still the only form of illumination, carvings of griffons and eagles stand guard over the oakwood snugs, Moorish pillars hold the arabesques of the vault in suspension above the mosaic-tiled floor, and the gilded bar with its high mirrors offers a good prop against which to reel in amazement at all this magnificence.

St Anne's Cathedral, Belfast.

The Grand Opera House just across the road is the flamboyant 1894 creation of Frank Matcham, one of the greatest British theatre designers. The building is a menagerie and cornucopia of animal and vegetal imagery set within a beautifully proportioned framework that recalls, on the one hand, the big top of the traditional circus, and, on the other, the pagodas and palaces of the East, from which Matcham derived much of his inspiration. From the turn of the century up to the 1950s this palace of dreams was host to many of the greats of opera, theatre, vaudeville, pantomime and music hall: Beerbohm Tree, Sarah Bernhardt, the Three Stooges, Orson Welles and Pavlova all appeared here in their day.

By the early 1970s both the Crown and the Opera House had declined almost to the point of no return, victims of neglect, bomb damage, changed times and changed tastes. Their more or less simultaneous restoration in the 80s, by the National Trust in the case of the pub and the Arts Council in the case of the theatre, made a strong symbolic contribution to the saving of Belfast as a living city.

The presence of Queen's University, and the spending power of its 10 000 students close

to the centre of town, also helped to keep Belfast's urban spirit alive. Founded originally as one of the constituent colleges of the University of Ireland, along with the university colleges of Dublin, Cork and Galway, Queen's became a degree-granting institution in its own right in 1908. Its neo-Gothic main building sits well back from University Road on an open, elegant, though somewhat restricted campus that from the 50s onwards has been spreading tentacles into the surrounding avenues. This scattering of outposts of learning within a half-mile radius of the Old Library imbues the whole area with the university spirit, which is most notable every October when the Belfast Festival at Queen's – the second biggest arts festival in these islands after Edinburgh – puts on a plethora of events in every hall the university possesses and in many downtown venues as well.

The Ulster Museum that stands in the Botanic Gardens just up the road from Queen's completes this scholarly ensemble. Through steady reformations over the last thirty years, and especially with the building of the new wing in 1971, the extensive collections of the museum have been made eminently legible. With particular strengths in the fields of industrial archaeology, the natural sciences and Ulster painting of the 20th century, the museum always repays a visit, whether it be to see ghoulish favourites of a Belfast childhood such as the Egyptian mummy, or more recent acquisitions like the gold hoard from the *Girona*, a ship from the Spanish Armada that was wrecked off the coast of Antrim in 1588.

The curvilinear Palm House built in 1839 by Richard Turner in the Botanic Gardens shelters bananas and bamboos, ferns and orchids, epiphytes and xerophytes, in a collection begun by the Royal Belfast Botanical Society in the days when every city worth its charter laid out such gardens and greenhouses for the edification of its citizens. These citizens have enjoyed the Botanic ever since, even if it is only to play chess or draughts in the pensioners' shelter or to court their lovers among its shrubberies and dells.

The back gates of the park take you to the area around Fitzroy Avenue known as the Holy Land because the streets are called after Jerusalem, Palestine, Damascus and other hallowed places of the Middle East. An early song by Van Morrison (1945–), Belfast's most illustrious rock 'n' roll musician, was inspired by this area.

A short descent through any of the side streets to the west brings you out onto the Stranmillis Embankment alongside the River Lagan. Downriver from here is the Ormeau Park, one of the many municipal parks that break up Belfast's Victorian streetscape of red-brick terraces. Upriver begins the Lagan towpath that once ran all the way to Lough Neagh in the days when Ulster capitalists pioneered the development of inland navigation and drew together factories, mills and farms in a network of canals and rivers that shifted raw materials and finished goods from all over the province out to the seaports of Belfast and Newry.

The Lagan Valley Regional Park, that has the towpath as its core, incorporates the woodlands, fields and lawns of three or four old estates, including Barnett's Demesne and Lady Dixon Park, and stretches from the centre of Belfast right out to Lambeg and Lisburn. Apart from the canal cuts and the

The gas-lit interior of the Crown Bar, Belfast.

lock chambers redolent of the slower-moving life of only a couple of generations ago, mill villages like Edenderry along its banks are evocative of a time when the linen frenzy whitened village greens and powered mighty looms all over the north of Ireland.

After it was sown and grown in the heavy Ulster clays which suited its cultivation perfectly, the raw flax for the linen was harvested by twisting hanks of it out of the ground. It was then retted in foul-smelling millponds for weeks on end to soften it, before being scutched in special beetling mills which stripped the fibre from the husk. The fibre was then sent off to the factories of Belfast to be made into yarn.

At its peak of production in the early 20th century the linen industry employed tens of thousands of people. The linen barons built enormous mills in which whole families from the surrounding streets of two-up two-down terraced houses toiled long hours in damp, noisy conditions to make fine lawn and cambric for the beds and tables of the well-to-do.

All this bygone life is recreated at the Ulster Folk Museum at Cultra near Holywood in County Down. As one of the first outdoor museums in these islands, Cultra has a well-laid-out collection of reconstructed houses, mills, churches and even a whole city street that give a sense of what life was like in an earlier Ulster. If it suffers a little from the whimsy which so often adheres to such enterprises, it is nonetheless instructive to know how the many different kinds of spades were made for different purposes and how they all had their distinctive local peculiarities, thus the expression 'he had a face as long as a Lurgan spade'. Spades were also right-footed or left-footed, depending on local tradition, so a man's religious affiliation could be told from whether he dug with the one or the other, a means of describing people's allegiance that has survived into the age of the tractor and the mechanical digger. In a stroll round the 136-acre site you can discover what griddle bread tasted like, what kinds of animals a prosperous 19th-century farm might have reared, or what hymns would have been sung in an 18th-century

Presbyterian church. The guiding spirit and founding father here is the Welshman Estyn Evans (1905–89), one-time professor of geography at Queen's University, whose *Irish Folk Ways* is one of the classics of modern Irish literature.

Not too far away from Cultra are the Parliament Buildings at Stormont. Inaugurated by the Prince of Wales (later Edward VIII) in 1932, this Palladian-style extravaganza stands at the end of one of the longest and most pompous entrance avenues in Christendom. After the separation of the two parts of Ireland in 1922, Stormont, ironically, became the seat of a form of Home Rule granted to the Unionists after they had armed to resist Home Rule being given to the whole island. This carbon copy of the Mother of All Parliaments, down to Black Rod and the Speaker's Mace, was abolished in 1972 as a result of a civil rights campaign that made headlines all over the world by exposing the inequities that had been perpetrated under its aegis in fifty years of unbroken rule by the Unionist Party.

From Stormont the drumlins of County Down roll away to the Mountains of Mourne to the south and Belfast Lough to the north. These rounded, low, glaciated hills – what generations of northern geography teachers and their students have called 'basket of eggs topography' – give the backbone to a productive, pastoral countryside where the cultivation of the earth is intense, especially along the milder coastal strips where frost is negligible and the sandy soil is particularly suited to potatoes and root crops in general.

Recently there has been a quickening of interest and concern for the unique marine environment of Strangford Lough, a straggling estuary of drowned drumlin islands which stretches almost to the gates of Belfast itself. Because of its peculiar geography – sheltered from the east by the Ards Peninsula, ripped through twice a day by cleansing and feeding tides bottled up by the narrow entrance between Strangford and Portaferry – Strangford Lough is one of the richest bird feeding grounds in Europe. It is also a haven for seals, pilot whales, porpoises, basking sharks and other marine creatures which feed on the extensive mud flats or hunt prey in the deeper waters. The National Trust runs a Strangford Lough Wildlife Scheme to protect this precious place, with organised hides at Castle Espie, Reagh Island and the Gasworks at Mount Stewart.

The mild maritime climate of County Down has favoured the creation of two great gardens at Mount Stewart and Rowallane, within an easy hour's reach of one another. Mount Stewart is the more elegant of the two. The lovely house at its centre was the ancestral home of Robert, Viscount Castlereagh, British War Minister and Foreign Secretary throughout much of the Napoleonic Wars. Each of the near sections of the garden is designed to reflect the room of the house from which it is visible, yet for all their formality the vistas and allées you see from the tall windows can also be quite frivolous, as Edith, Lady Londonderry, wished them to be when she first laid them out in 1921. One of the sunken Italian-style terraces, the Dodo Garden, even has fanciful statuary and topiary to represent the animals and mythic creatures whose names she gave to various of her fashionable London friends, including one of Winston Churchill as a warlock. The shrubberies and woodlands of the extensive

park, with its mausoleum and artificial lake, make a botanical treasure house of tender rarities like mimosa, eucryphia and acacia, along with many different species of rhododendrons and tree heaths. The Temple of the Winds, a replica of the original in Athens, enjoys panoramic views of Strangford Lough right across to Scrabo Tower, the most prominent landmark in this part of County Down.

Rowallane on the other side of the Lough is another paradise for the botanist, though for the stroller, too, its walled gardens, dense woods and umbrageous avenues offer ravishing walks. Its founder, the Reverend John Moore, was infected by the Victorian passion for plant collecting. His heir, Hugh Armitage Moore, reorganised the gardens better to show off the glories of the acid-loving plants that thrive in the light soil of County Down, especially when sheltered as they are here by the swathes of beech, pine, holly and laurel which have been planted round the boundaries. Rowallane is also the headquarters of the National Trust for Northern Ireland which has done so much with limited resources to preserve the best of the built and natural heritage of the six counties of Northern Ireland, to an extent

The Dodo Garden at Mount Stewart, County Down.

The Mountains of Mourne dominate the beach at Newcastle, County Down.

The Mournes themselves are very thinly populated, with Hilltown being the only village actually in the mountains. After that the rich brown tracts of bog and bracken are broken only by the green fields around isolated farmsteads. These laboriously won patches of grazing are connected by a tracery of dry stone walls that disappear over ridges in the foreground and then reappear miles away still marching up the steep hillsides like a hill-walker determined to do his five peaks before dark. The Brandy Pad, a smugglers' track from the coast to Hilltown, and other paths like the Black Stairs and the Trassey Track that were once used by quarrymen who worked the Mourne granite, offer points of repair for explorers of this wilderness.

Coming down out of these hills into Newcastle provides a bracing plunge into the hugger-mugger of a seaside resort. Breezes from the Irish Sea blowing across its miles of ridged sand give an infectious lift and jangle to the brash music of the fairground rides and the rattle and whirl of the coin arcades that line its main street. All is not godless amusement here though. As with many resort towns in the north of Ireland, there are Temperance hotels all along the seafront and in summer little knots of Revivalists often gather at sheltered spots along the promenade to sing the Lord's praises.

The clement aspect of Tollymore Forest Park on the flanks of Slieve Donard (the highest peak of the Mournes at 2796 feet) has allowed it to grow some fine specimens of cypress, sequoia and other conifers. Castlewellan Forest Park nearby is the National Arboretum of Northern Ireland. The most tender plants can be grown outdoors in its 15-acre walled garden and the further 1100 acres spread over the foothills of the Mournes. One of the enormous Wellingtonia redwoods was planted here in 1854, just one year after their seeds were first brought to Europe from the northwest coast of America. It now looms over the native forest like Gulliver among the Lilliputians. It is a testimony to the horticultural fame of this part of Ireland that its two best-known local nurseries, Slieve Donard and Daisy Hill, sent plants named after them to all the great Irish

that is much envied in the Republic.

Downpatrick, where St Patrick is buried under a massive monolith in the cemetery of the cathedral, is the urban equivalent of these carefully planned and executed gardens. The doorways and windows of the terraces of Georgian and Victorian houses, elegant and imposing buildings like the Judge's Lodgings, the Downe Hunt Club, the Southwell Charity Almshouse and the Assembly Rooms, all testify to the prosperity of this market town, whose human history is evoked in the names of its streets: Irish Street, English Street, Scotch Street.

For all its ordered docility, the landscape of County Down has a backdrop of alternate mystery and grandeur in the Mourne Mountains that by times stand blue and coy in the middle distance, and on other days come and go brown and black, blasted by cloud and wind on the far horizon. The Kingdom of Mourne, one of the few places in Ireland to enjoy this royal distinction, has the compact self-sufficiency of a mountain principality, from the fastnesses of its high, heather-clad hills to the bedlam of 'brawling townlands' that squabble to the sea on the coast between Warrenpoint, Rostrevor and Newcastle.

gardens, as well as to many others abroad.

It is worth making the complete circuit of the Mourne coast right to Newry, for this is a country of myth and magic, where Cuchallain once roamed, where the Vikings raided, returned, and eventually settled, and where a salty memory lingers of all the seafaring peoples who have made their homes here. The land has been divided and subdivided so often that the inhabitants have always had to supplement the livings from their farms with the fruits of the sea. Kilkeel, the biggest fishing port in Northern Ireland, brims with boats and tackle in various states of repair, and always reeks strongly of the sea bottom.

Rostrevor is a sedate watering place of ivy-clad houses around the ford of the river of the same name. The harmonious terrace of Victorian shop and pub frontages along Bridge Street leads onto the tree-lined mall of the Hilltown Road. For all its peaceable air, this place produced one bellicose hero, Major-General Robert Ross, who captured Washington and burnt the White House in 1814 during the Anglo-American war. The 100-foot-high obelisk to his memory that stands along the coast road to Warrenpoint looks somewhat incongruous now among the seaside villas that surround it, but the Major-General stares indomitably out to sea regardless.

The rapid development of Warrenpoint over the last twenty years has spread a space station of warehouses and industrial estates right back along the now defunct ship canal all the way to Newry. It did, though, have a previous heyday in the 50s as a destination for day trippers from Belfast who would take the ferry from Warrenpoint across Carlingford Lough to Omeath in the Republic in the days when drink and cigarettes were cheaper in the south and you could get a skinful of beer and whiskey there and bring it back in your belly without the customs men being able to charge you duty on it. That ferry still runs, somewhat eccentrically, in the summer months, and the publicans of Omeath still welcome the odd bit of northern trade to their one-time pilgrimage place whose cult of cheap booze has fallen into disuse. And, while you are on that side of the Lough, it is well worth exploring Carlingford itself, a beautiful medieval town, and the Cooley Mountains behind it.

Newry is a border town that has known how to adapt and change with the times. Always a trading place, its greatest prosperity came when the first canal in the British Isles

Warrenpoint and Carlingford Lough, County Down.

was built in 1741 to link Lough Neagh to Carlingford Lough. Some of the warehouses and chandlers' shops built to serve this trade are still to be seen around the Town Hall that stands on stone arches over the Clanrye River. Newry can also boast the first Protestant church in Ireland, St Patrick's, built by Nicholas Bagenal in 1578, as well as – by pure coincidence – the first Roman Catholic cathedral to be built after Catholic Emancipation, St Patrick and St Colman's, a Perpendicular-style edifice whose striking prickly outline was completed in 1829.

As an outward-looking and progressive town, Newry's shops gladhand Irish punts and British sterling with equal dexterity. Up until January 1993, when the single market of the European Union began eroding the last fiscal differences between the North and the South, its true bible was the customs and excise regulations of the Republic of Ireland and Northern Ireland, which was also the unofficial religion of the region of South Armagh and Monaghan that straddles the border from here westwards. This was Ireland's Rio Grande and Ruritania all rolled into one.

South Armagh was one of the last areas in Ulster to be planted. Even then the Undertakers, agents working on commissions from the Crown, did not manage to establish much more than a few bridgeheads like Newtownhamilton and Hamiltonsbawn, that to this day have an air of being places under siege. This was also a country of legend, song and story. Around the town of Forkhill there is a vigorous tradition of singing and in September it hosts a singers' weekend to which enthusiasts flock from every part of the north and south to hear ballads about events that have survived in the memory simply because they were committed to verse.

Here and there across this rough countryside the ordnance survey maps indicate more sections of the Black Pig's Dyke, that, confusingly, changes its name here to the Dorsey. In one area near Crossmaglen it is plainly visible as a square fortification enlarged out of the run of the dyke itself, with very deep ditches on either side, the whole commanding access to the Gap of the North. For all its impressive height and width, this straggling Worm Ditch – yet another of the names it goes by – must have been as difficult to defend in its entirety as the present loose and leaky border is now.

Coming out of the rough country around Slieve Gullion, you descend into the more pastoral parts of County Armagh. The moderating effect of the vast waters of Lough Neagh on the local climate allows apple orchards to flourish along the shores; some cider is made locally. In this most pleasant and fruitful of Irish counties the old houses recall the *bawns*, or fortified mansions, of the first English and Scottish settlers, each with its own orchard and kitchen garden, the home fields and the farm all around.

The city of Armagh reflects this hinterland in its solid grandeur. Along the Mall, Georgian mansions look down into the tree-lined park that was once the racetrack and cockpit of a gamier city than today's. Francis Johnston, the architect responsible for many of the great buildings of Dublin, was a son of Armagh, and this mall and the courthouse which stands at one end of it are his legacy to his home town.

For all its rather English air – the British chain stores, little tea shops, antique shops, art galleries and bookshops of its town centre recalling a sort of bomb-battered Bath – Armagh is a very Irish town, even down to its divisiveness. The Church of Ireland cathedral of St Patrick stands on one of the town's twin drumlins looking straight across at the Roman Catholic cathedral, also of St Patrick, on the other, giving an ecclesiastical rivalry to the skyline of the place where St Patrick himself founded a church in the fifth century to usurp the power of the old competing pagan deities. Thus it is that there are two archbishops of Armagh, one of them the head of the Protestant Church of Ireland, the other the Roman Catholic Primate of Ireland, who is also usually a cardinal. This history of faith is interpreted and explained in St Patrick's Trian, which takes its name from what the old quarters of the town were called. This absorbing complex includes a 'Lilliput' display in honour of Jonathan Swift's connection with the locality.

In the Protestant cathedral military flags, banners and other memorabilia of the local grandees and yeomen hang limp and dusty between the stained-glass windows – a celebration of the secular alongside the sacred that goes back to the time of the Irish King Brian Boru, who defeated the Vikings at the Battle of Clontarf in 1014, and whose remains are buried in the cemetery. The 19th-century Roman Catholic cathedral is a triumph of Irish Gothic. The arrayed hats of the dead cardinals, that are traditionally hung above the main altar when their wearers pass on, add a touch of the macabre to its soaring interior.

The area around the Church of Ireland cathedral is steeply stepped up past the public library, founded by Archbishop Robinson in 1771. The Archbishop's Palace, a Georgian blockbuster of a house, stands about a mile from the cathedral in grounds of its own. Now the offices of the County Council, its yard and stables have become a cultural centre that is often host to visiting theatre and music groups, especially during the Armagh Festival in October. For even more stellar entertainment and enlightenment, the Observatory, founded by the same Archbishop Robinson in 1791, puts on regular dioramas of the movements of the heavens.

You have to leave the city of Armagh and travel only a few miles west to understand why St Patrick chose this part of Ireland, which was neither central nor obvious, to found his first church. For 5000 years before Christ, Emain Macha (also called Navan Fort), a 16-acre enclosure within a massive earthen mound, was at the core of the Irish Celtic world.

We can only speculate about the rituals that bound this pre-Christian society together, but there is no doubting Emain Macha's importance, even if it was only as a site pre-eminent among the many other hilltop raths that make detailed maps of these border counties look like they have been randomly dotted with moon craters. We can say with certainty that this was a society of cattle-rearers rather than tillage farmers. Emain Macha on one level is merely a bigger version of a tribal stockade – presumably to enclose the large herds of a powerful chieftain – that over time would have taken on other ceremonial significances as the power which derived from ownership invested the whole place.

A new interpretative centre slightly removed from the site itself explains how Emain Macha might have looked in its heyday and the kind of life that revolved around it. In its time this was Ulster's Camelot, with Cuchalainn as King Arthur and Lancelot rolled into one, Deirdre as Guinevere, the Druids as Merlin and Queen Maeve as the enemy without.

Smugglers' stories are the modern-day equivalents of the heroic tales spawned by the Celts. For the fifty or sixty years up to 1993, smuggling was the lifeblood of a clandestine commerce that flowed across the Irish frontier. The ingenuity of these entrepreneurs is celebrated in song and story, from the pettiest acts of defiance – when freelancers would dangle packets of contraband butter out of train windows on lengths of string to avoid the eye of the boarding customs men – to more organised frauds whereby lorryloads of livestock would be shunted back and forth from the North to the South in order to swindle agricultural subsidies on either side.

With increased vigilance by the British Army and the blowing up or blocking of many of the border bridges and roads during the 25 years of the Northern Troubles, traffic used to be restricted to the few approved roads – less than a dozen along the whole length of the border – so the scope for any kind of serious smuggling was considerably diminished even before the killjoy threshold of January 1993 and the establishment of the Single Market. With the reopening of most of these minor roads in 1994, a web of local connections has begun to be knitted back together, and the traffic, carrying more or less what it wants, has begun to pass freely once again from North to South and vice versa.

For all the eagerness with which one usually cranes to see the differences after traversing any kind of frontier, thinking of all the myths about the hard-working North and the easy-going South, the fields on either side look much the same. What real differences there are are the creation of the last seventy years of separation. Post boxes, for all that they might be emblazoned with such archaic imperial echoes as *Victoria Regina* or *Georgius Rex*, no matter which side of the border they might be on, are still painted red in the North and green in the South. Road signs in the South are bilingual in English and Irish – often with the new ones rather confusingly marked in kilometres and the older ones in miles. Most of these differences are skin-deep, the result of symbolic tinkerings which have merely scratched the surface of a common culture that unites more than it divides.

In County Monaghan the population is nearly as mixed between Protestants and Catholics as in the southern parts of Armagh, Tyrone and Fermanagh which border it. Though there has been considerable Protestant emigration from the Republic over the last half century or so, most of the Protestant churches in Monaghan and Cavan still have respectable congregations of a Sunday, even if, as elsewhere, one pastor must look after three or four parishes on a monthly roster.

The population here is one of the most scattered in Ireland. More people live out in the countryside than in the towns. Maps of the region are as complex as Clones lace, with roads snaking up to isolated dwellings on the leeside of hills from which often no other human habitation would be visible. There are those who say that living in these little bowls of hills without much intercourse with their fellows gives a closed cast to the character of the people but – on a good night, in the right pub, the ice broken with a few pints – you will find these drumlineers as garrulous as any oceanic gabbler from the West, albeit perhaps somewhat more guarded in matters of religion and politics, more out of respect for their neighbours than from any bigotry or fear.

This scattered population, scratching a living out of relatively poor land that can only be made productive as a result of major capital investment, has favoured the creation of home-based agricultural industries. The countryside is dotted with silos and long, low sheds where pigs and poultry, including vast numbers of turkeys, ducks and even quails, are reared intensively. Mushrooms, too, are grown in houses that look like upended boat keels, covered with black polythene and rearing up from behind hedges or in field bottoms in the most unexpected places.

The sylvan elegance of Armagh.

At one time this was a county of 100 000-acre estates. The towns of Monaghan are nearly all the creations of landlords who built to the Planter pattern of diamond, market house, courthouse and church. Some of the market houses have survived as grain stores or as outposts for the county library, as in Carrickmacross and Castleblayney, but many of them are now redundant, waiting for Social Employment Schemes to renovate them as community centres, now that cattle trading has moved to the vast corrugated-iron marts outside the towns.

Monaghan town itself is perhaps the most successfully transformed of the old towns. Through some enlightened town planning in the 1980s, and with the help of grants from the International Fund for Ireland and other agencies, the old and the modern have been made a bit easier in one another's company. In Old Cross Square at one end of the town a three-sided, cupped stone that may have been a sundial stands sentinel over the space where the market and butchers' shambles used to be. The long curve of Dublin Street ends in the diamond that was laid out by the Lords Rossmore, whose one-time estate just outside the town is now a forest park.

Monaghan is the cathedral town for the Catholic diocese of Clogher that straddles the border between County Monaghan and County Tyrone. The cathedral of St Macartan's which dominates the town from every direction is a jewel of the Irish Gothic Revival, designed by J.J. Mc Carthy (the 'Irish Pugin') between 1861 and 1892. Its beautiful interior has recently been restored and repainted, to glow the glory of the Lord on even the dullest drumlin day.

Much of the enhanced awareness of the importance of history and conservation that is evident in Monaghan can be traced to the presence on Hill Street of the county museum, which was awarded the Council of Europe Museum Prize in 1980. Along with its extensive collections of old artefacts, of which the 15th-century Cross of Clogher is the pride, the museum is also a storehouse for the tools of the industries and crafts that were once practised in County Monaghan. The growing of flax and the making of linen were very important here in the late 19th and early 20th centuries, part of the linen boom which extended into every part of Ulster. There are, too, many beautiful samplers of Clones and Carrickmacross lace, the two best known of the many different styles that developed from the original techniques introduced in the early 19th century by the Sisters of Saint Louis and other philanthropic ladies who wished to give local employment. Others samplers in these diverse styles can be seen in the Heritage Centre at the Saint Louis Convent.

The social improvement based on self-reliance brought by these craft industries would have been actively encouraged by the Big Houses of the county, of which a few still survive, mostly by dint of themselves finding other ways of making a living now that their estates have been reduced to the few hundred acres of the home farm more or less as bounded by the demesne walls. The tour of Castle Leslie near Glaslough is enlivened by tales of the proud eccentricity of its denizens since the 'fighting bishop' John Leslie took a strong hand in the suppression of the Catholic uprising of 1641, before going on, presumably fortified by his warlike labours, to marry a girl of 18 when he was 70 and father 10 children with her.

Hilton Park near Scotshouse is part of the Hidden Ireland network of big houses that offer the choicest of accommodation and cuisine at prices which compare very favourably with what you would pay in an ordinary hotel. Annaghmakerrig House, one-time home of the theatre director Sir Tyrone Guthrie, is now a workplace for artists from all over the world.

Apart from the many artists who now visit County Monaghan on account of the Tyrone Guthrie Centre, there is a strong indigenous literary tradition here which found its most resounding expression in the work of Patrick Kavanagh (1905–67), the son of a cobbler-cum-small farmer, whose poems, novels, reviews and articles crystallised the poverties and yearnings of an Ireland that he described most poignantly in his epic *The Great Hunger* (1942). Kavanagh's native village of Inniskeen has a well-signposted trail around places associated with his work, with an interpretative centre dedicated to him in the parish church of St Mary's.

The town of Clones has suffered much from being cut off by the border from its natural hinterland of south Fermanagh and has a rather dejected air that sits oddly with the gracious buildings of its diamond that were once the seats of local government for the whole county. You have only to enter the old graveyard of St Tighearnach's, though – still, as Tiernach, a common Christian name for boys in Monaghan – to find yourself a thousand years removed from its present plight amidst the rude humilities of an earlier time. The 'quaint' 18th-century gravestones in the churchyard are vernacular descendants of the medieval carvings of the monasteries around the Lough Erne basin. They depict skulls and crossbones, hourglasses, bells and coffins in a *memento mori* that is both chilling and winsome.

The neighbouring county of Cavan, for all that it is often lumped with Monaghan, is very proud of its distinctiveness. As so often in Ireland, with the shift of only a few miles across the county boundary, the accent changes and the outlook with it. There is a great pride in the area's one-time precedence as the Kingdom of Breffni, a name that is to be seen in various spellings over shops and cafés and bars. When it was the stronghold of the O'Reillys – who built the now disappeared castle at one end of the town and a monastery at the other – Cavan even had its own mint. The town's ancient origins can still be traced in its wayward topography that follows more the lie of the land and the tramp of the human foot than any benevolent landlord's pencil-and-paper plan.

North Cavan is a rugged landscape whose bleak moorlands are dominated by the whaleback of the Cuilcagh Mountain rearing out of the oceanic swell of drumlins. The romantically named Swanlinbar, often abbreviated to Swad by the locals, had a brief popularity in the 19th century as a spa town where the gouty gentry came to take the acrid waters which bubble up from deep springs carrying minerals leached out of Slieve Anierin, the Hill of Iron, nearby. This same iron was the raw material for an iron smelter set up by Messrs Swann, Linn and Barr – thus the strange name of the town – that went into decline when the surrounding woods that supplied the charcoal for fuel became exhausted.

The Cavan Way, a branch of the Ulster Way that encompasses the North, begins here and takes you sixteen miles or so, over a landscape where the wind flattens the heather tight to the scalp of the hills, to Glangevlin in the Kingdom of Glan and on to Dowra, a village built at an awkward kilter to the first major bridge over the River Shannon that rises in the Shannon Pot only a few miles away.

Looking down into the strongly flowing, already deep, peat-brown water of Ireland's major river, you can search for the drowned tresses and listen for the cries of Sionna, granddaughter of the sea god Lir, who tried to capture the salmon of knowledge at the river's source and was swept away by the boiling waters into the bowels of the earth for her presumption. Her memorial is the name of the river itself.

On nearby Lough Allen, not too far from Dowra, another bit of the Black Pig's Dyke appears – here called the Worm Ditch because it was fancied that it was gouged out by an enraged snake fleeing St Patrick when he banished the reptiles from Ireland. At the Burren near Blacklion, a limestone upland that shimmers with flowering plants in spring, there is an ancient conurbation of wedge tombs, court tombs, passage graves and dolmens, one of which is called the Druid's Altar for its six-ton capstone perilously perched on two uprights.

Against the wall under one of the delicately latticed windows of the Church of Ireland

The Shannon Pot, County Cavan, source of Ireland's greatest river.

church in Ballyconnell is propped the Tomregon Stone, a door arch from an earlier church a couple of miles away, to which it may have been added from some even earlier monument. It has been interpreted as, on the one hand, a male fertility figure or *Seamas-na-Gig*, down to the tracing of the genitals, or, on the other, as a depiction of a piece of primitive surgery by St Bricin, a renowned local sawbones in his day.

County Cavan is the ancestral home of the novelist Henry James (1843–1916), whose forebears were tenants of Bailieborough estate, homeplace of Richard Brinsley Sheridan (1751–1816), author of *A School for Scandal*, and of Percy French (1854–1920), composer of 'The Mountains of Mourne', 'Slattery's Mounted Foot', 'The West Clare Railway', and hundreds of other popular ballads that he sang in recitals all over the British Isles which made him one of the most successful entertainers of his day.

Since the county town is by no means centrally situated, Cavan has a lot of other towns of almost equal consequence in terms of size, each the centre of its own sphere of influence. Belturbet, at the southernmost navigable point on the Erne, straddles its drumlin in a Baltic profusion of brightly painted, tall houses, many of them with pubs or fishing tackle shops on their lower storeys – for the angling trade and the people on shore from the cruisers bring the bit of a roughness of money about the town. There is a very fine town hall overlooking the diamond that would not be out of place in Riga or Tallinn, and a 1904 post office whose elegant brick and stone lines express the reassurance that all the correspondence, sentimental or otherwise, committed to its

care will be dealt with promptly and efficiently.

Beyond the Cuilcagh Mountain that dominates so much of the landscape of County Cavan and County Fermanagh, a series of mountain ridges runs from Lough Erne to the Atlantic through north Leitrim, Sligo and Donegal, to make some of the most dramatic landscapes in Ireland. Donegal especially – for all that it is, humanly speaking, quietly spoken and courteous – is a geographically rough braggart of a place. Everything natural here is large-scale, oceanic, turbulent, challenging. Mankind clings for survival to the crannies of thin soil along the jagged coast or in the deepest recesses of the long, brown, boggy valleys that intersect the steep and unyielding mountains.

Donegal town shapes itself in most comely fashion around its diamond yet it has none of the air of pure commerce that other Planter towns exude. It is, rather, a discreet and decent place, full of country people talking and shopping, making the best of a good day out, that might end with a cup of tea in one of the nice hotels on the Diamond or something a bit stronger in one of the quiet pubs.

The stone obelisk with its simple engraved cross in the middle of the Diamond honours the Four Masters who wrote their *Annals* – a compendium of the history of Ireland going back to the time of Noah – in Donegal Abbey, whose ruins stand beside the seaweed-clogged harbour. The Four Masters bookshop on the Diamond takes its name from these long-dead scholars and manages, for all its bright, modern layout, still to have something of the atmosphere of a monastic scriptorium. In Magee's, a veritable temple of tweed, you can linger over and finger well-tailored clothes made from the wool of the hardy Donegal sheep whose population density out on the hills easily exceeds that of humans.

Throughout Donegal Irish tweed is as much part of the landscape as the heather, ling, bracken and gorse which inspire its colours. Every town and village has its tweed shop and along the roads you come upon signs exhorting you to visit annexes to cottages

Belturbet, southernmost navigable point on the River Erne, County Cavan.

The beetling cliffs of Slieve League, County Donegal.

and bungalows where the cloth is woven on traditional hand looms. There are factories, too, where it is produced under the auspices of Gaeltarra Eireann, a state company established to bring industry to the *Gaeltachts* where Irish is still the native tongue. Many of these factories have shops attached where the tweed can be bought quite cheaply by the yard, the metre or the bolt.

The other main occupation of the people here is fishing. Some of the richest fishing grounds in Europe lie off this coast on the continental shelf that stretches as far as Rockall to the north and the Aran Islands in the south. With increasing competition from vessels from other EU countries, the trawlers from Killybegs, Ireland's busiest fishing port, now have to go further and further to get their share of diminishing catches. Heavy investment by Bord Iascaigh Mara, another state company set up in the 50s to foster fishing and its ancillary industries, has allowed the more enterprising fishermen to buy ocean-going trawlers the size of small car ferries that can spend weeks at sea catching and processing prized species such as cod and hake, as well as the horse mackerel and gurnet destined for the markets of the Far East. Smaller boats still fish the inshore waters for catches that weigh in by the box rather than the ton. In the seasons when the shoals run, the daily auction of the fleet's catch can have the bustling expectancy of a Klondike Gold Rush.

Yet, for all the stories one hears of fortunes blown in wild drinking sprees, the captains' villas and deckhands' more modest bungalows that dot the hills all around Killybegs are testimony to the basic good sense of the Donegal people. Fishing and its related processing industries have brought solid prosperity to this whole region, and a number of local entrepreneurs who have set up processing factories have ensured that some of the added value stays there.

From One Man's Pass over Slieve League, the highest sea cliffs in Europe, you might be lucky enough to see the whole Killybegs fleet steam out of a summer evening towards reports of fishy bonanza that are relayed in codes from boat to boat on their short wave

radios, but it is more likely that you will be deepening your foothold against the wind that always seems to be blowing over the crest of these beetling cliffs, as you apprehensively eye the choughs and fulmars soaring on the updraughts from the seething sea hundreds of feet below. Retreating, honour and bones still intact, to Carrick, you might savour your brush with eternity in the Sliabh Liag bar, where the challenge is the more pleasurable one of wondering how you might drink your way through the hundreds of liqueurs of the world that adorn its shelves.

The smell of turf that always lingers in the Donegal air, or catches you in downdraughts as the wind snatches it from the chimneys of the close-packed houses in these Donegal towns, is conducive to seeking out the comfort of the great indoors. Often, in pubs like Nancy's Kitchen in Ardara, on the wet days which can suddenly assault this soggy sea-bottom of a landscape in even the most temperate summers, you will find other travellers becalmed there, their rucksacks, coats and instrument cases piled steaming in a corner while they go through all the diffident rituals that prefigure a session of music-playing and drinking that will get its first wind in the afternoon and might still be blowing strong at two o'clock in the morning.

Donegal, though, will always lure you back out, to expiate your sins of excess if nothing else. At Glencolumbkille, a toehold of a place in the midst of a wilderness of rock and water, there is a penitential round that begins at midnight on 9 June – feast day of its patron saint, Columba of Iona, who lived here for a time in the sixth century – and takes the pilgrims on a three-mile tour of the 15 holy sites in the vicinity. These include chapels, cairns and graveslabs, some of which may have pagan significance, for many Irish pilgrimages have their origins in pre-Christian practices.

The admixture of Planter and Gael that prevails in the rest of Ulster peters out here, in these rough western reaches, to a fairly homogenous Catholicism where Protestant churches are rare and what few there are are usually semi-abandoned. In the Rosses and neighbouring Gweedore – sprawling townlands of houses and smallholdings that stretch almost uninterruptedly from Dungloe to Dunfanaghy – the two Catholic churches are recent, designed by the Derry architect Liam Mc Cormick. He has managed to capture in their soaring slate roofs and spires something of the nature of the place and of the human presence within it, where traditional three-roomed thatched cottages are dug into their sheltered sites like seasoned soldiers in their foxholes, awaiting the worst the Atlantic might throw at them.

The capital of the Rosses is Dungloe, even though 'capital' seems a rather inflated title for a town that really only lives up to it for the annual Mary of Dungloe Festival. For the rest of the time it is a mild-mannered resort whose chief advantage is that all roads pass through it, making it an almost inevitable place to stop. From there you might go to Burtonport, the second fishing village of Donegal and the port of embarkation for Aranmore Island. The little ferry, sallying out as weather and passengers permit, plies through an archipelago of islands which are richly fertile with seaweed and wrack up to the tideline and barren and bare of all but lichens and mosses above it. Like most Irish islands, especially those which do not have Garda Siochana living on the premises, there is a happy sense of primitive anarchy on Aranmore, of people regulating their own lives as they see fit. This has the advantage for native and visitor alike that the pubs close more or less when they list, or, as the old joke has it, on Christmas Day and Good Friday. Even with a stable population of 900 or so, Aranmore in the off season does not have much call for the pubs before ten or eleven o'clock at night. One of the blessings and reliefs here for city-dwellers is that no-one ever clashes a tray in your ears or snatches your drink off the table to drive you out at closing time.

From Bunbeg and Derrybeg – joint capitals of Gweedore, though it is next to impossible to tell where the one ends and the other begins – the awesome quartzite cap of Errigal Mountain, Donegal's highest peak at 2466 feet, lures you inland. It overlooks Dunlewy's

Poisoned Glen, so named for the legend that God laid poison there, which is why no birdsong is ever heard within its silent bourne. You do hear the occasional wren rasping its territorial imperative from a brake of brambles, but it is a forlorn place that has never offered much succour to man or beast.

The thirst that this boggy landscape engenders is not only for drink but also for greenery, for any living thing that stands more than three feet off the ground and is not bent and twisted into agued shapes by the withering west wind. This thirst can be slaked in the oasis of Glenveagh Castle and Gardens, a Scots baronial house that lies at the heart of Glenveagh National Park whose 10 000 acres are home to a herd of native Irish red deer. The house and grounds were presented to the nation in the 1970s by Henry Mc Ilhenny of Philadelphia and the Tabasco Sauce fortune, who himself lived there on and off for forty years. Into the elaborate tiered gardens he had built up over years with soil that had to be brought in on muleback to get it up to the highest terraces, he brought plants, bulbs and seeds from his extensive travels, as well as bringing to the house as his guests such human exotics as Greta Garbo and Clark Gable. The restoration of this property to the Irish people makes amends for the time in the 19th century when the Adairs, the original owners, evicted hundreds of their tenants from their smallholdings and put them on boats for America, merely in order to improve the view from their new castle's windows!

Only a few miles away is the Glebe House and Gallery, one-time home of another inveterate traveller, the painter Derek Hill. As well as moving in the best cosmopolitan society and making portraits of its luminaries, Hill spent many of his youthful summers in a rough hut without water or electricity on Tory Island, where he discovered and encouraged the artistic talents of some of the natives, since known as the Tory Island School of painters. Some of their haunting primitive paintings are on view in the Glebe Gallery, along with an extensive collection of works by Hill and his many artist friends.

Tory Island itself, two hours by boat from

The stained glass
windows of the
Guildhall, Derry City.

Bloody Foreland, is famed as having been a dumping ground for outlaws. This gave the word 'Tory' to the English language to describe those royalists who supported the claim of James, Duke of York (later James II) to the English and Scottish thrones during the 'Exclusion Crisis' of 1679–81 in opposition to the Whigs and subsequently became the nucleus of the Conservative Party. It was also said to be the home of Balor, the one-eyed Celtic god of darkness. Tory Island is often cut off from the mainland for weeks on end in winter, when reports of the plight of its inhabitants make the rest of Ireland grateful to be on dry land.

The three easterly Donegal peninsulas of Rosguill, Fanad and Inishowen can also sometimes seem a little aloof from the rest of the world, even though they are all perfectly accessible by scenic drives that take in views north to Tory, inland across the beautiful Mulroy Bay and east to the beaches and headlands of County Antrim.

Here we are back in the land of the Planters. Rathmelton, where the River Leannan joins Lough Swilly, was a stronghold of Scottish and Welsh settlers who came here under the aegis of Sir William Stewart, the founder of this market town in the 17th century. For a long time it prospered through dealing in all the produce of the locality: fish, iodine-rich seaweed, pigs, cattle and grain. These goods were exported from the solid, stone-built Fish House that still stands on the quayside among other well-preserved 17th- and 18th-century buildings such as the old Presbyterian Meeting House that is now a heritage centre and museum called the Makemie Centre.

Rathmullan is lorded over now by a battery fort built in 1810, when Napoleonic hysteria struck Ireland and many such strongplaces and Martello towers were built around the coast to repel the hordes of Bonaparte who never came. It also holds pride of place in Irish lamentation as the port from which the Earls of Tyrone and Tyrconnell took to sea with their families and a small band of retainers to seek succour from Philip III of Spain for the catastrophic defeat of the native Irish aristocracy at the Battle of Kinsale in

1602. As so often in Irish history, the winds took a hand and blew them to France instead, from where they made their way to Rome. The Flight of the Earls Heritage Centre in the town commemorates these events and explains the Plantation of Ulster which followed in their train.

The legacy of this plantation is much in evidence on the beautiful Inishowen Peninsula where a 100-mile drive takes you from Buncrana to Ireland's most northerly point, Malin Head, which features on shipping forecasts as a place only slightly less stormy than southeast Iceland. This hammer of land thrust up into the Atlantic's craw is scattered with ancient monuments: the Bocan Stone Circle and Cloncra High Cross near Culdaff, the castle at Greencastle built by the Norman Richard de Burgo in 1305, the 18th-century Buncrana Castle where the patriot Wolfe Tone was held after his capture in 1798, right down to the immense fort at Dunree with its Martello tower outflankers that was last used in World War I to protect the Allied convoys that mustered there for the dangerous passage to North America.

This area has in its time been a refuge for many people needing to escape from their enemies. Bonnie Prince Charlie hid out here for a while after the failure of the 1745 Rebellion in Scotland, which is only 30 miles away by sea. After the Siege of Derry in 1689 some of the remnants of James II's army settled here and created the neat little town of Malin, whose village green even yet looks like a parade ground on which the veterans might troop their colours.

The most spectacular monument on the peninsula is the Grianan of Aileach, a stone-stepped amphitheatre whose baleful omphalos dominates Lough Swilly and the surrounding countryside. With walls 17 feet high and 13 feet thick forming an enclosure 77 feet in diameter, it must have been a place of considerable ritual importance in its day. After the arrival of Christianity in Ireland it became for a time the royal residence of the O'Neill kings of Ulster and was attacked over and again in the almost endless succession of their wars. After many centuries of disuse, it was restored in the 1870s and what we see

THE OLD TOWER ST. COLUMBA'S COLLEGE A.D. 546

ST. COLUMBA in the OAK GROVE

RICHARD DE BURGHO

NORTHBURGH OR GREENCASTLE A.D. 13

BURT CASTLE A.D. 1601

today is really just an antiquarian's idea of the Grianan, put back together out of a puzzle of collapsed masonry.

Ironically enough, from the much-tumbled walls of the Grianan of Aileach you can see the Maiden City of Derry, so called because its walls have never been breached. Originally founded as a monastery by St Columcille, it is one of the many places in Ireland to take its name from *doire*, meaning an oak grove. Raided repeatedly by Vikings from the ninth to the eleventh centuries, its abbey was burnt to the ground in 1195. The town was the victim of many tussles between the Irish and the English in the succeeding centuries until it was completely destroyed by Cahir O'Doherty in 1608. Shortly afterwards it was granted by James I to the Irish Society of London 'for the promotion of religion, order and industry'. This group of merchants and adventurers rebuilt the town and surrounded it with strong walls. This was when the city acquired 'London' as part of its title, a bone of contention to this day.

These walls were tried twice and not found wanting, first of all in the rebellion of 1641 and then in the Cromwellian wars of 1649. They faced their greatest test in 1689 when 13 apprentice boys closed the gates against the Catholic armies of James II. Thus began the siege of Derry that lasted 105 days until the boom across the river was broken with the arrival of ships bringing food and reinforcements. This was a turning point in the Williamite wars which were fought on Irish soil as an important sideshow to the strategic wrangling then going on between the great powers of England and France for control of Europe.

On 12 August every year the Apprentice Boys, members of a Protestant society with members almost as numerous as those of the Orange Order, march round the walls in vindication of the heroic deeds of their ancestors who ate rats and dogs rather than submit to Popery and superstition. The stained-glass windows of St Columb's Church of Ireland cathedral depict scenes from the siege. Flags and tablets in its interior and objects and documents in its Chapter House continue the story in a dusty, dowdy sort of

way. The Tower Museum near Guildhall Square gives an altogether more balanced and graphic account of the same events in a sophisticated series of audiovisual presentations that take some of the hurt and triumphalism out of that history and make it once again the inheritance of all the city's citizens.

While the walls are well preserved, it is only possible these days to walk along sections of them. They had become a vantage point from which the more virulent element of the Apprentice Boys and other Protestant irredentists could rain insults, pennies and worse on the people of the Bogside. This Catholic enclave still has a gable end painted with 'YOU ARE NOW ENTERING FREE DERRY',

from its own siege in 1969 when the people held out for a week against repeated assaults and baton charges by the Royal Ulster Constabulary and the infamous 'B' Specials until the British Army had to be drafted in to restore order in a 'temporary' peace-keeping role that has lasted to this day.

Over the last decade or so Derry City Council has been fostering cultural activities in which all its people can join, not by pretending differences do not exist, but by exploring them through music, theatre, dance and other art forms to find the parts of history that they can all share. For ten years the Field Day Theatre Company, founded by the playwright Brian Friel (1929–) and the actor Stephen Rea (1950–), premiered a new play every year in the Guildhall. The Orchard Gallery has an outstanding reputation for showing avant-garde work by international artists who are attracted to Derry by its frontier status. Many of these exhibitions and events reflect the fact that the city has served through the ages as the port of embarkation for tens of thousands of emigrants who left for America, or merely departed for the season to be tatie-hokers picking crops in the fields of lowland Scotland.

The city of Derry has a warm intimacy partly born of its centre being contained within the solid walls, giving it a medieval feel, and partly because its people have developed a resilient irony and good humour that have stamped themselves on the distinctive local accent that can often be heard on the radio and television stations of both the North and the South. Derry has always faced, and addressed itself, both ways.

The counties of Derry and Tyrone have a kind of homogeneity that makes it natural to consider them together and see their arbitrary border through the Sperrin Mountains as even more of a cartographer's convenience than is usual in the shiring of Ireland. While this might seem a little unfair to Omagh, capital of Tyrone, whose most remarkable feature is the lopsided Catholic Church of the Sacred Heart with its two spires of unequal heights, it is easier to think of the whole area between the western shore of Lough Neagh, the River Foyle and the coast of Lough Foyle

as one tract of land that over the centuries of the Plantation of Ulster was parcelled out in large lots to various Undertakers who created estates and towns on a New World scale. The Guilds of the Haberdashers, Fishmongers and Skinners settled in the valley of the Roe, while Clothworkers, Tailors, Ironmongers, Mercers, Vintners, Salters, Goldsmiths and Grocers parcelled out the valley of the Foyle between them.

It was from these regions that many Protestants emigrated to Canada and America in the 18th and 19th centuries. Since they were not forced into exile by the same needs as compelled their Catholic compatriots to flee famine and oppression, and were often younger sons going off with nest eggs to make their fortunes in the lands of plenty, their energy and connections, not to speak of their religion, made it relatively easier for them to make their way in 'Amerikay'. Thus, long before John F. Kennedy, the first American president of Catholic Irish descent, there were many presidents of Ulster Protestant lineage, such as John Adams, James Monroe, Andrew Jackson, Ulysses S. Grant, Grover Cleveland and Woodrow Wilson.

The contribution of these people to the development of America is documented at the Ulster American Folk Park near Omagh, where the ancestral home of the Mellon family of industrialists has been reconstructed, along with a replica of the two-storey Pennsylvania log farmstead in which they lived when they landed in the New World. The virtues celebrated here are thrift, hard work, self-reliance and resourcefulness, such as the Mellons would have learned and practised in this hard country around the Strule river for many generations. Just as the furniture straightened and the work toughened their bodies, the Bible and pious tracts would have stiffened their minds with resolve. It was this sterling stuff of which they were made that enabled them to amass one of the great American fortunes by making Pittsburgh the steel capital of the United States.

Strabane is another place with strong connections to the New World. John Dunlap,

THE GLENS OF ANTRIM AND THE ANTRIM COAST ROAD

The Glens of Antrim are a rough and isolated country whose only egress, until the Antrim Coast Road was built in the mid 19th century, was seawards to Scotland or landwards over the high passes to the interior. Irish was still commonly spoken here until early in this century, and in the 40s and 50s folklorists like Estyn Evans found many traditions still extant here which had died off in other parts of the island.

The nine glens are worth naming, as they trip off the tongue, though it is always a mite problematic to know if you have seen them all on any one visit, or if there were not some cleft you mistook for one of the less dramatic ones that was not a true glen but only a hanging valley, for they are not all equally imposing. Some are mere declivities with small streams wearing their tireless way through the basalt of the Antrim plateau, while others are wide, steep swathes that gush water from the wounds left by the blunted sword ruthless Nature used to hew them out. Glentaisie, named after the Princess Taisie, and Glenshesk, the glen of the sedges, run down to

Ballycastle. Glendun, the brown glen (for its abundance of heather and gorse), meets the sea at Cushendun, with Glencorp, the glen of the slaughter from some forgotten battle, running into it higher up. Glenann, the steep-sided glen, and Glenballyeamon, the glen of the town of Eamon, meet at Cushendall. Glenariff, the ploughman's glen, debouches in the sandstone of Red Bay with its strange arches and deep caves. Glencloy, the glen of the hedges, gathers Carnlough Bay at its foot, and Glenarm, the glen of the army, marches into the sea with all the brave determination of the Light Brigade.

From the Antrim Coast Road heading north from Larne, the headlands of the Glens contain a sea which sometimes seems a brimming cauldron whose rims are the edge of the Antrim Plateau and the coast of Scotland. This is the nearest the island of Ireland gets to its neighbour and, as the coast road winds round the blunt muzzles of the headlands, Scotland and Rathlin Island come and go like mirages on the near horizon.

Glenariff, the ploughman's glen, County Antrim.

The villages at the feet of the Glens have just the right amount of commerce for the glen-dwellers from higher up who might come in of a market day: one branch of one bank, a small post office that might also sell a few groceries or bits of stationery, a couple of pubs, and some hopeful concession to the summer trade in the form of a bucket and spade emporium or a simple craft shop. Tourism here is very basic, lacking the sophistication of the Ring of Kerry or the Dingle Peninsula, and even in July and August visitors are few and far between. It is, though, all the more charming for the lack of congestion. Much of the time you have the place to yourself and the few people you do share it with are likely to be either locals or visitors from the rest of Northern Ireland.

Glenarm is a bright and cheery village connected by a drawbridge to the portcullised gate of the O'Donnell castle whose Jacobean tudorings can only be glimpsed from the road through the forest park that now takes up much of what would have been its estate. As everywhere on the north coast of Ireland, the O'Donnells have been a major influence on the place's development, dictating the neat Scottish look of the village and setting up the limestone-crushing industry that has covered the whole area with a fine white patina of its dust. From time immemorial this area has been inventive and industrious, as the Harvard Archaeological Expedition of 1934 discovered when they unearthed a large cache of flint instruments that were probably traded from here all over northern Celtdom.

The same O'Donnells – in the much more re-spectable and presumably more peaceable person of the Marchioness of Londonderry – built the Londonderry Arms Hotel in Carnlough as a coaching station and developed another lime-stone quarry with its own single-gauge railway to a toytown harbour that now shelters only pleasure craft, for maritime trading and even serious commercial fishing have almost died out along this coast. St Mac Nissi's College, also called Garron Tower, was another one-time home of the same Marchioness of Londonderry, that was no sooner built in the latest Scots baronial style than she abandoned it to live elsewhere. The John Hewitt Summer School, dedicated to the memory of the founding father of the movement in northern poetry which has flourished in the last twenty or thirty years, is held here every July. It affords its devotees a chance to see and hear the best contemporary poets read their work, to listen to inspiring talk, to meet and mingle among themselves, and to get to know better through field trips and excursions this fascinating part of the country to which John Hewitt (1907–8) was dedicated all his life.

John Hewitt is buried beside Ossian's Grave, a court cairn which dates from at least 3000 BC, near Cushendall, the capital of the glens. This highland town converges on itself in a rush from four directions around the eccentric Garrison Tower that only local pride manages to keep upright. Its worn and pitted red sandstone looks like the next good shower of rain will wash it all to powder. Its funny little protuberances, embrasures, holes for pouring down boiling oil and all, make it seem older than its two hundred years.

printer of the American Declaration of Independence and the publisher of America's first newspaper, *The Pennsylvania Packet*, was born in Meeting House Street in 1746. He is said to have served his apprenticeship in Gray's Printers, whose Georgian façade still survives on the main street of the present town. The printing works are preserved by the National Trust for their collection of old presses, including one with a heraldic American bald eagle perched imperiously on its cross rod. Fonts and casts of both wooden and lead letters lie in cases and on benches as if the printers were just about to strongarm the machines into action again, just as in days gone by when Strabane's printing industry kept ten different presses and two newspapers going.

Over the centuries many attempts have been made to give prosperity and life to these towns and this countryside. The linen industry once thrived here along the brimming rivers that brought water down from the Sperrins to drive the machinery of the factories in places like Sion Mills, a model village created by the English architect William Unsworth, designer of the Shakespeare Memorial Theatre at Stratford-upon-Avon. Supported by the brothers Herdman, founders of the mill, he was able to give full rein to his mock-Tudor fantasies by creating a little England of half-timbered houses clustered around the Romanesque Church of the Good Shepherd. Any one element of this whimsical confection would be astonishing in its own right but the ensemble of gatehouse, mansion house, factory, church and workers' houses is redolent of a benevolent, all-embracing paternalism of another age. The fact that the new linen factory in the town is one of the most modern and efficient in Europe gives hope that the old buildings in need of restoration might one day benefit from its prosperity. For all that there are occasional rumours of gold finds in the Sperrins, from which the lustre is usually taken when it is learned that as much as a ton of ore would have to be mined and chemically processed to yield half an ounce of the true metal, the area husbands a steady and respectable livelihood from the trade that clusters around Draperstown, Stewartstown, Cookstown, Fivemiletown and other villages set up by the City of London livery companies. Many of the great estates of Plantation Ulster remain intact: the Brookes at Brookeborough, the Stronges at Tynan Abbey, the Alexanders at Caledon, all preserving their houses and their lands with the tenacity of the military castes from which they derive.

There is another, more ancient history here that you have to go off into the forest to find or scramble up brackeny hills to stumble across in the mist. The Clogher Valley, comprising the towns of Augher, Clogher and Fivemiletown, and sprawling on into the valley of the Blackwater proper that takes in Benburb and Moy, is an antiquarian's happy hunting ground. The Clogher Historical Society has for decades been burrowing into burial chambers, dolmens, attics, presbyteries and graveyards, anywhere in which another few names or facts or artefacts might be unearthed, and *The Clogher Record*, their journal, is a paragon of this kind of local historical scholarship.

The Kings of Oriel once reigned from the fort that stands just behind the cathedral of St Macartan in Clogher, giving their royal title to streets, shops, parks and football clubs all over this diocese, which takes in parts of Monaghan too. From the same hilltop you can see Brackenridge's Folly, a mausoleum built by a local squire who wished that the gentry who ignored him in life might be reminded of him in death as they went to their services of a Sunday. At Augher you can have tea and buy keepsakes of Ulster linen in the old train station of the Clogher Valley railway that has not run here for fifty years, though now every last scrap of memorabilia associated with it is treasured.

If the Sperrin Mountains fall just short of being another of the Irish Kingdoms, dominating the landscape but not overwhelming it, they still have their own integrity. From their modest heights, looking out to the Blue Stacks and the Derryveagh Mountains in Donegal to the west and across Lough Neagh to the Mournes in the east, you can feel yourself at the heart of a very old Ulster, whose stone circles and passage graves hold the bones and the secrets of the same people who left their marks around the Cooleys and Slieve Gullion and at Emain Macha and the Cave Hill. It could perhaps be said that Ulster is all that can be seen in a 360-degree gaze on a good day from the summit of Sawel Mountain in the Sperrins, with all the irregularity and haziness that entails.

This great sweep would also take in the volcanic cone of Slemish mountain in County Antrim, east of the Bann, where St Patrick, after being captured as a boy and made a slave in an Irish raid on the coast of Wales, is supposed to have tended sheep and goats for a local chieftain called Miluic. He preached at Saul in County Down. He prayed at Station Island on Lough Derg in County Donegal and thus founded Ireland's most popular, and perhaps most penitential, pilgrimage. Thousands of the faithful still follow in his steps every year, fasting on black tea and dry toast as they walk barefoot round the Stations of the Cross, pray at St Patrick's stony bed and perform other devotions over three hard days and nights of very little sleep.

The Scottish-seeming towns of North Antrim, many of whose public buildings are hewn from the pitch-dark local granite, have a sombre, somewhat forbidding air. Ballymena was created by William Adair, a Scottish planter, as a market town in the middle of the rich Antrim plains. A number of important industries have grown up around the town and many fairs and agricultural shows take place here. It is hyperbolically called 'the city of the seven towers' even though only four of these remain. One of them, Adair Castle, was demolished to make way for the Seven Towers Leisure Centre.

The O'Neills are the dominant landed family in the region, though their estates are much diminished from the time when they ruled almost all of Ulster as descendants of the High Kings of Tara. Shane's Castle near Antrim is still the family seat, from which Terence O'Neill emerged to be one of the last Prime Ministers of the old Stormont government from 1963 to 1969. The more colourful and warlike Mc Donnell clan of the Glens of Antrim were the great rivals of the O'Neills. The scraps and standoffs between these two families in the 15th and 16th centuries kept the Glens in a state of Sicilian agitation and rumour. Then and since these valleys have always been a world of their own, likely to be called a kingdom indeed if the fact that there are nine had not given them individuality and independence enough.

Coming out of the enclosure of the Glens to travel to Ballycastle is like leaving a close embrace in a warm, intimate room well stocked with family mementos to face a cruel world where Torr Head and Fair Head take the full brunt of the fierce gales from Scotland and the Mull of Kintyre, with little shelter anywhere along their steep descent to the Irish Sea. Murlough Bay seems to slip and erode even as you look at it, especially on a day of wind, so that the sheep fences at its edge have to be hauled further back from the

brink every year. The Ballymena patriot, Roger Casement (1864–1916), hanged as a traitor by the British, is commemorated here with a stone cross looking out across the same treacherous sea that did not bring the German help he hoped and schemed for in the Easter Rising of 1916.

Built as it is at the foot of Glentaisie, the most northerly of the Glens, Ballycastle was as constricted a settlement as its sister towns in the other Glens until, in the 18th century, the local landlord, Hugh Boyd, remade it as a substantial town of fine churches, houses and memorials gathered round an ample diamond.

The Sir Randall Mc Donnell who built the first castle here on the site where Holy Trinity Church now stands, was granted a charter in 1606 permitting him to hold six fairs in the town. These have now become the one and only Auld Lammas Fair whose fame was revived by the song written in its praise by John Macauley just as it would have been dying out like so many of the other markets and fairs of Ireland. Nowadays relatively few cattle, sheep and horses are bartered at the Fair, but there is no shortage of dulsk, an edible seaweed, yellow man, a jaw-breaking form of toffee, and Bushmills whiskey to wash them down.

For those who are not prey to vertigo – nor too burdened with common sense – the swaying challenge of the Carrick-a-Rede rope bridge near Ballintoy is hard to resist. This spider's web of rope and planks is thrown across the gulf from the mainland to Carrick-a-Rede island every spring by commercial salmon fishermen. These men and their ancestors have been taking their tithe of sea-fed fish for hundreds of years with nets staked to the cliffs.

There is a clannish closeness in the Glens of Antrim, a sense that something ancient has clung on here. The town of Bushmills, spread prosperously around its famous distillery, has maintained a whiskey-making tradition from 1608. As you sit over a dram (as you almost want to call it) in one of the town's neatly scrubbed public houses where alcoholic pleasure comes in sips and nips rather than long slaking swallows, you and the inebriating potion that sits in vats of

Carrigfergus Castle,
County Antrim.

The Auld Lammas
Fair, Ballycastle,
County Antrim.

The basalt grandeur of
the Giant's Causeway,
County Antrim.

thousands of litres just up the road are mellowing together in the same damp air that blows across the Highlands and the Islands of Scotland.

These winds have recently brought golden eagles and buzzards, from their strongholds in the Scottish Highlands, to colonise the cliffs and uplands of the north of Ireland after an absence of more than a hundred years. Ornithologists have been much heartened by seeing descendants of these birds prospecting for territories as far south as Monaghan and Leitrim.

This Scottish connection is most spectacularly apparent in the Giant's Causeway, the mythic basalt road that plunges under the sea on the north coast near Bushmills and re-emerges on the Scottish island of Staffa. This eighth wonder of the world has been much eulogised, painted and photographed, and yet still manages – for all that it is the most visited tourist attraction in Northern Ireland – to preserve an air of mystery. The endearing anthropomorphic explanation, that the regular geometric columns were laid down as stepping stones by the giant Finn MacCool as he hurried to Scotland in pursuit of a foe, continues to delight the children who come there in busloads on organised trips. You can see their attention waning as the teacher then gets on to the hard stuff about volcanoes and cooling lava and flues and pipes and all the geological fact that is described in the well-laid-out interpretative centre at the start of the trail.

Even though access to the Giant's Causeway is carefully monitored by the National Trust, which now owns what is one of Ireland's two World Heritage Sites, you somehow miss the busking importunacy of the old guides and conmen who ran this stretch of the coast as a private racket for many years and gave names like the Wishing Chair, the Honeycomb, the Giant's Loom, the Giant's Organ, the King and his Nobles, to the most prominent of the rock formations.

The *Girona*, a galley of the Spanish Armada which foundered here in October 1588 with 1300 men on board, was not the first nor the last vessel to come to grief off this coast, for the North Channel that runs between Antrim and Argyll constrains all the traffic heading north from the Irish Sea between its Scylla and Charybdis. The winds of history have forced many adventurers through this bottleneck and shipwrecked some of them on its shores. After his defeat by the English at Perth in 1306 Robert Bruce holed up in a cave on Rathlin Island. From watching a spider patiently swinging backwards and forwards to find purchase for its web, he himself mustered the resolve to go back and fight again, this time victoriously at the Battle of Bannockburn.

John de Courcy arrived on this coast in 1157 and secured the first Norman bastion on a basalt promontory at Carrickfergus. In 1689 the castle he built was garrisoned by King William of Orange. A Williamite trail now follows the first fateful footsteps of this Dutch king in Ireland, and from his landing place, from which nowadays you can watch the Larne Stranraer ferries that ply the three-hour crossing to Scotland a few times a day, you can let your imagination follow his further travels, to Derry, Aughrim, Limerick and the Boyne, where he created a tortured legacy that haunts Ulster and Ireland to this day.

MUSTS IN ULSTER

* The Twelfth of July.
* Dunree Fort & Museum in Donegal.
* Derry's Walls.
* An Ulster fry for breakfast; a heart attack on a plate.
* A Sunday sermon in the old style.
* A drink of water from the Spelga Dam in the Mournes.
* Roscoff's Restaurant, Donegall Pass, Belfast.
* Radio Ulster.
* A book of poems by Seamus Heaney.
* The pilgrimage to Lough Derg.
* A visit to Rathlin Island.
* A session of traditional music, accompanied maybe by set dancing.
* The Landbooks by the Appletree Press on everything from birds to stone walls.
* Crossing the border.
* The model plane enthusiasts at Nutts Corner, Crumlin, on a Sunday.
* Gable ends.
* Mussenden Temple on the coast near Coleraine.
* Belfast Castle and Cave Hill.
* The Orange Museum in Loughgall, Co. Armagh, where the order was founded in 1795.
* Peatlands Park on the shores of Lough Neagh.
* Castlewood House near Strangford.
* Marble Arch Caves.
* Caledon Village.
* The train to Derry.
* A sunset on Bloody Foreland.
* The Pig House Museum, County Cavan.
* The Butlersbridge Inn and Museum, County Cavan.

6 The Erne and the Shannon

Colm Tóibín with Bernard Loughlin

COUNTIES

FERMANAGH

LEITRIM

ROSCOMMON

LONGFORD

WESTMEATH

OFFALY

CLARE

LIMERICK

Ireland is a very watery place. Of the hundreds of millions of gallons of rain that fall on the island every year, much of it ends up in the Shannon and Erne systems. The lakes and bogs and callows these two great rivers form stretch from Donegal and Fermanagh in the north to Kerry and Clare in the far south, making a natural frontier between the east and the west of the island that almost divides it in two.

With Ireland further divided by a man-made border between North and South that runs along the watershed of the Erne and the Shannon, around these hundreds of square miles of deep channels, backwaters and shallow bays human histories merge and flow into one another like the myriad tributaries that swell the mother rivers.

These waterways were the first roads into the interior of the island that man ever explored. Those who left the most enduring memorials to their passage were the monks of the early Irish Church who would have quested for sites in skin-covered boats not unlike the curraghs that can still be seen along the west coast. Over a thousand years ago these ascetic men built churches and living places on many of the islands. These tiny-seeming jewels of the most robust Irish Romanesque were the earliest outposts of the new religious order that would eventually spread to the whole of Ireland and change its moral and social character out of all recognition.

The accepted piety is that these hermits and holy men sought out the peace of the islands in order to pray. Another school of thought, given respectability in the 1950s by the great Welsh geographer Estyn Evans (1905–89) in his book *The Personality of Ireland*, would have it that it was to escape the suspicion and resentment of the Druids who still dominated the civic life of those distant times. As you wade through the umbellifers and long wet grass that have overtaken some

of these sites, you try to imagine how rude and simple must have been the lives of these pioneers, and still do not grasp its breathtaking austerity. Following the earliest and harshest of monastic rules, long before Benedict or Francis or Dominic ever codified them, they would have harvested enough from small plots of gardens, supplemented by fish or game from the lake and the land around, to afford a frugal and basic diet.

The redoubts of these first Irish followers of the One True God have been in slow decay ever since. More than a thousand years of Atlantic weather and the searching fingers of the native vegetation have reduced some of them to little more than moss-covered piles of rubble.

Apart from the monasteries on Devenish Island and at Clonmacnois, all the others are tiny in comparison to the abbeys that were built a few centuries later on more favoured sites inland. Only a handful of men would have lived on any of the smaller islands at any time, their days measured in matins, lauds and vespers, and by the flow of the river or the moods of the lakes. These holy brotherhoods were not to enjoy their peace for long.

At the turn of the first millennium Norsemen keelhauled their boats over the shallow stretches at the estuary ends of both rivers and sailed – unhindered, it seems – over the expanses of Lough Derg and Lough Ree in the south and Upper and Lower Lough Erne in the north, for the natives had no military or naval organisation with which to resist them. The Vikings' ruthless depredations – as many as eight separate raids on Clonmacnois between 832 and 1163, according to the annals – forced the building of the round towers that are still points of repair in this watery wilderness.

After the Vikings came the Normans – though overland this time by horse on roads that were just beginning to grow from the

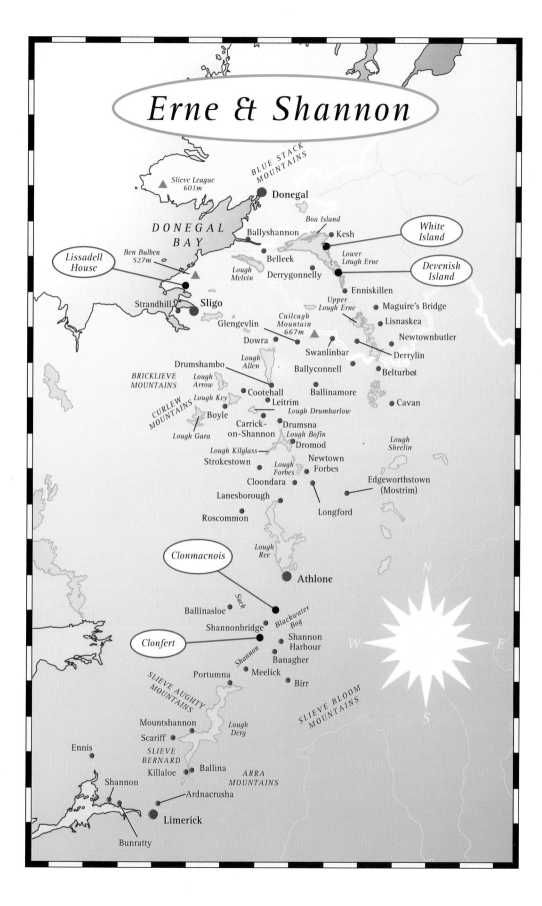

Erne & Shannon

Slieve League 601m

BLUE STACK MOUNTAINS

Donegal

DONEGAL BAY

Boa Island

Ballyshannon

Kesh

White Island

Lissadell House

Ben Bulben 527m

Belleek

Lower Lough Erne

Devenish Island

Derrygonnelly

Lough Melvin

Enniskillen

Strandhill

Sligo

Upper Lough Erne

Maguire's Bridge

Glengevlin

Cuilcagh Mountain 667m

Lisnaskea

Dowra

Newtownbutler

Swanlinbar

Derrylin

Drumshambo

Lough Allen

Ballyconnell

Belturbet

BRICKLIEVE MOUNTAINS

Lough Arrow

Ballinamore

Lough Key

Cootehall

Ballinamore

CURLEW MOUNTAINS

Leitrim

Cavan

Boyle

Lough Drumharlow

Lough Gara

Carrick-on-Shannon

Drumsna

Lough Bofin

Lough Sheelin

Dromod

Lough Kilglass

Newtown Forbes

Strokestown

Lough Forbes

Edgeworthstown (Mostrim)

Cloondara

Lanesborough

Longford

Roscommon

Lough Ree

Clonmacnois

Athlone

Suck

Ballinasloe

Blackwater Bog

Shannonbridge

Shannon Harbour

Clonfert

Shannon

Banagher

Portumna

Meelick

Birr

SLIEVE AUGHTY MOUNTAINS

SLIEVE BLOOM MOUNTAINS

Mountshannon

Lough Derg

Scariff

SLIEVE BERNARD

Ennis

Killaloe

Ballina

ARRA MOUNTAINS

Shannon

Ardnacrusha

Limerick

Bunratty

N E W S

tracks tramped by many generations of human feet and the hooves of animals – and then all the other waves of Cromwellians and Jacobites and Orangists. From the fortified town of Enniskillen to the bastion at Athlone and King John's Castle commanding the rapids at Limerick, these invaders set about securing the river crossings. Even now there are fewer than thirty bridges along the more than three hundred miles of the two rivers. They have always been of crucial importance to any plan of conquest.

A century and a half ago the Erne and the Shannon systems were further tamed and controlled by the monumental works that made the rivers navigable from end to end and connected them to one another and to the major towns of the coast. There is a strong sense of the British Empire during the reign of Queen Victoria in these public works undertaken by the Board for Congested Districts, that employed over 20 000 people at the peak of their construction. The new breed of civil engineers worked out elaborate and ingenious hydraulic schemes to make these waterways accessible for vessels of up to 120 feet long. Their intention was to open up the interior of Ireland to trade, as in the other colonies overseas. The relics of this

Sunset over Lough Erne, County Fermanagh.

mercantile optimism are the magnificent quays with their bollards and iron rings, big enough to tie up ocean liners, that stand by every bridge, often overlooked by derelict warehouses into which no cargoes have been discharged for many years. First the railways dispersed many of these goods faster and cheaper, and then road transport took the rest.

While the Grand Canal saw thousands of boats pass through its locks over its century of operation, the later canals were redundant almost as soon as they opened. The Guinness Company, the last to move its product by water – which some claim made for a better pint of stout – sold off the last of its commercial fleet in the 1960s. It is only the development of pleasure cruising in the last twenty years that has made it worthwhile to keep the navigation open and maintain the buoys, markers, locks and bridges which make it possible. This timely revival has been zealously promoted by the Inland Waterways Association of Ireland that has been campaigning for many years for the preservation of this inheritance.

For all that their navigations were improved around the same time, the Erne and the Shannon remain quite different in character. Around the settled shores of Lower Lough Erne old houses stand in substantial grounds, often with tennis courts or their own few holes of golf, a jetty and a boathouse maybe by the lake, as in Germany or Scandinavia. Yet, beyond its seeming peacefulness, this is a fraught and mythic landscape. This is the Kingdom of Breffni, that was fought over by the O'Rourkes and the O'Donnells long before the Protestant/ Catholic schism was ever invented.

The Lower Lough is very wide and open. On some days during the summer heat hazes create a timelessness out of its immensity of still, flat, oily water; a conflation of lake and sky out of which the Magho cliffs on the western shore loom like a mountain range in another country entirely. On other days, that are scoured clear by the wind from the north or the east, it is possible to see right out across Lower Lough Erne to Donegal Bay, where it embraces the Atlantic with the arms of the Bluestack Mountains and Slieve League to the north and Ben Bulben to the south. For all the intimacy of its back roads and boggy reaches, Fermanagh always remains somehow spiritually open to the sea, even though it is one of the few Irish counties without a coastline.

The Magho cliffs on the southern shore are part of a series of limestone outcrops running west from Benaughlin through Lough Macnean to Lough Navar and the rough countryside around it. Swallow holes and caves honeycomb this whole area, most notably at the Marble Arch Caves that mine dozens of square miles between Derrygonnelly and Tully Castle. First explored in 1895 by the Frenchman Edouard Martel, using only primitive potholing equipment and a collapsible canvas canoe, these caves are now open to even the least adventurous public. The guided tour includes a trip by boat over a sepulchral underground lake and a walk across a Moses path that seems to be cut through the very water itself.

The flora of these free-draining chalk uplands is nearly as diverse as that of the Burren in County Clare. Many of the same Lusitanian species are found here, including wintergreen, orchids, gentian and a rare form of Welsh poppy, *Meconopsis cambriensis*. So steep are the slopes of this side of the lake that there are no towns or villages, only scattered farms that cling close to the shore amid vestigial stands of native woodland. Predators and scavengers – hen harriers, peregrine falcons, ravens and choughs – quarter the uplands among the scrub hazel and willow, their cries resonant in the emptiness.

The Erne flows into the sea at Ballyshannon along a course that was much dredged and banked in the 1950s to make one of Ireland's early hydro-electric schemes. Before this canalisation the bridge at Ballyshannon had ten arches to span its last unruly rush to meet the sea. The modern bridge has one span of reinforced concrete for a river reduced to half its old width. However, wild salmon still swim under it on their return from their long migrations, to clamber up through the fish weirs of the

dam on their way towards their spawning grounds in the streams that feed the Erne out of the Sperrins.

Ballyshannon has grown up on the ancient border between the Kingdom of Breffni and the Earldom of Tyrconnell. After its incorporation in 1611 it became a British garrison town. The 18th-century barracks have long since been abandoned to the jackdaws, but it is still awesome to behold in its mantle of green ivy looming imperiously over the river crossing.

The town itself is grandly planned around a triangle of streets of fine Georgian houses and public buildings. The poet William Allingham (1824–89) is commemorated by a bust and plaque in the Scots baronial edifice that was once his home and now belongs to the Allied Irish Bank. The bridge is also named after him.

For pleasure craft the Erne is navigable only as far west as Belleek, a seemly village renowned for the delicate porcelain pottery made in the factory at its west end. This industry was founded in 1857 by a local landlord, John Caldwell Bloomfield. Having studied the manufacture of fine china in places like Dresden and Meissen, Broomfield recognised the same sparkling finish – from the local deposits of felspar and kaolin (the raw material of bone china) – on the mud walls of his estate cottages, and brought in foreign craftsmen to teach local people their skills. For many years, among certain classes, a piece of Belleek was an obligatory part of a young Irish bride's trousseau, to be kept as a treasure in the parlour china cabinet as the beginnings of a collection that was added to on subsequent special occasions. The factory also made complete dinner services for grander houses and commemorative pieces of various kinds for national events, such as the greyhound-and-round-tower figurine that became their trademark.

Local mythology would have it that the owners of the factory once had the border specially redrawn to leave the factory on the South side when that was more fiscally convenient, but for many years now it has been firmly in the North, while the rest of the village continues to enjoy its ambiguous and not unprofitable status as not quite the one or the other.

Eastwards of Belleek are the estate and ruins of the 17th-century Castle Caldwell, ancestral home of the founder of the pottery. The grounds of the castle are one of the oldest state forests in Ireland. Their mature oak and beech woodlands shelter a rich variety of wildlife; there is a bird-watcher's hide by the lake shore from which it is sometimes possible to see common scoters, a marine duck for most of the year, whose main Irish breeding grounds are on the lough in the summer.

At the gates of the demesne stands a monument in the shape of a stone fiddle, which commemorates a local fiddler called Denis Mc Cabe who, in the 1760s, was summoned to play on a pleasure barge for the Caldwells, drank too much wine, fell overboard and was drowned. The inscription on the fiddle says: 'On firm land only exercise your skill/That you may play and safely drink your fill.' In later times the Caldwell family, ever enterprising, were the first to introduce steam transport on the lakes.

Boa Island, while a true island in every other sense, is joined to the mainland by a bridge on either side. The absence of a sign telling the visitor where the famous Boa Island figure is to be found is a deliberate policy: you have to know to look for Caldragh Cemetery, a weed-grown, grave-collapsed burial place where this Janus creature squats beside a smaller figure brought here from nearby Lusty More Island. It is even harder to find the cemetery from the water, where a boat has to grope its way in to a tiny landing place, but the spine-chilling thrill of discovering this mysterious figure and its diminutive doppelgänger is all the greater for the effort required to find them. The carvings are powerful in their simplicity yet astonishing in their modernity. The pagan sculptor made an image of Man as God, or God as Man, for which no precedents existed in the Ireland of two thousand or more years ago. The nomadic migrations that brought this artist's people here had carried only memory with them, not stone. Yet this graven image prefigures in the fullest sense the rational, refined, Romanised imagery that crowds the later high crosses, and shows that a style that might be called 'Lough Erne' already existed here. This singular sculpture stands at a threshold of human invention, looking far into the dark past and somewhat more blindly into the darker future. Knowing that Bronze Age weapons and implements found on the island are now in the Ashmolean Museum in Oxford gives an added poignancy to the Boa Island figure's integrity and self-absorption, standing still where it was made to stand, the original Ulster Not-An-Inch.

While most of the monastic sites of Lough Erne are on the islands – for the obvious protection they afforded from the monks' enemies – there are also a few lakeshore sites which are important. In the graveyard of the Yellow Church at Killadeas, a few miles west of Castle Archdale, is the Bishop's Stone dating from the seventh or eighth century. For all its cryptic crudity this is unmistakably a religious sculpture, albeit with stylistic links to the Boa Island figure. One side simply shows a moonface with an open mouth, that might be a brother of the Lusty More Island man, while on the other side a cleric walks along, head down, intent on the Lord's business, armed with bell and crozier to ring and to smite. Episcopus Killadensis stands just on this side of the same threshold where pagan and Christian image-making meet.

The best stone carvings in the whole Lough Erne area are on White Island in the bay of Castle Archdale. The low door of the ruined church makes you duck in reverence as you pass under its beautiful Hiberno-Romanesque carvings, though this may be more because the floor level has risen with the accumulated debris of the years than that the people of that epoch were as squat as the door's height might suggest.

Inside the ruin, under a stone shelter built out from the north wall, are eight figures that were found on the island at different times, dating from the ninth, tenth and eleventh centuries. Collected here in a jumbled, not at all hierarchical pantheon, cemented to a stone wall, they both disturb and amuse.

Mary Rogers in her book *Prospect of Erne* risks identifying some of the characters in this dumb show of uneasiness as St Patrick, possibly St Columba, King Leary and his son Enna, and another as an abbess. Whatever their names, they look like passengers stuck together willy-nilly in the compartment of a train bound for eternity. The two largest figures embody the stern pomp of a Church imposing its will. Their bells and croziers still surge from the stone with great authority. Another of them, the last in the row, looks positively unhappy, as if he were about to call the guard and have the others removed. He is perhaps outraged by the *sheelagh-na-gig* lewdly displaying her pudenda at the other end of the compartment. The fixed grin on her face and her bulging, chortling cheeks are glee-full of lust, like a bawdy contemporary commentary on the new profession of celibacy. There is speculation that she may have come from an earlier pagan edifice and been put here to frighten temptation away, on the principle of the gargoyles on medieval cathedrals spewing all the evil outwards.

As you navigate back out across the lough again, your head ringing with the ceremony and ritual that once ruled here, the crude but majestic 14-feet-high cross that rears above the ruins of the sixth-century monastery on Inishmacsaint suddenly appears out of the densely wooded landscape like a piece of Cubist sculpture. The design is rough and plain, as though the makers had tired of Celtic carvings and had decided simply to hew the mystery of the cross in its most minimal abstraction. Legend has it that it rotates three times on Easter Sunday morning, the old pagan feast having not yet been completely subdued by Christianity.

In the summer months a ferry goes regularly from the Round O Jetty in Enniskillen to Devenish Island, the monastic capital in its day of all of southwest Ulster. Within the strong fence that surrounds the site proper, the grass has been cut to a close sward around the shored and mortared lower walls of the monastery founded by St Molaise in the sixth century. Outside this precinct, sheep and cows graze the rougher pasture. From the top of the soaring round tower, 85 feet above the ground, you see the ground plan of the monks' habitations and praying places, just as they are laid out in the diagrams of the excellent museum nearby. This is about the size of a largish cottage, and its thatched roof is a reminder that at one

The round tower, Devenish Island, County Fermanagh.

time all of these buildings would have been roofed with straw, as would most buildings of the epoch. This partly explains their rapid disintegration once the roof has rotted.

After all the encounters with monastic settlements and ancient statues on remote islands, coming to Enniskillen is a refreshing earthly pleasure. Here you can get good pints in any number of decent pubs, buy fishing tackle in two or three specialist shops, purchase books from Hall's, one of the best bookshops in the Irish provinces north or south, and on a Sunday find English newspapers, fresh bread, Italian food at Franco's Pizzeria, as well as religious services of all denominations in the many churches and chapels of the town.

Even though the town is built on an island between the Upper and Lower loughs, there are no streets actually giving onto the waterfront. Presumably for safety from flooding in the days before the flow of the Erne was controlled as it is now, the main street turns its back on the river and meanders in a long, snaking progress over the backs and through the hollows of the hills that form the island. Narrow alleys that seem like afterthoughts lead down to the river from between the houses that are of two or three storeys on the town side and as many as six or seven on the water side, so great is the difference between the two levels.

The 15th-century castle of the Maguires with its early 17th-century Watergate dramatises the landscaped parkland that runs along the river's shore. The recently enlarged County Museum in the courtyard of the fort explains the strategic importance of the castle in the early days of the Plantation of Ulster. Enniskillen was always a garrison town and

the Regimental Museum of the now disbanded Inniskilling Fusiliers in the same complex recalls those days of glory. The Maguires lost their hold on the town when James l granted it and the lands around to Sir William Cole. The statue on the top of the plinth that dominates the town is of Sir Galbraith Lowry Cole, one of Wellington's generals in the Peninsular War. It is known by the locals as Cole's Pole.

Among the many shops and pubs that have preserved their old façades – including that of the local paper, *The Impartial Reporter* – the outstanding monument to the social virtues is William Blake's, a magnificent public house situated in the dip called The Hollow opposite the Church of Ireland on the main street. With an open fire in one of the snugs, lustrous old woodwork and lamps that once worked on gas, the narrow bar fosters intimacy and badinage between staff and clientele. On market days and weekends the crowded area near the door is a hive of coming and going, greeting and leave-taking. In the rituals of Irish pub-going Blake's is cathedral rather than low church, ministered to by a prebendary of curates and canons who often emboss shamrocks on the foamy heads of the glasses of Guinness.

Once shopping ends at six o'clock, Enniskillen empties of people, so that it can be a shock when you come out of Blake's or one of the other pubs and find yourself the only person in the street. Memories here do not need to be long: on Remembrance Sunday in 1987 an IRA bomb exploded at the cenotaph in Enniskillen just before the wreaths were to be laid. Eleven local people were killed and many others injured. In the painful yet hopeful aftermath of this outrage, the Enniskillen Together movement founded an integrated school that children of all the traditions in the town now attend.

As well as the Portora Royal School that was founded in the 17th century and boasts Oscar Wilde and Samuel Beckett among its distinguished alumni, the hinterland of Enniskillen has nurtured other great houses, legacies of the plantation, three of which are now owned by the National Trust and open to the public.

The 17th-century Watergate on the banks of the River Erne, Enniskillen, County Fermanagh.

Florencecourt was the seat of the same Cole family who became the earls of Enniskillen. It is pre-Palladian in style, more square and gaunt than its neighbour, Castle Coole, but with a more dramatic setting against Benaughlin and the Cuilcagh Mountains. In the brief *pax britannica* of the 18th century the planters brought in architects and craftsmen to build mansions that befitted their newly landed state. Gardeners laid out the grounds with French and Italian formality in allées and vistas around big, broad, confident axes. Now that the families which once owned these palaces have mostly died out or gone to live elsewhere, it is a constant struggle to keep the landscaped grounds – with their pergolas and ha-has and other embellishments – from succumbing to the wildness of the Irish climate.

In the park of Florencecourt stands the famous Florencecourt yew, a unique fastigiate or upright form of *Taxus baccata* from which have been propagated the thousands of sombre sentinels that stand in churchyards the length and breadth of the island. With her tattered branches from which so many cuttings have been taken, this long-suffering tree could be yet another candidate for the title of Mother Ireland.

Castle Coole was designed by James Wyatt in the late 18th century as a place where, as he said himself, one could 'step from a hayfield into a mansion'. The bulky, wide-winged house sits in a congested parkland without much of a view of anything. Recently restored in a complex technical operation that involved the dismantling of the massive Ionic portico and putting it back together stone by stone with new stainless steel clamps to replace the iron ones that had

begun to rust and shatter the stone, it has been beautifully refurbished within as well.

The third great house in the vicinity, and the only one which is still inhabited by descendants of its original builders, is Crom Castle near Lisnaskea. While the house itself remains private and must be skirted on a long path that leads through woodland along the shores of one of the many inlets of Lough Erne, the turf house, boathouse and other outlying buildings of this estate – in its heyday almost exclusively supplied from the water – give a strong sense of its past importance, which is well documented in the new visitors' centre.

From the heights of the Cuilcagh Mountain you can survey Upper and Lower Lough Macnean, renowned fishing waters that hold the legendary gillaroo trout, and the sprawl of Upper Lough Erne, so completely different from the stretch of water between Enniskillen and the sea. Mary Rogers, in *Prospect of Fermanagh*, describes the difference perfectly: 'There is an indescribable beauty, tinged with sadness, about the upper lake. The water is often very shallow, meandering and sluggish, great houses and cottages alike stand in ruin, but water lilies and tall reeds, plaintive bird-call and silence, make it a remote and eerie otherworld.' Upper Lough Erne, more enfolding and intimate than the Lower Lough, is a maze of shallow inlets and cul-de-sacs of bays that wind among densely wooded islands, on some of which cattle are left to graze for the whole summer. There are said to be 154 islands between the two loughs. In their time they have been retreats for anchorites, bivouacs for soldiers, haunts for poachers and *poitín*-makers, sites for castles, churches and tombs. Nowadays they are picnic places for boaters and studies for scholars.

A pleasure craft on the great expanse of the lower lake has to hug the lee shore in high winds, since the lough is wide open to the west and can be treacherous at times. But the upper lake is more manageable, at times closer to a river than a lake, and it is here you find Fermanagh at its most verdant and romantic. Carry Bridge and Craigavon Bridge are the only crossing points in the dozens of

The 18th-century façade of Castlecoole, County Fermanagh.

square miles of a drowned landscape that stretch from Kinawley and Derrylin in the west to Maguiresbridge and Lisnaskea in the east.

There is no better place to understand this land than the Olde Barn Family Museum near Lisbellaw. A pikestaff brought from lowland Scotland by the Carrothers family to defend their first grant of land in 1769 holds pride of place among a collection of artefacts, deeds, letters and other papers which chronicle the subsequent history of these typical planters, some of whose descendants later emigrated to settle among the large Ulster diaspora in the province of Ontario in Canada. Many of the male Carrothers fought in World War I with the Royal Inniskilling Fusiliers, who are commemorated in Ontario in the name of a fine wine.

The country round about is haunted too by the ghosts of all the tribe of Maguires who once held sway here. Their ancestral burial ground at Aghalurcher Church is guarded by an ancient yew which is said to excrete drops of blood in autumn in memory of the time in 1484 when a Maguire killed a kinsman on the altar, though a rationalist would say that these are merely the tree's fruits, whose purple-red flesh is sweet to suck but whose pips are deadly poisonous.

The islands on Upper Lough Erne are mostly used as pastureland these days, relict rights of the homesteads that once occupied them. There were crannogs here too, artificial islands like those on the estuary of the Tigris in Mesopotamia, that were built to give safe refuge to the first inhabitants. At the site of the one-time monastery on Galloon Island, close to Newtownbutler, are two impressive but badly weathered high crosses which depict scenes from the Old and New Testaments. The same ghoulish, though somehow jocular, 18th-century motifs of skull and crossbones, coffins, bells and sandtimers are to be found on some of the gravestones in this cemetery as one finds in Clones, also founded by St Tighernach in the sixth century – a reminder that long before the present border existed these parts of Fermanagh and Monaghan drained by Lough Erne were not only contiguous but were in

some way continuous with one another in terms of their topography and culture.

The old Erne navigation upstream ended at Belturbet. Somewhere along the way you cross the invisible line between Northern Ireland and the Republic. There is no checkpoint in the water, just an old sign much peppered with duck shot asking anyone with goods to declare to report to a customs post that does not even exist any more.

The Erne and the Shannon, and incidentally the North and the South of Ireland, are now joined through the old Ballinamore Ballyconnell Canal which lay dormant and leaking for years until work began in 1990 to restore the link between Ireland's two great waterways. In its first phase this was the shortest-lived and least successful of all the canals in Ireland, though the one at Cong in County Galway between Lough Corrib and Lough Mask may have a counter-claim here, since it did not even hold water when it was first opened. Be that as it may, the Ballinamore Ballyconnell Canal only collected £18 in tolls in its nine years of operation, which was not much of a return on the £500 000 that had been invested. The recent reconstruction cost more than £30 million but is well worth every penny to make the combined waterway one of the longest and most varied in Europe. During its reconstruction a great effort was made to preserve the ecology of the canal by working from one bank only. The restored towpath makes a pleasant walking route, as indeed do the towpaths of many of the other canals that wind through the depths of the Irish countryside.

While the monks and Vikings and other adventurers of the early days were able to push and pull and roll their boats over the shallower parts of the river, it was not until the 1760s that the entire Shannon became navigable, and not until the reign of Queen Victoria that the monumental locks were put in place. As on Lough Erne, most of the boats on the Shannon are new; there are hardly any of the old-fashioned barges you see on English and French canals. The Shannon, like Lough Erne, remains *terra incognita* for most Irish people, a part of Ireland better known to tourists than it is to the natives. This is particularly true of the county of Leitrim, which is a byword in the rest of the country for a sort of blameless backwardness due to its landscape being super-saturated and more or less hopeless for agriculture. If the county had a plant for an emblem it would have to be the rush, which stands in groves all along the rivers and around the lakes, and appears in clumps in the midst of even the steepest fields, for the heavy clay here is almost impossible to drain. It is said that the land here is sold not by the acre but by the gallon. It is for this reason that Leitrim is the most thinly populated county in Ireland, with one of the highest rates of emigration.

The Ballinamore–Ballyconnell Canal joins the Shannon at Leitrim village, one of the rare Irish towns that carries its county's name but is not its capital. This unassuming little place with its few quiet pubs will probably take whatever bit of prosperity the renewed canal link with the Erne might bring with the same shrug with which it has absorbed every other novelty that has passed its way.

A plaque on the ruins of Leitrim Castle by the beautiful canal bridge recalls the ordeal of O'Sullivan Beare and his followers after the defeat of the Irish forces at Kinsale: 'Here on January 14th 1603 Brian Og O'Rourke welcomed Donal O'Sullivan Beare and his followers after their epic march from Glengariff in fourteen days. Though one thousand started with him only thirty-five then remained, sixteen armed men, eighteen non-combatants and one woman, the wife of the chief's uncle, Dermot O'Sullivan.' A couple of miles upstream is Battlebridge, so called after the skirmishes there during the 1798 Rebellion, when General Humbert's French divisions and their motley Irish followers passed this way to their defeat and slaughter at Ballinamuck. Battlebridge used to be the most northerly navigable point on the river until the re-opening of the old canal to Lough Allen. It is well worth toiling through the few locks of the narrow canal by way of Drumshambo and Acres Lake to get to this inland fjord. Lough Allen is so deep and its sides are so steep it has no islands at all. It is overlooked on one side by Arigna, once the site of one of Ireland's two coal mines, and on the other by Slieve Anierin, the Iron Mountain, from which ore was mined and smelted in the 18th and 19th centuries.

At the point where the Rivers Shannon and the Boyle merge to form the inland estuary of Lough Drumharlow – a shallow sheet of

The village of Ballinamore, County Leitrim.

water that seems to have submerged the land only yesterday – you are again at the meeting of two different worlds. The Anglo-Irish ascendancy was once predominant in this area but is now withered to a last few stalwarts who linger on in the *Götterdämmerung* so affectingly recorded by David Thomson (1914–88) in *Woodbrook*, an account of the years from 1932 to 1942 that he spent as a tutor to Phoebe, daughter of a local landowner, Major Kirkwood. Near Lough Oakport – a little oculus of a lake shrouded by billows of the fine deciduous trees planted by the Kirkwoods – is Cootehall, homeplace of another great Irish writer, John Mc Gahern (1934–), who has become in many ways the chronicler of the class which superseded the Anglo-Irish.

When you arrive in Cootehall by boat it is at first hard to descry any village at all from the bridge until you walk up a bit and discover the little clump of a few houses and Henry's public house opposite the church. Of a Saturday evening the local renegades might gather in the front bar to watch and comment upon the people filing in to mass, before gulping down the last of their drinks and hurrying over themselves to be seen to be doing the decent thing, always a preoccupation in rural Ireland. It is *de rigueur* in Henry's to sign the visitors' book, now in its umpteenth edition, and then to come back years later and laugh at the daft things you all wrote under the influence of the drink and this good-tempered, quietly spoken public house, one of the 'moral' pubs of Ireland.

The Boyle river above Cootehall is narrow and winding, overhung by alder and ash, beech, oak and hawthorn in a dense canopy that throws deceptive shadows on the water,

creating phantom channels and spectral markers that can lure the unwary into dangerous shoals. The two massive stone bridges you meet along the way always come as a shock as they draw you deep into their womblike embraces and then propel you out into a bath of aqueous colour and movement on the other side.

Clarendon Lock, just above Knockvicar Bridge, is not to be rushed either, for here you can see the prodigious hydraulics of the navigation system at its most easily understood. The lock and its weir stand side by side and can be inspected at close range by walking over the gates. Lock-watching is a time-honoured occupation all over the hinterland of the Shannon, where often whole families come out of a Sunday to watch a few boats go through.

After the verdant confinement of the River Boyle, Lough Key seems like an inland sea. On certain days its wooded islands appear to float and shimmer above its surface like so many phantom vessels, with the aged, bearded goats that have been abandoned on them as their eerie figureheads. It is only the ecclesiastical and civil remains that dot these islands and the shore that hold Lough Key firmly fixed in history. In these piles of stone can be seen many of the elements that govern Lough Erne. The monastic churches and dwellings are all in ruins now but still give a sense of the importance of these waterways in the medieval world. There are reminders, too, of the wars between the Gaelic chieftains and the English settlers. Just as the Castle at Enniskillen was built by the Maguires and later fortified by the Planters, Castle Island on Lough Key was once owned by the MacDermotts of Moylurg, and later by the

Cruising at Cootehall, County Roscommon.

The wooded islets of Lough Key, County Roscommon.

King-Harmon family who had a Gothic fantasy erected there to improve the view from their seat at Rockingham House. It was on this island in 1541 that Tadgh MacDermott gave a great feast for the poets of Ireland, which probably inspired W.B. Yeats to imagine a place 'where a mystical order would retire for a while for contemplation'.

As a kind of end point to the monastic expansion that worked its way up along the Shannon and the Boyle rivers, Lough Key has given its name to annals written on Castle Island in the 11th century by the monk chroniclers. In a kind of Domesday Book of the era they recorded the goods and deeds and battles of the MacDermotts and other clans who disputed ownership of the land.

At a later epoch the Rockingham estate, which once bounded the whole southern shore of the lake, was one of the grandest and richest in Ireland in its day. Rockingham House, designed by John Nash (1752–1835), burned to the ground in 1957. In the years after the fire it was, according to Hugh McKnight, 'a gaunt but romantic ruin standing high above the lake in an exquisite park'. But the ruin was demolished in the 60s and the extraordinarily ugly, bare concrete Moylurg Tower was erected in its place as a look-out post that remains locked for most of the year because it was found to be dangerous to let people up it on their own and there were never the resources to pay a full-time guardian.

L.T.C. Rolt was invited to have a bath and a meal in the big house when he was making his Shannon journey in 1949. 'The chief splendour of Nash's Rockingham, to my mind,' he wrote, 'was the suite of three rooms, a long drawing room, the circular drawing room and the dining room whose windows look out over the lake. In the circular drawing room which was, as it were, the focal point of the house, there were three pairs of great mahogany doors having curved surfaces to conform with the curve of the wall. I have seldom seen finer examples of the joiner's craft. Such was the spacious and sophisticated splendour of these rooms that to turn my eyes from them and see the wild

beauties of Lough Key beyond the windows instead of the trees of Hyde Park or the squares of Bath gave me quite a shock of surprise.' The house has gone, then, and the only traces of it now are a few outbuildings, including the mandatory ice house that many such big houses used to store their perishables, and the network of tunnels that used to service the mansion in such a way that its denizens never had to see their servants carrying up the provisions from the lake shore. The estate itself preserves many of its best features, such as a bog garden, extensive plantings of rare trees (including some massive redwoods) and a long avenue of limes leading to the main road under the arch of a fanciful Gothic gatehouse. Faery bridges still span the private canal system that was used for bringing turf for the mansion's many open fires but the channels are all silted up. The ruins on Castle Island, Trinity Island and Hog's Island are also worth exploring by rowing boat that can be hired at the little harbour.

The nearest town to Lough Key is Boyle, about three miles away. A veritable ruck of public houses jostles round its square and the ornate stone clock tower which stands oddly off-kilter in one of its corners. The mansion built by Sir Henry King MP in the early 1700s to a design by Sir Edward Lovett Pearce, the great Palladianist, once so dominated the town that the main street was designed as an avenue leading up to it. After a brief period in the 19th century in use as a barracks, the mansion lay neglected for many years, but has recently been restored as a community and cultural centre.

Just outside the present town the ruins of Boyle Abbey stand on a rich, well-watered mead. This abbey was the most important in medieval Connaught. On its remaining walls – all that was left standing after the ravages of the occupying Cromwellian forces in 1659 – you can still trace the various stages of its building from its foundation in 1161 to its consecration in 1218. Among the ruins, that in places have had to be shored up with strong buttresses to stop whole arcades collapsing, there are kitchens, a gatehouse, a cloister, dormitories and a room known as the

Drummans Bridge,
Lough Key Forest
Park, Boyle, County
Roscommon.

calefactorium, the only place in the whole abbey where there was a fire for the monks to warm themselves. The main church was added to and altered between the 12th and 15th centuries and is an interesting example of the transition from the Romanesque to the Gothic style, with rounded and pointed windows standing side by side. Even though it has no roof, the church still exudes great power and mystery, built as it is to the rigorous Cistercian plan then being executed all over the continent of Europe. The whimsical carvings of human figures, beasts and foliage on the capitals of the pillars make it all a mite less solemn.

The Curlew Mountains that overlook Lough Key are an outcrop of old red sandstone that makes the water of the lake brown and peaty. Across the watershed the Bricklieve Mountains are of limestone, which imparts a marvellous clarity to the waters of Lough Arrow, one of the best trout-fishing lakes in Ireland. The megalithic monuments on the slopes of the Bricklieves are part of the extensive ancient remains that are scattered throughout Sligo. A day's browsing through this tumbled necropolis, exclaiming at the extent and complexity it gradually reveals, makes believers in ley-lines and ancestor worshippers of even the most sceptical.

Carrick-on-Shannon is the capital for this part of the Shannon and the principal town in County Leitrim, just as Enniskillen is for Lough Erne and Fermanagh. Its main street, now well supplied with supermarkets and other shops catering to the river trade and selling such delicacies – unthinkable twenty years ago – as Veuve Cliquot champagne and snails in their shells, runs up in a long curve from the Shannon, as it is always referred to by the locals, never as simply 'the river'. The street turns at J.P. Flynn's bar that was closed for many years and only recently opened again, more or less as it had been in the 50s. Beside it is the smallest memorial chapel in Ireland, measuring just 15 feet 9 inches by 11 feet 9½ inches by 29 feet 6 inches, which was built in 1877 to house the coffins of Edward Costello and his wife who are buried under glass on either side of the tiny nave. Near the altar entwined hearts carved in

The 12th-century
ruins of Boyle Abbey,
County Roscommon.

stone attest to their undying love, a most untypically Irish romanticism that is touching to behold.

South from Carrick-on-Shannon you come to see the river's strategic importance, the sense that if you could control the river crossings then you could control the country for miles around. The dual heritage – Gaelic and English – is amply illustrated in the names and histories of places like Jamestown. Originally the site of an ancient earthwork called the Dun, a walled town was founded here by Sir Charles Coote in 1622 to protect the Shannon crossing. The Catholic hierarchy met in the Franciscan Friary in 1650 to decide on a strategy to defend the Catholic Church against the onslaught of the Cromwellians. The village is now sunk in a deep torpor that is only broken by lorries changing down to negotiate the bottom half of a narrow gateway, on the main Dublin road, that is all that remains of the fortifications.

After the rush of the narrows at Drumsna, the Shannon's last surge of youthful friskiness before it settles for its sedate meander to the sea more than a hundred miles away, it spreads into an Everglades of inner lakes in Carnadoe Waters, Grange Lough, Kilglass Lough and the narrow Mountain River which fingers up into the rushy hills of Roscommon. These shallow lakes are refuges for otters, roosting places for cormorants, boltholes for all that is wary and easily startled. Reed buntings, snipe, great crested grebes, dabchicks, redshanks, grasshopper warblers, all kinds of duck and other wildfowl, are here to be found in abundance. To spend the night with the boat tied to the bank in these callows is to be

surrounded by the rushes and gulps of a natural world that is as near to undisturbed as it gets in the very humanised landscape of Ireland.

From the little piers that stand at the end of these intricate waterways it is possible to walk to Strokestown, the nearest major town. Its magisterial main street leads straight to the gates of Strokestown House, built by the Pakenham-Mahon family in the 17th century. Ireland's only Famine Museum has recently been established in converted buildings in its yard. The story of how the house itself had deteriorated almost beyond repair until it was bought by the proprietor of Westward Garages in the town, because he did not want to see this inheritance slip away, is a salutary tale that acts as an anecdotal antidote to all the other tragic ones of similar houses that were lost. There are tours of the house and the museum, as well as the chance to see the longest herbaceous border in Ireland in the old walled garden, where a number of contemporary artistic interventions give a lively and ironic twist to the restoration.

The lands to the west and east of the Shannon around Lough Bofin and Lough Forbes between Dromod and Lanesborough are the least topographically interesting on the whole of the Shannon, but are nonetheless rich in their own midlands history. On the western side, in the plains of Roscommon which for thousands of years have fattened strong-boned kine on their limestone pastures, you can just about make out the overgrown remains of Rathcrogan, seat of the kings of Connaught. It was from here that Queen Maeve marched out with her hosts of warriors to capture the Brown Bull of Cooley in the cattle raid that became the basis of the Irish epic *Táin Bó Cuailgne*.

On the eastern side of the Shannon, in County Longford, are the places associated with Oliver Goldsmith (1728–84), scapegrace son of the rectory at Pallas, who wrote *She Stoops to Conquer* and *The Deserted Village* based on his youthful experiences in these parts before he went off to Dublin, Edinburgh and London. The writer Maria Edgeworth (1767–1849), who wrote *Castle Rackrent* out of indignation at the extortionate rents charged by some of the landlords of her time, was a daughter of the big house at Edgeworthstown (now Mostrim). Her father was an enlightened and benevolent parson, scientist and inventor, who did all he could to foster prosperity among his tenants.

South of the estate of Castle Forbes, that

Carrick-on-Shannon, County Leitrim, home to the smallest memorial chapel in Ireland.

also gives its name to Newtownforbes and Lough Forbes, there is another opportunity to go off the beaten track along the Camlin River to Richmond Harbour – a name which seems to suit this somnolent place better than its old one of Cloondara – where the Royal Canal meets the Shannon. Built between 1799 and 1817 by a company set up by a shoemaker called Inny who had fallen out with the promoters of the Grand Canal further south, the Royal Canal bankrupted many of its shareholders. It was at one time possible to navigate from here through Longford and Mullingar to Dublin but this waterway was finally closed in 1961 when it was no longer possible even to drag a shallow boat over some of the silted stretches. The old warehouses, mills, lockhouses and dry docks of the glory days of inland navigation seem to be awaiting a magic wand to rouse them from their slumbers. At one time the distillery here, now a tanning mill, produced 70 000 gallons of whiskey a year, some of which must have gone to lubricate the tears of the emigrants who landed on the flyboats from Dublin on their way to the ports of the south coast and the hazardous sea voyage to America. Their voices haunt this backwater still.

Lanesborough is the last river crossing before the Shannon opens out into Lough Ree. Even in mildly windy weather this 20-mile-long body of water, with its many treacherous shallows and rocky places, can be as choppy as the open sea. Boaters are advised not to venture onto it at all in any kind of strong wind, so that even in summer if you travel through Lanesborough by road you can see boats tied two or three deep under the bridge at the quay opposite the turf-fired electricity generating station, patiently waiting for the weather to clear. The bestormed mariners can contemplate the constant coming and going of the narrow gauge trains whose wagon loads of milled turf are lifted straight up the side of the incinerator to feed its voracious hunger with over 400 000 tons of peat a year.

Lough Ree, like Upper Lough Erne, is full of small islands. Inchclearaun (also called Quaker Island after a Mr Fairbrother who brought a curse on all the animals of the place through stealing stones from the ruins of the sixth-century monastery founded by St Diarmid) gets its Irish name from Clethra, sister of the famous and fierce Queen Maeve of Connaught. It was here that Maeve was supposed to have been killed, while she was

Remains of an ancient bog road, County Longford.

peaceably bathing, with a slingshot flung by Forbaid, son of the King of Ulster, from the shore a mile away. Like much else that is said about Maeve and her associates, attributable perhaps to the fact that she was originally the Celtic Goddess of Drunkenness, this feat is not verifiable in *The Guinness Book of Records.*

Hare Island, Nun's Island, Inchbofin and Saint's Island all have interesting ecclesiastical remains, some of which are associated with St Ciaran who expended some of his youthful energy proselytising in these parts before he moved south to found Clonmacnois.

Inchmore is the largest island on Lough Ree, where almost 200 people lived at the turn of the century. The Marquess of Westmeath built Inchmore Lodge with a walled garden and a road leading up to it from the shore. Only holidaymakers live there now for a few months of the summer, in old houses that they have rescued from dereliction. This means that no island on the Shannon, from Killaloe to Lough Allen, is inhabited all the year round.

Hare Island is where St Ciaran lived as a hermit. Around him a small monastery grew up that in time became rich enough to attract the marauding Vikings. The largest hoard of Viking gold ever found in western Europe was uncovered here in 1802. The Dillon family, who were very powerful on the Longford shore, built a lodge here and planted the island with a varied collection of trees, plants and shrubs. The buckthorn that was part of this horticultural imposition is the major food plant of the yellow brimstone butterfly small flocks of which, on a calm day, might flicker around your boat if you went close enough to the shore.

The southern part of Lough Ree around Ballykeeran, Coosan and Hudson's Bay is a hearty, yachty sort of place with fine bars and restaurants catering for those who go out on the big lake in ships and return with fierce hungers and thirsts. Like the district around Enniskillen in the north, it seems that every commanding view afforded by the small hills in this otherwise flat country has been occupied by a new house with picture

windows looking out on expanses of open water and marshland.

Athlone itself is one of the many frontier towns that divide up Ireland's interior. There used to be an inscription, on the old wooden bridge that the present handsome stone structure has replaced, saying: 'Here Civilisation ends and Barbarism begins', meaning Leinster and Connaught. During the centuries when Ireland was being colonised this crossing was much fought over. In the tenth and eleventh centuries the local kings had their headquarters close to the site of the present castle and in 1129 the High King of Ireland built a fort to protect the bridge across the Shannon. Until the end of the 12th century there were constant battles over possession of the fort and control of the river crossing. By the end of that century the Anglo-Normans had captured it, but the castle they built was subsequently sacked and destroyed by the native Irish.

In the 1641 uprising – one of the last revolts of the dispossessed Irish against the planters – the town and its English garrison were under siege for 22 weeks, but early in 1642 the town was taken by the native Irish, then re-taken by Cromwellian forces in 1650. Forty years later Athlone was attacked by 10 000 Williamite soldiers, but was successfully defended by Jacobite forces. The following year – June 1691 – the Williamites returned in earnest: 21 000 of them versus a garrison in Athlone of only 1500. The Williamites had 50 cannon and eight mortars. They are reputed to have fired 600 bombs and 12 000 cannon balls in the most intense bombardment of a town in the whole of Irish history. The castle we now see was much extended around 1800 to meet the threat

The Aghnacliff Dolmen, County Longford.

from the French that never transpired.

Athlone is quiet now, having left its bellicose past behind to be commemorated only within the confines of the Castle Museum, a suitably dark and dowdy home for such bloody memories. The town's winding streets have their fair quotient of characterful old shops and good pubs – like Sean's Bar on the quays, much favoured by the old salts who ply the river.

Athlone is home every year to the All-Ireland Amateur Drama Finals. Theatre groups from all over the country converge for a strongly contended competition when the standards can be as high as in the professional theatres of the cities. The amateur drama movement is very active in Ireland, part of the inheritance left by the literary renaissance of the early 20th century led by W.B. Yeats and Lady Gregory. In almost every town and village in the country there will be a group of dedicated thespians putting on some kind of a show over the winter months that they might then take on the circuit of regional competitions in the hope of building up enough points to qualify for the 'am-dram' Parnassus of Athlone in May.

When it is illuminated at night, the flamboyant basilica of Saints Peter and Paul looks like an unidentified flying object detained for further inspection. By day it is well worth visiting to see the stained glass windows by Sarah Purser and Harry Clarke. On the esplanade between the church and the river there is a bronze bust of Count John Mc Cormack (1884–1945), Ireland's most famous tenor, whose birthplace in the town itself is also open to visitors.

South of the massive lock and the riotous weir at Athlone, the Shannon is at its most meandering and sluggish, forming the Shannon Callows that in spring and autumn are the lifeline and compass for thousands of migratory water birds like widgeon, golden plover, whooper swans, barnacle geese, godwits and greenshanks. L.T.C. Rolt, in his book *Green and Silver*, wrote of this sere plain that merges with the Bog of Allen: 'the country is so flat that in clear weather it is possible to stand on Athlone bridge and see

quite distinctly the shape of the Slieve Bloom mountains 30 miles and more away to the south. The great river winds tortuously through reed-fringed levels of water meadows interspersed with patches of bogland which, in time of winter flood, become a great inland sea.' The vegetation of these callows, relatively undisturbed by man because of their tendency to flood in winter, is one of the richest of its kind in Europe. The dense thickets of reed along the shore give way to forests of sedge. The hay meadows behind grow dense and lush with flag irises, marsh marigold, cuckoo flower, buttercup, bedstraw, ragged robin, meadowsweet and other plants that provide a diverse summer nesting and feeding place for birds like skylarks, pipits, black-headed gulls, snipe, curlews and herons. This is one of the last places in Europe where corncrakes are abundant. Farmers here are given grants by the government to cut hay late in the year, starting from the centre of the fields and working outwards, so as not to kill the corncrakes on their nests.

If you are travelling by river, this quiet, unspectacular landscape, where human beings are a rare sight, leaves you completely unprepared for the impact of Clonmacnois suddenly surging into view at the end of the ridge of eskers that rears from the surrounding bog. These eskers are gravel ridges left behind by the melting of glaciers. They were washed out here into a shallow ford that would always have been an important crossing point for all human and animal traffic, where there is no other crossing through the swamp.

The visitors' centre at the road entrance to Clonmacnois is modest and unobtrusive, a help rather than a hindrance to understanding the place. For the rest, the stones have been left to speak for themselves, so that you can feel that you are discovering them for yourself.

The monastery was founded by St Ciaran in 548 or so. It quickly grew in importance as it was endowed by the chieftains and kings who seemed to have vied with one another to be its benefactors. For the next thousand years it was raided over and over again until finally, in 1552, when the Dissolution of the Monasteries and the English conquest of Ireland coincided, Clonmacnois was abandoned for the last time. It was, in its day, the most important ecclesiastical site in Ireland after Armagh, and throughout the medieval period it would have been an influential centre of learning, with students coming from all over Ireland and from abroad to study in its schools.

Clonmacnois produced, among other manuscripts, *The Book of the Dun Cow* and the *Annals of Clonmacnois*, as well as a great number of other treasures. Accounts of the attacks on Clonmacnois give us some idea of the wealth of the place. In 1129 among the objects stolen by raiders from the high altar were a model of Solomon's Temple, an engraved silver chalice decorated with burnished gold, a drinking horn, a silver cup and three gifts from Turlough O'Conor, High King of Ireland: a silver goblet, a silver cup adorned with a gold cross and a drinking horn embellished with gold. In a raid fifty years later – a contemporary chronicler reports – 105 houses were burned down. The last raid, by the English garrison at Athlone, took place in 1552, when 'not a bell, large or small, or an image, or an altar, or a book, or a gem, or even glass in a window, was left which was not carried away'. What has survived, then, is what is strong, what could not be burned or stolen or smashed up: the stone. As you stand among a seeming jumble of churches, graveslabs and crosses, your mind's eye fills all the spaces with the bustle of human activity there must have been in 'Ciaran's city fair'.

In recent times, more graves have been dug in the area of the monastery, whose new headstones stand out rawly against the mossed and tumbled medieval monoliths. The altar designed for the visit of Pope John Paul II in 1979 is another rather unhappy addition to the site, recalling a bus shelter more than the glories of the past, and already beginning to crack along its concrete seams. But these are small distractions, minor irritations against the grandeur of what remains at Clonmacnois: the ruins of eight churches, three high crosses, two distinctive round

towers and more than four hundred early tombstones. The ruins show a mixture of styles. Little survives of the 904 cathedral but the figures of St Dominic, St Patrick and St Francis over the east doorway stand out from the hodge-podge of remodellings that were wreaked between the 11th and the 15th centuries.

Teampall Rí, or the King's Church, has a Western Transitional east window with plain mouldings, an early Gothic lancet window and a late Gothic doorway. The humbler, smaller oratories stand at awkward angles to these later structures. Ciaran himself is said to be buried at the east end of Temple Ciaran. Miraculous properties are ascribed to the soil from round his grave, which must be why there is so little of it that you have to scrape in the cracks in the rock to get enough even to anoint yourself.

The high crosses are the chief glory of Clonmacnois. The carvings on the Cross of the Scriptures, directly in front of the ruined cathedral, show scenes from the Bible such as the Crucifixion and the Last Judgment, with whimsical secular details – such as cats and birds and a man playing a musical instrument – making the story more human and warm. The High King of Ireland, Conor Mc Carthy, is shown on one of the panels helping St Ciaran to erect the first pillar of his church, in the earliest known example of a political PR opportunity.

The Nuns' Church – completed in 1167 by the Dervorgilla whose affair with Dermot MacMurrough brought the Normans to Ireland – lies a chaste quarter of a mile away along the Pilgrims' Road that follows the ridge of the esker. Its magnificent Hiberno-Romanesque doors and chancel arch brim with chevrons and interlacings. The grotesque beasts on the capitals of the west door were probably meant to ward away evil from the holy sisters praying within.

Clonmacnois was built in the desert of the mind the early monks sought. A primeval God broods in these immense spaces of the Irish midlands. Just as on the rocky fastnesses of the west coast, the holy men and women who lived in communion with this savage landscape were in touch with its deepest

The basilica of St Peter
and St Paul overlooks
the River Shannon,
Athlone, County
Westmeath.

forces, and the stone monuments they have left us are a testimony to the power of the faith that sustained them.

From Clonmacnois the river winds slowly south to Lough Derg by way of Shannonbridge and Shannon Harbour, the first close to the confluence of the Shannon and the River Suck, the second at the confluence of the Shannon and the Grand Canal. Shannonbridge has one of those irreplaceable, inimitable, small-town grocer's – Killeen's – where you can buy groceries until the pub closes. Its relaxed and friendly atmosphere as the town's unofficial headquarters is further enlivened by all kinds of jokes about Irish snake sticks and shillelaghs that are stuck up around the walls for the passing tourist trade. The bridge at Shannonbridge is especially narrow and beautiful, with little embrasures to shelter pedestrians from passing traffic. It leads to an elaborate 19th-century fortification on the west side of the river, another of those built to keep at bay the Napoleon who never came. Shannon Harbour, a few miles south, has the remains of one of the Georgian canal hotels from the early 19th century when the Grand Canal was not just an important trade route from Dublin into the middle of Ireland but was also a highway for the thousands of passengers who were carried along it on horse-drawn barges.

Banagher is where Anthony Trollope (1815–82) was based when he worked as a deputy surveyor for the Post Office in Ireland. He came to know the area well from touring it on horseback and used his experiences in his first two novels: *The Kellys and the O'Kellys* and *The Macdermots of Ballycloran*.

While many of the old railway lines have disappeared – including the line connecting Portumna to Birr which went bankrupt so quickly that the creditors moved in and removed the rails, the sleepers and even the railway station – there is a new passenger service called the Clonmacnois and West Offaly Railway which travels at 12 miles an hour and offers the visitor a 40-minute trip around Blackwater Bog which, at 7000 acres, is the largest bog in Ireland, supplying a million tons of turf a year to the peat-

The 6th-century Cross
of the Scriptures,
Clonmacnois, County
Offaly.

burning electricity station at Shannonbridge.

Meelick, between Banagher and Portumna, was an important ford across the Shannon and was thus heavily fortified throughout the ages. The first castle was built here by the Norman William de Burgo in 1203 and the first monastery by the Franciscans in 1404. This has recently been restored. At Long Island, south of Meelick, is the spot where O'Sullivan Beare with his followers crossed the Shannon in 1602 on his way to Leitrim. The Shannon was in flood when they reached the crossing, and they had to kill their horses to make boats from their skins.

Portumna is the gateway to the last of the great Shannon lakes – Lough Derg. This is where the scenery of the Shannon is at its most spectacular as the now mighty river cuts through the last obstacle of mountains on its way to the sea. It is said that only for the difference of a couple of hundred feet the Shannon might have met the sea at Galway Bay, which would have changed Ireland's geography out of all recognition, and probably her history too.

Around Lough Derg, the contrast between all the Irelands that merge around the great Irish waterways is at its most pronounced. To the west are the rough hills of Clare where generations of subsistence farming have eaten into the very bones of these hungry hills, that become ever more stark and barren until they meet the sea in the scraped moonscape of the Burren itself. But all around Lough Derg, and especially on the Tipperary shore, there are opulent estates, many of them revived with money from the industries which have come to cluster around Shannon Airport. Partly because of the airport's presence, the main ports of call around the lake – Terryglass, Dromineer and Garrykennedy – are quiet little villages that yet have excellent public houses which serve food and drink with a cosmopolitan grace and style.

Mountshannon is the most decorous of these Dergside villages, slumbering in an easy gentility all its own. In days gone by the village was the stopping place for pilgrims making their way to Iniscealtra or Holy Island which sits with its old churches, high crosses

and round tower like a mystical omphalos in the middle of Scarriff Bay. When St Colm arrived here in the seventh century to lead a solitary life, he is said to have dislodged an earlier hermit called St Mac Creiche, who may in fact have been some kind of pagan deity who would still have been honoured by the local people through pilgrimage. The usurping Christian ritual grew in popularity through the ages. Like many of the old pilgrimages, it was undertaken at night so that people would be on the island at dawn. This nocturnal foray became too licentious for the Church so, with the onset of Catholic puritanism in the 19th century, it was made a daytime pilgrimage, after which all the fun went out of it and people stopped going.

Just as further north the Shannon has sideshows – smaller streams which are navigable for a few miles up to a sheltered harbour well away from the main river thoroughfare – here there is a small stretch of the Scarriff River which can be navigated up to a little marina a short walk from the village of Scarriff. And just as the Shannon around Cootehall is associated with John McGahern and his writing, this part of County Clare was the birthplace of the novelist and short-story writer Edna O'Brien (1932–). It is a sign of the changed times that in the old church in the village which has become the East Clare Heritage Centre, Edna O'Brien's books, once banned for their imputed obscenity, are now proudly on display as part of the area's 20th-century history.

The twin towns of Killaloe and Ballina at the southern end of Lough Derg stand like the Pillars of Hercules where navigation for pleasure boats on the Shannon effectively ends. Wedged between Slieve Bernagh on the Clare side and the Arra mountains in Tipperary, with a canal running alongside the river, Killaloe is one of the most picturesque little towns in Ireland. It has a riverside of marinas, hotels, yacht club and fish weirs under the old stone bridge, and then a hidden inner town that spreads up along the steeply climbing street that lurks behind. The interior of the 12th-century cathedral has a splendid Hiberno-Romanesque doorway taken from an earlier church that stood on the same site.

Alongside this door stands a fragment of a high cross that has inscriptions in ogham (an early form of writing made up of strokes), in old Irish and in Norse Runic. In the grounds of the cathedral there is a stone-roofed church dedicated to St Flannan and, just for balance and fairness, in the grounds of the Catholic church at the other, higher end of the town there is another corbelled-roofed oratory from Friar's Island further downstream that was drowned with the making of the Ardnacrusha dam.

In some ways the hydro-electric scheme at Ardnacrusha, the biggest engineering job undertaken in the early years of the State, completed between 1925 and 1929, had a more profound effect on the development of the Republic than all the moral and censorious legislation that was being enacted in the Dáil of the time. With the rural electrification programme that this project ushered in, the Irish countryside was changed irrevocably, never to revert to the pre-electric simplicities that had sustained its people for so long. Yet, strangely enough, around the Shannon Estuary is evoked another Ireland, that is now a fast-fading memory: at the Craggaunowen Project, where a full-scale replica of a lake crannog has been built and the leather-skinned boat used by Tim Severin to recreate the voyage of Brendan the Navigator has been preserved; at Bunratty, Knappogue and Dunguaire where medieval banquets are held; in the Bunratty Folk Park; at Durty Nelly's pub; and at other smaller crafts shops and tourist projects dotted around this area which is often the first place visitors see after landing at Shannon.

Limerick city itself, which for the most part turns its back on the Shannon, is the meeting place of many of these contradictions. For many years King John's Castle, which overlooks the rapids where the Abbey River and the Shannon meet, was so little appreciated that the Corporation built an ugly jumble of municipal housing within its 13th-century walls. These tenements have now been cleared away and a spanking new, and not entirely uncontroversial, interpretative centre has taken their place. For a long time, too, the magnificent Georgian squares and terraces of the city seemed to be in terminal decline as people moved out into the suburbs and to the resorts along the coast, but recently, with events such as the Treaty celebrations of 1991, Limerick has begun to take proper pride in the elegant spaces of its city. The Municipal Art Gallery promotes an annual Exhibition of Visual Art that is one of the most respected group shows in the country. The Belltable Arts Centre puts on theatre, music and exhibitions, and a number of private galleries, such as the Riverrun, manage to survive by selling the work of local artists. Limerick has come a long way from its old image as Sodality City, supposed to embody all the worst kinds of Catholic reaction.

And this is only as it should be, for Limerick is the last great strategic, historical and sociological crossing point that the Shannon makes. Here Munster meets Connaught, with the richness of the one and the wildness of the other giving the city a kind of well-off rakishness. There is a robust independence about its people too, partly inspired perhaps by the knowledge that their ancestors resisted one of the great sieges of the Williamite wars in 1691. It only ended when Patrick Sarsfield, the nearest we have to a true military hero, was persuaded to surrender by the offer of safe passage out of the city for himself and his 10 000 men. The terms of the treaty he had agreed with General Ginkel were not observed. Ever afterwards Limerick has been known as the City of the Broken Treaty.

As the Shannon opens up and eases out into the Atlantic between the pastoral lowlands of Clare and Kerry, it carries with it a weight of memory and history that hangs like silt in its dark waters. 'The broad, majestic Shannon', as the old song has it, has dissolved all of Irish history in its molecules, and here in its estuary – which has seen the first transatlantic flying boats land at Foynes, that is traversed by one of Ireland's very few internal ferries from Killimer to Tarbert, where Irish treasures like the Ardagh chalice and the Bell of St Senan were preserved from the raiding Norsemen – the old river gratefully consigns its corpuscles to the salt ocean, from which to be born again.

Anyone who has made the great journey, then, from Kesh on Lough Erne, through Enniskillen, and then along the repaired Ballyconnell canal to Leitrim, Carrick-on-Shannon, Athlone, Portumna and Killaloe, has passed through the heart of Ireland, a heart she is happy to reveal to anyone who comes to look for it with patience and understanding.

The Dergside village of Mountshannon, County Clare.

The River Shannon at Limerick City.

MUSTS ALONG THE ERNE AND SHANNON

* A feed of Mullingar beef.
* Sunset over the Bog of Allen.
* The ancient site of Uisneach, to the west of Mullingar, another of the dead centres of Ireland, where the pre-Christian feast of Bealtaine was celebrated on 1 May.
* Bog botany, especially the insect-eating plants like sundews.
* Birr Castle Gardens and Science and Technology Park.
* The Hill of Tara, seat of the High Kings of Ireland.
* Trim Castle.
* A recording of harp tunes by Turlough O'Carolan (1670–1738).
* A remastered recording of John Mc Cormack.
* The President Douglas Hyde Interpretative Centre at Tibohine, five miles west of Frenchpark.
* A cattle mart on auction day.
* A long drift on a slow boat.
* Dishes made from freshwater fish such as pike, perch, bream, eel or rudd.

Index

Abbey, National Theatre	27
Achill Island	115, 188, 199, 121
Act of Union	24, 26
Adair, William	155
Aghalurcher Church, County Fermanagh	168
Ahenny	39
Aherlow, Glen of	58, 59
Ailwee Caves, County Clare	111
Allihies	69
Allingham, William	163
Annaghmakerrig House, County Monaghan	141
Anne, Queen of Great Britain and Ireland	8, 14
Annestown	60
Antrim Plateau	152
Antrim, Glens of	152–153
Antrim Coast Road	128, 152
Apprentice Boys of Derry	132
Aran Islands	99, 104
Aranmore Island	147
Áras An Uachtaráin	26
Arbutus Lodge Restaurant, Cork	73
Ardagh Chalice	23, 187
Ardara	146
Ardmore	62
Ards Peninsula	128, 134
Arigna	169
Armagh	44, 138
Arra Mountains	184
Ashford Castle, Cong, County Mayo	120
Athenry	107
Athlone	162, 177-8, 180-1
Athy	38, 44
Augher	154
Aughrim	107
Auld Lammas Fair, Ballycastle, County Antrim	155
Avondale	32
Bailieborough	143
Balbriggan	29
Ballina	116, 121, 184
Ballinagaul	61
Ballinamuck	116, 169
Ballinasloe	107, 108
Ballinrobe	117
Ballintemple	72
Ballintoy	155
Ballintubber Abbey, County Mayo	117
Ballybunion	90
Ballycastle	155
Ballycotton	61
Ballyferriter	89
Ballyhack	43
Ballyhoura Hills	77
Ballykeeran	178
Ballymaloe House, County Cork	68, 79
Ballymena	155
Ballymoney	51
Ballynahinch	105
Ballyporeen	43, 55, 58, 120
Ballyshannon	163
Ballyvaughan	111, 114
Ballyvourney	66
Balscadden Bay	31
Banagher	182
Bandon	71
Bann, River	128
Bannow Bay	42
Banville, John	51
Barna	102
Barrow, River	38, 43, 47
Barry, General Tom	71
Barry, Sebastian	28
Barry, Commodore John	49
Battlebridge	169
Béal na mBláth	71
Beara Peninsula	70
Becket, Thomas à	49
Beckett, Samuel	6, 18, 35, 166
Belleek	163
Belltable Arts Centre, Limerick	186
Belturbet	143, 168
Ben Bulben	122, 123
Benaughlin	167
Benburb	154
Bennettsbridge	44
Berkeley, Bishop George	17, 47, 79
Bewley's Oriental Cafés	25
Bianconi, Carlo	55, 58
Birr	182
Bishopstown	72
Black Preceptory, Order of the	132
Black Pig of Ulster	128, 138, 142
Black Abbey, Kilkenny	46
Blackfriars Gate, Kilkenny	46
Blacklion	142
Blackrock	72
Blacksod Bay	115
Blackstairs Mountains	38, 47
Blackwater, River (County Cork)	38, 51, 62, 77
Blackwater, River (County Tyrone)	154
Blanchardstown	10
Blarney Castle	19
Blasket Islands	89
Blennerville	90
Bloody Foreland	148
Bloom, Leopold	18, 31
Blue Stack Mountains	154, 162
Boa Island	164
Bogside (Derry)	150
Boleyn, Anne	55
Bolton, Theophilus	59
Bonny Prince Charlie	148
Boolavogue, Father Murphy of	48
Boole, George	74
Booterstown Marsh, Dublin	31
Boswell, James	30
Botanic Gardens, Belfast	133
Botanical Gardens, Dublin	29
Bourn-Vincent Memorial Park, Killarney	84
Bowen, Elizabeth	77
Boycott, Captain	117
Boyle, Richard	63
Boyle Abbey	174
Boyle, River	170
Boyne, Battle of the	30
Boyne Valley	33
Bray	8, 31
Brazen Head pub, Dublin	15
Breffni, Kingdom of	142, 162
Brian Boru	111, 139
Bricklieve Mountains	174
Broken Treaty, The City of the (Limerick)	187
Brookeborough	154
Browne, Noel	27
Browneshill Dolmen	36
Bruce, Robert	159
Bryce, Annan, MP	71
Bull Ring, Wexford	49
Bulloch Harbour, Dublin	31
Bunbeg	147
Bunclody	47
Buncrana	148
Bunmahon	60
Bunratty Castle and Folk Park	98
Burke, Edmund	17
Burke, Theobald	116
Burne-Jones, Edward	63
Burntcourt Castle, County Tipperary	58
Burren, The	97, 108
Burtonport	147
Bushmills Distillery	155
Butler Family	44, 45
Butler, Hubert	46
Butler Gallery	46
Buttevant	79
Caherdaniel	80
Cahir	43, 55, 58
Cahirciveen	80
Cahirmee Horse Fair	79
Caldragh Cemetery, Boa Island	164
Caldwell, John Bloomfield	163
Caldwell, Castle	164
Caledon	154
Calvinists	36
Cape Clear	70
Cappoquin	62

Caragh Lake	80	Cloondara (Richmond Harbour)	177
Carlingford	128, 137	Cloyne	75
Carlingford Lough	137, 138	Cobh	79
Carna	105	Cockburn, Claud	82
Carnadoe Waters	175	Cole, Sir William	166
Carnlough	153	Coleman, Michael	122
Carraroe	102, 105	Coleraine	128
Carrauntoohill	85	Coliemore	31
Carrick	146	Colligan Glen	60
Carrick-a-rede	155	Collins, Michael	71
Carrick-on-Shannon	174	Comeragh Mountains	54
Carrick-on-Suir	39, 55	Commitments, The, by Roddy Doyle	28
Carrickfergus	159	Cong	120
Carrickmacross	141	Connemara	105
Carrigastyra	70	Connolly, James	27
Carrowmore	122	Conolly, William	32
Carson, Sir Edward	130	Conolly's Folly	33
Casement, Roger	155	Cook Street, Dublin	10
Cashel, Rock of	59	Cooke, Barrie	44
Cashel	38, 44, 54	Cookstown	154
Casino at Marino, Dublin	29	Coole Park	107
Cassells, Richard	32, 119	Cooley, Cattle Raid of	28
Castle Leslie	141	Cooley Mountains	154
Castle Coole	167	Cooneyites	36
Castle Archdale	164	Coosan	178
Castle Forbes	177	Coote, Sir Charles	175
Castlebar	117	Cootehall	170
Castleblayney	141	Corcromroe Abbey, County Clare	110
Castlecomer	36	Cormac's Chapel, Cashel	59
Castlegregory	88	Corofin	114
Castlereagh, Viscount	135	Corrib, River	99,
Castletown House, County Kildare	32	Costello, Edward	175
Castletownbere	70	Courtown Harbour	51
Castletownshend	68	Craggaunowen Castle	97
Castlewellan Forest Park	136	Craig, Maurice	19
Catholic Emancipation Act	77	Crawford Art Gallery, Cork	73
Cavan Way	142	Croagh Patrick, County Mayo	97, 114, 121
Cave Hill, Belfast	154	Croke Park, Dublin	50
Ceide Fields, Mayo	94	Crom Castle	167
Celtworld, County Waterford	60	Cromwell, Oliver	46, 52, 77, 95
Chambers, Sir William	30	Cross, Eric	68
Chandler, Raymond	54	Crossmaglen	138
Cheekpoint	43	Crown Bar, Belfast	132
Chester Beatty Library	30	Cuchulainn	27, 137, 139
Chichester, Sir Arthur	130	Cuilcagh Mountain	142, 143, 167
Christ Church Cathedral, Dublin	10, 13	Cultra	134
Churchill, Winston	135	Curlew Mountains	126, 174
City Arts Centre, Dublin	24	Curracloe	51
Claddagh	101	Curragh, The, of Kildare	33, 34
Clancy, William	113	Cushendall	153
Clanrye River	138	Custom House, Dublin	19
Clare Island	116	Dáil Eireann	23
Clarke, Harry	24, 25, 69, 74, 178	Dalcassians	111
Clew Bay	97, 105, 114, 115	Dalkey	29, 31
Clifden	97, 105	Dalkey Island	29
Cloch Labhrais, County Waterford	36	DART, the	31
Clogher Valley	154	Davis, Thomas	60
Clogher	141	Davitt, Michael	117
Clonakilty	71	de Courcy, John	159
Clonea	60	de Burgo, Richard	148
Clones	142, 168	de Burgo, William	184
Clonfert	108	de Valera, Eamon	112
Clonmacnois	62, 160, 177, 179, 184	Delaney, Edward	22
Clonmel	54, 57	Delphi	96
Clontarf, Battle of	111, 139	Democratic Left	23
Derry	150		
Derrybeg	147		
Derrygonnelly	163		
Derrylin	168		
Derrynaflan Chalice	23		
Derrynane House, County Kerry	80		
Derryveagh Mountains	154		
Dervorgilla	182		
Devenish Island, Lough Erne	160, 165		
Devil's Bit, Slieve Bloom Mountains	59		
Devonshire, Dukes of	63		
Dingle Peninsula	88		
Donegal Abbey	143		
Donegal Town	143		
Doneraile	77		
Doogort	119		
Dooney Rock, County Sligo	122		
Doonican, Val	54		
Dorsey, The	138		
Douglas Hyde Gallery of Modern Art, Dublin	17		
Downpatrick	136		
Dowra	142		
Dowth	33		
Doyle, Roddy	6, 28, 31		
Doyle, Jack	79		
Draperstown	154		
Dromana	62		
Dromineer	184		
Dromod	176		
Druid Theatre, Galway	102		
Drumcliff	122		
Drumshambo	169		
Drumsna	175		
du Maurier, Daphne	69		
Dublin, Battle of	10		
Dublin Zoo	26		
Dublin Castle	10, 17		
Dublin Writers Museum	19		
Dublin Bay	10		
Dufferin and Ava, Marquess of	130		
Duiske Abbey, County Kilkenny	40		
Dun Aengus, Aran Islands	95		
Dun Cow, Book of The	179		
Dún Laoghaire	31		
Dún an Oir	89		
Dunbrody Abbey	42		
Duncannon	41		
Dundalk	31, 34		
Dunfanaghy	147		
Dunganstown	43		
Dungarvan	36, 51, 60		
Dungarvan Bay	60		
Dungloe	147		
Dunguaire Castle	107		
Dunlewy	147		
Dunloe, Gap of	85		
Dunmore East	60		
Dunquin	89		
Dunree	148		
Durcan, Paul	74, 75		
Dursey	70		
Dwan's of Thurles	57		
Dysert O'Dea	111		
Dzogchen Beara	70		

Easky 127
Eason's Bookshop, Dublin 8
Edenderry 134
Edgeworth, Maria 176
Edward VIII, King of Great Britain and
  Northern Ireland 134
Edwards, Hilton 21
Elizabeth I, Queen of England 17, 97, 116
Emain Macha, Navan Fort 139, 154
English Market, Cork 72
Ennis Abbey 113
Ennis 113
Enniscorthy 49
Enniskillen 162, 165
Ennistymon 114
Errigal Mountain, County Donegal 147
Erris Peninsula 121
Evans, Estyn 134, 160
Everard, Sir Richard 58
Eyre Square, Galway 99
Faerie Queen, The, by Edmund
  Spenser 49, 62, 77
Fair Head 155
Fairyhouse Race Course 34
Famine, the Great 33, 70, 96
Fanad 148
Father Mathew Bridge, Dublin 10
Feather Bed 30
Fermoy 77
Ferrycarrig 47
Fethard 42, 51
Fianna Fáil 23
Fine Gael 23
Finnegans Wake 10
Fir Bolgs 60, 111
Fishamble Street, Dublin 11, 13
Fitzgerald, George Robert 118
Fitzgibbon, Marjorie 23
Fivemiletown 154
Florencecourt, County Fermanagh 167
Flower, Robin 90
Foley, John Henry 27
Ford, Henry 72
Forkhill 138
Forty Foot, Dublin 31
Fota Island, County Cork 79
Four Courts, The, Dublin 24, 27
Foxford 117
Foyle, River 128
Francis Street, Dublin 15
French, Percy 143
Friel, Brian 28, 151
Gaelic Athletic Association 50, 76
Gainsborough, Thomas 55
Gallagher, Rory 75
Gallarus Oratory 89
Galloon Island, Lough Erne 168
Galtee Mountains 43
Galvin, Patrick 74
Galway Races 100
Galway Blazers 106
Galway City Museum 100
Galway Arts Festival 99
Gandon, James 19
Gap of the North 138

Garnish Island 71
Garrykennedy 184
Garter Lane, Waterford 54
Gate Theatre, Dublin 21
Gealtarra Eireann 146
Giant's Causeway 128, 158, 159
Giraldus Cambrensis 38
Girona 133, 159
Glangevlin 142
Glasnevin 29
Glebe House, County Donegal 147
Glenariff 152
Glenarm 152, 153
Glenballyeamon 152
Glenbeagh 80
Glencar 122
Glencloy 152
Glencolumbkille 146
Glencorp 152
Glendalough 30, 62
Glendun 152
Glengarriffe 71
Glenisheen Collar 110
Glennan 152
Glenshesk 152
Glentaisie 152, 155
Glenveagh Castle and National Park 147
Gogarty, Oliver St John 102
Goldsmith, Oliver 176
Gore-Booth, Eva 124
Gorey 48
Gougane Barra 67
Grafton, Duke of 8
Grafton Street, Dublin 8, 26
Graiguenamanagh 40
Grand Canal 25, 44, 182
Grand Opera House, Belfast 132
Grand Parade, Cork 72
Grange Lough 175
Grattan's Parliament 26
Graves, Alfred P. 80
Graves, Robert 80
Graves, Charles 80
Greencastle 148
Gregory, Lady 27, 107, 178
Grianan of Aileach, County
  Donegal 148, 150
Grubb, Major Samuel 65
Guinness, Robert 59
Guinness, James Arthur 15
Guinness Brewery, Dublin 15
Gurranabraher 72
Gweedore 147
Haigh Terrace, Dublin 31
Ha'penny Bridge, Dublin 23
Hall, Mr and Mrs 68
Hamiltonsbawn 138
Handel, Georg Friedrich 11, 13
Hare Island, Lough Ree 177
Harland & Wolff Shipyard, Belfast 130
Harrow, The, County Wexford 48
Haughey, Charles J. 23, 89
Hawkins Street 10
Hazelwood 122, 126
Heaney, Seamus 6, 13, 48

Helvick 61
Helvick Head 51
Henry, Paul 102, 126
Henry VII, King 52
Henry II, King 49, 63
Hewitt, John 153
High Street, Dublin 13
Hill, Derek 147
Hilltown 136
Hilton Park, County Monaghan 141
Holy Cross Abbey, County Tipperary 42
Holywood 134
Honan Chapel, University College Cork 74
Hone, Evie 126
Hook Peninsula 51
Hook Head 36
Horan, Monsignor James 117
Howth, Hill of 8
Howth Castle 31
Howth 31
Hudson's Bay 178
Hugh Lane Gallery, Dublin 24
Huguenots 52
Humbert, General 116, 121
Hungry Hill 69
Inch 88
Inchbofin 177
Inchclearaun 177
Inchiquin, Earl of 59
Iniscealtra, Lough Ree 184
Inisfallen Island, Killarney 85
Inisfallen, Annals of 85
Inisfree, Lake Isle of 122, 124
Inishbofin 106, 115
Inishmacsaint 165
Inishowen Peninsula 148
Iniskilling Fusiliers 166
Inistioge, County Kilkenny 44
Ireland's Eye 29
Ireton, General 52
Irish Museum of Modern Art, Dublin 19, 24
Irish National Heritage Park 47
Irish Sketch Book, by W.M. Thackeray 62
Iveagh Markets, Dublin 15
James I, King 150, 166
James II, King 107, 123, 148, 150
James, Henry 143
Jamestown 175
Jerpoint 40
John, Augustus 107
John, King 63
John Paul II, Pope 26, 117, 182
Johnson, Dr 30
Johnston, Francis 138
Johnstown Castle 47
Joyce, James 6, 10, 18, 22, 35
Kavanagh, Patrick 6, 25, 141
Kean, Edmund 54
Keane, John B. 6, 43, 106
Keating, Seán 102
Kells, County Kilkenny 40
Kells, Book of 18, 23
Kelly, Oisín 71
Kelly, the Boy from Killane 48
Kenmare 80

Kennedy, President J.F. 43, 49, 101, 151
Kenny's Bookshop, Galway 101
Kilbarrack 31
Kilcash 42
Kildare, Earls of 59
Kilfenora 111, 114
Kilglass Lough 175
Kilgreany 36
Kilkee 114
Kilkeel 137
Kilkenny 38, 44, 45, 46
Killadeas 164
Killala Bay 115, 116
Killaloe 113, 184
Killane 48
Killarney National Park 84
Killary Harbour 106, 115
Killimer 187
Killiney Bay 31
Killiney 31
Killorglin 80
Killybegs 146
Kilmainham Jail, Dublin 27
Kilmakedar 89
Kilmore Quay 36, 51
Kinawley 168
King John's Castle 162, 186
Kingstown 31
Kinsale, Old Head of 79
Kinsale, Battle of 116, 123
Kinsella, Thomas 35
Kintyre, Mull of 155
Knock 117
Knockaheany 72
Knockmealdown Mountains 36, 54, 60, 65
Knocknarea 122
Knockvicar Bridge 171
Knowth 33
Kylemore Abbey 105
Kyteler's Inn, Kilkenny 46
Labour Party, Irish 23
Lagan, River 133
Lagan Valley Regional Park 133
Lake, General 116
Land League 117
Lanesborough 176, 177
Lanyon, Charles 130
Larne 155
Lavery, Sir John 24
Laytown Strand 30
Lee, River 67
Leenane 96
Leinster House, Dublin 10, 23
Leinster, Duke of 23
Leitrim Castle 169
Leitrim 169
Leland, Mary 74
Lemass, Seán 97
Leopardstown Race Course 34
Lettermore 103
Lettermullan 103
Liberty Hall, Dublin 28
Liffey, River 8, 10, 13, 20, 25
Limerick 162, 186
Linenhall Library, Belfast 130

Lir, Children of 121
Lisbellaw 168
Lisdoonvarna 113
Lismore Castle 63
Lismore, Book of 63
Lismore 36, 57
Lissadell 124
Listowel 92
Loftus Hall 51
Londonderry, see Derry
Londonderry, Lady 135
Long Valley Bar, Cork 73
Longford 177
Loop Head 113
Lough Allen 142, 169
Lough Bofin 176
Lough Bray 30
Lough Carra 115, 120
Lough Conn 115
Lough Corrib 108
Lough Derg 113, 154, 182
Lough Drumharlow 169
Lough Forbes 176, 177
Lough Foyle 151
Lough Gill 124
Lough Key 170
Lough Macnean 163, 167
Lough Mask 108, 115
Lough Neagh 138, 151, 154
Lough Oakport 170
Lough Ree 177
Lough Swilly 128, 148
Lough Tay 30
Loughlinstown 10
Louisburgh 96, 116
Lovett-Pearce, Sir Edward 174
Lughnasa 114
Lugnaquilla 30
Lusitania 24, 79
Lynch's Memorial, Galway 101
Lynch's Castle, Galway 101
Maamturks 115
Mac Cumhaill, Finn 27, 89, 123, 158
Mac Liammóir, Micheál 21
MacConghail, Muiris 90
Macken, Walter 103
MacMahon, Brian 93
MacMurrough, Diarmuid 123, 182
Macnas 99
Macroom 70
Maeve, Queen 123, 177
Magho Cliffs, County Fermanagh 163
Mahony, Francis Sylvester
  (Father Prout) 73
Malahide 30
Malin 148
Malin Head 148
Mallow 76
Malone, Molly 8, 23
Marble Arch Caves, County Fermanagh 163
Maritime Museum, Dublin 31
Markieviecz, Countess Constance 123
Marley Park, Dublin 30
Marsh's Library, Dublin 14
Marshall, William 43

Marstrander, Carl 90
Martel, Edouard 163
Martin, Richard 'Humanity Dick' 105
Martin, Violet 69
Martyn, Edward 27
Master McGrath (greyhound) 60
Matcham, Frank 132
Maxwell, Lady Lucy 47
Mc Cracken, Henry Joy 130
Mc Gahern, John 170
McBride, John 27
McCarthy, J.J. 141
McClure, Sir John 51
McCormack, John 79, 178
McCurtain, Thomas 74
McDonnell, Sir Randel 155
McGonigal, Maurice 102
McGuinness, Frank 28
McIlhenny, Henry 147
McKenna, Jackie 22
McSwiney, Terence 74
Meelick 184
Mellon family 151
Menapia 36
Merriman, Brian 113
Midleton 79
Milesians 88
Milltown Malbay 113
Mitchelstown 76
Mitchelstown Caves 55
Model Arts Centre, Sligo 126
Moher, Cliffs of 112
Molloy, M.J. 102
Monaghan 141
Monasterboice 35
Monavullaugh Mountains 54, 59
Montenotte, Cork 72
Moore, John 116
Moore Street, Dublin 15
Moore, Thomas 46
Moore Hall 120
Moore, George Henry 121
Moore, George 27, 120
Moore, Christy 28
Morrison, Van 133
Mount Gabriel 70
Mount Leinster 38, 47
Mount Mellary 62, 77
Mount Eagle 89
Mount Usher Gardens 32
Mountain River, County Roscommon 175
Mountsandel 128
Mountshannon 184
Mountstewart 135
Mourne Mountains 31, 34, 128, 134
Mourne, Kingdom of 136
Moy River 117, 154
Moytura 115
Muckross House, Killarney 84
Mullaghmore 97, 127
Mullet, the 121
Mulligan, Buck 31
Mullingar 177
Mulraney 118
Mulroy Bay 148

Murlough Bay 155
Murphy, Tom 28, 102
Murphy, Séamus 68
Napoleon Bonaparte 182
Nash, John 58, 170
National Gallery, Dublin 23, 24
National Museum, Dublin 10, 13, 23, 115
National Library, Dublin 23
Natural History Museum, Dublin 23
Navan Fort, Emain Macha 139
Navan 34
Nelson's Pillar, Dublin 28
Nephin Beg Mountains 115
New Ross, The Walling of 42
New Ross 44
New Geneva 36
Newcastle 136
Newgrange 33, 34
Newmarket-on-Fergus 114
Newport 118
Newry 137
Newtownforbes 177
Newtownhamilton 138
Ní Dhomhnaill, Nuala 88
Nire, River 60
Nore, River 38, 43, 44, 46, 47
Normans 39, 42
Nun's Island 177
Ó Buachalla, Tadhg 68
Ó Docherty, Cahir 150
Ó Criomhthain, Tomas 90
Ó Dalaigh, Cearbhall 80
Ó Suilleabháin, Muiris 90
Ó Rathille, Aogan 84
Ó Conaire, Padraic 101
O'Brien, Vincent 60
O'Brien, Edna 6, 184
O'Brien, Kate 6
O'Brien, Murrough 59
O'Briens of Thomond 111
O'Casey, Sean 27, 28, 107
O'Connell, Daniel 8, 27, 80, 111, 113
O'Connor, Frank 74
O'Connor, Rory 123
O'Connor, Sinéad 28
O'Connor, Turlough 120
O'Doherty, Eamonn 22
O'Faolain, Sean 6, 72
O'Malley, Grace 97, 105, 116, 119
O'Neill, Terence 155
O'Neills (Earls of Tyrone) 148, 155
O'Riada, Seán 66
O'Riordan, Seán 66
O'Shea, Kitty 112
O'Sullivan Beare 169, 184
Old Barn Family Museum, County Fermanagh 168
Oldgrange 33
Olympia Theatre, Dublin 28
Omagh 151
Omeath 137
Orange Order, The 33, 132
Oranmore 106
Orchard Gallery, Derry 151
Oriel, Kings of 154

Ormonde, Marquess of 46
Osborne, Walter 24
Ossian's Grave 153
Oughterard 108
Oulart, County Wexford 48
Ox Mountains 115, 121
Pakenham-Mahon family 176
Paradise Hill, County Tipperary 58
Parliament House (now Bank of Ireland), Dublin 24
Parnell, Charles Stewart 8, 32, 112, 117
Parnell Square, Dublin 21
Parthelonians 60
Passage East 36, 43
Patrick Street, Dublin 14
Patrick Street, Cork 72
Pearse, Patrick 8, 27, 105
Peto, Harold 71
Phoenix Park, Dublin 26
Piers 45
Pike, The, County Waterford 60
Plassey Technology Park, Limerick 97
Poddle, River 10, 11
Pontoon 121
Portaferry 134
Portlaw 55
Portora Royal School, Enniskillen 166
Portumna 107, 182, 184
Powder Tower, Dublin Castle 11
Powerscourt House, County Wicklow 32
Progressive Democrats 23
Prospect of Fermanagh 167
Ptolemy of Alexandria 36, 72
Puck Fair, Killorglin 80
Pugin, Augustus 36, 73
Purser, Sarah 74, 178
Pyle, Hilary 74
Queen's University, The, Belfast 132
Queenstown (Cobh), County Cork 79
Quilty 113
Rafferty, The Blind Poet 107
Railway, West Offaly 184
Raleigh, Sir Walter 63, 82
Rathcrogan 176
Rathfarnham 29, 30
Rathlin Island, County Antrim 152
Rathmelton 148
Rathmullan 148
Rea, Stephen 151
Reagan, Ronald 43, 120
Real Charlotte, The, by Somerville and Ross 69
Reginald's Tower, Waterford 54
Renvyle House 103
Reynolds, Sir Joshua 55
Richard III, King of England 100
Richard II, King of England 54
Richmond Harbour (Cloondara) 177
Ring 36, 61
Ring, Christy 75
Ring of Kerry 80
Riverrun Gallery, Limerick 185
Robinson, Tim 103
Robinson, President Mary 17
Roche, Billy 51

Rockingham House 170
Rogers, Mary 165
Rolt, L.T.C. 170, 179
Rosmuc 105
Ross, Major General Robert 137
Rossaveal 103
Rosses Point 124
Rossguill 148
Rosslare Harbour 54
Rosslare 47, 51
Rostrevor 136, 137
Roth House 46
Rotunda Hospital, Dublin 21
Rowallane Gardens, County Down 135
Royal Canal 25, 177
Royal Hospital, Kilmainham 19
Royal Dublin Society 29
Russborough House 32
Russell, George 126
Rynhart, Jeanne 22
St Anne's Cathedral, Belfast 131
St Audoen's Church, Dublin 13
St Brendan the Navigator 98, 108
St Bridget 34
St Canice's Cathedral, Kilkenny 44, 47, 59
St Ciaran 177, 182
St Columbcille 150
St Dominic 182
St Finbarr 67, 72
St Francis 182
St Gobnait's graveyard 66
St Kevin 30, 32
St Kevin's Church, Glendalough 30
St Macartan 141, 154
St Michan's Church, Dublin 13
St Molaise 165
St Mullin 42
St Nicholas of Myra, Church of, Galway 101
St Patrick 97, 114, 131, 136, 138, 139, 154, 182
St Patrick's Cathedral, Dublin 14
St Patrick's Hall, Dublin 17
St Senan, Bell of 187
St Tighearnach's graveyard, Clones 142
Saint's Island, Lough Ree 177
Sally Gap, County Wicklow 30
Salthill 102
Sandycove 31
Santry 10
Sarsfield, Patrick 187
Saul 154
Saw Doctors 99
Sawel Mountain, Sperrins, County Tyrone 154
Sayers, Peig 90
Scarrawalsh 48
Scarriff, River 184
Scarriff Bay 184
Schull 70
Scrabo Tower, County Down 135
Seanad Eireann 23, 68
Selskar Abbey, Kilkenny 49
Severin, Tim 98
Shandon 73
Shane's Castle, County Antrim 155

Shankill, County Dublin 31
Shannon Harbour 182
Shannon Airport 114
Shannonbridge 182
Shaw, George Bernard 6, 107
Shee Alms House, Kilkenny 46
Sheeffry Mountains 115
Sheehan, Canon 77
Shergar (racehorse) 34
Sheridan, Margaret Burke 117
Sheridan, Jim 106
Sheridan, Richard Brinsley 143
Siamsa Tire, National Folk Theatre, Tralee 90
Sidney, Sir Henry 116
Simnel, Lambert 52
Sion Mills, County Derry 154
Sirius 79
Skellig Michael 80
Skerries 29
Skibbereen 60
Skreen 122
Slaney, River 38, 48, 49
Slea Head 89
Slemish 154
Slieve League 146, 162
Slieve Bloom 59, 179
Slieve Gullion 138, 154
Slieve Anierin 142, 169
Slieve Donard 136
Slievenamon 36, 42
Sligo Art Gallery 126
Sligo Abbey 126
Slobs, the, Wexford 51
Smithfield Market, Dublin 15
Sneem 80
Soloheadbeg 58
Somerville, Edith 68
Spancil Hill 113
Spanish Point 114
Spanish Arch, Galway 100
Spenser, Edmund 48, 54, 62, 77
Sperrin Mountains 151, 154
Spiddal 102
Staffa 158
Staigue Fort, County Kerry 80
Stella (Esther Johnson) 14
Sterne, Laurence 55
Stewartstown 154
Stormont 134
Strabane 151
Stradbally 60
Straide 117
Strandhill 122, 126
Strangford Lough 134
Strokestown House 176
Strokestown 176
Strongbow 43, 52

Stuart, Francis 74
Sugarloaf Mountain, County Wicklow 29
Suir, River 36, 38, 43, 55
Sutton 31
Swanlinbar 142
Swift, Jonathan 14, 18, 47, 138
Synge, John Millington 18, 28, 30, 99, 102, 118
Taibhdhearc Theatre, Galway 102
Tain Bo Culainge (Cattle Raid of Cooley) 176
Tallaght 10
Tara Hill 44, 48
Tara Brooch 23
Tarbert 187
Temple Bar Gallery 24
Temple Bar 28
Terryglass 184
Thackeray, William Makepeace 83, 119
Thin Lizzy 28
Tholsel, Kilkenny 46
Thomas Street, Dublin 15
Thomastown 44
Thompson, George 90
Thomson, David 170
Thoor Ballylee 107
Three Rock Mountain 29
Thurles 42
Tintern Abbey 42
Titanic 79, 130
Tivoli 72
Tobercurry 126
Tolka, River, Dublin 29
Tollymore Forest Park, County Down 136
Tomregon Stone, Ballyconnell 143
Tone, Theobald Wolfe 46, 148
Toomebridge 128
Tor Head 155
Torc Waterfall, County Kerry 85
Tory Island 147
Tourmakeady 126
Tralee 90
Tramore 60
Trinity College, Dublin 10, 17
Triskel Arts Centre, Cork 73
Trollope, Anthony 182
Tuatha de Danaan 60, 88, 115
Turner, Richard 29, 133
Twelfth of July, The 33, 132
Twelve Bens, County Galway 99, 102
Tynan Abbey 154
Tyrconnell, Earl of 148
Tyrone, Earl of 148
U2 28, 99
Ulster Cycle 128
Ulster Folk Museum, Cultra 134
Ulster Museum, Belfast 133
Ulster American Folk Park, Omagh 151
United Irishmen 130

University of Limerick 97
University College, Dublin 18
University College, Cork 74
University College, Galway 101
Valentia Island 80
Vanessa (Hester van Homrigh) 14
Vee, The, County Tipperary 65
Victoria Road, Cork 72
Victoria, Queen of Britain and Ireland 19, 74, 79, 85, 130, 162, 168
Vikings 8, 10, 13, 30, 52, 120, 123
Vinegar Hill, County Wexford 48, 57
Wadding, Luke 52
Walcott, Derek 30
Wallace, William 54
Warbeck, Perkin 52
Warrenpoint 136, 137
Waterford, Lords of 55
Waterford Glass 52
Waterford 43, 51, 52
Wellesley Terrace, Cork 72
Wellington Road, Cork 72
Wellington Monument, Dublin 26
Westport House 119
Westport 119
Wexford Opera Festival 51
Wexford Historical and Folk Museum 48
Wexford Wild Fowl Reserve 51
White Island 164
Whitegate 113
Wicklow Way 30
Wicklow 29, 30
Wilde, Oscar 6, 166
William of Orange, King 30, 107, 123, 129, 132
Wood Quay, Dublin 10
Woodbrook, by David Thomson 170
Worm Ditch 138, 142
Wyatt, James 119, 167
Yeats, Jack Butler 24, 102, 124, 126
Yeats, John 126
Yeats Memorial Museum 126
Yeats Summer School 126
Yeats, William Butler 6, 27, 28, 54, 107, 121, 122
Yola 36
Youghal 61, 82
Young, Arthur 83

Picture Acknowledgements
The Publishers widh to thank Bord Fáilte and the Northern Ireland Tourist Board for their kind permission to reproduce pictures in this book.